Collateral Damage Autocracy?

DEVELOPMENT ECONOMICS AND POLICY

Series edited by Joachim von Braun,
Ulrike Grote and Manfred Zeller

Vol. 81

PETER LANG

Collateral Damage Autocracy?

On the Impact of Economic Sanctions on the Political System

Tobias Lechner

PETER LANG

Bibliographic Information published by the Deutsche Nationalbibliothek
The Deutsche Nationalbibliothek lists this publication in the Deutsche Nationalbibliografie; detailed bibliographic data is available in the internet at http://dnb.d-nb.de.

Library of Congress Cataloging-in-Publication Data
A CIP catalog record for this book has been applied for at the Library of Congress.

Printed by CPI books GmbH, Leck

ISSN 0948-1338
ISBN 978-3-631-80238-0 (Print)
E-ISBN 978-3-631-82386-6 (E-Book)
E-ISBN 978-3-631-82387-3 (EPUB)
E-ISBN 978-3-631-82388-0 (MOBI)
DOI 10.3726/b17039

This publication has been peer reviewed.

www.peterlang.com

For Mina and Ginnie

Contents

Part II Designing

List of abbreviations

AU	African Union
BAFA	Bundesamt für Wirtschaft und Ausfuhrkontrolle (German Federal Office for Economic Affairs and Export Control)
CV	control variable
DPRK	Democratic People's Republic of Korea (North Korea)
DV	dependent variable
ECOWAS	Economic Community of West African States
EEAS	European External Action Service
EU	European Union
EUR	Euro (€)
FDI	foreign direct investment
FRY	Federal Republic of Yugoslavia
FH	Freedom in the World Index; Freedom House 2018
GCC	Gulf Cooperation Council
GDP	gross domestic product
GIGA	GIGA sanctions dataset; Portela & Soest 2012
GNP	gross national product
GWF	Autocratic Regimes Dataset; Geddes, Wright, & Frantz 2014
HDI	Human Development Index; United Nations Development Program 2018
HRO	human rights organizations
HSEO	HSEO sanctions dataset; Hufbauer, Schott, Elliott, & Oegg 2007
IGO	international governmental or intergovernmental organization
IRGC	Islamic Revolutionary Guard Corps
IR	International Relations
IRI	Islamic Republic of Iran
IV	independent variable
MEPV	Major Episodes of Political Violence; Marshall 2018
NAFTA	North American Free Trade Agreement
NGO	non-governmental organization
OAU	Organisation of African Unity
OECD	Organisation for Economic Co-operation and Development
OPEC	Organization of the Petroleum Exporting Countries
OSCE	Organization for Security and Co-operation in Europe
PIV	Polity IV Index; Marshall, Gurr, & Jaggers 2017

SFIM	State Fragility Index and Matrix; Marshall & Elzinga-Marshall 2016
SWIFT	Society for Worldwide Interbank Financial Telecommunication
TIES	TIES sanctions dataset; Morgan, Bapat, & Kobayashi 2014
TSC	TSC sanctions dataset; Biersteker, Eckert, Tourinho, & Hudáková 2018; cf. Biersteker, Hudáková, & Tourinho 2016
UN	United Nations
UNGA	United Nations General Assembly
UNICEF	United Nations Children's Fund
UNSC	Security Council of the United Nations
U.S.	United States of America
USD	United States Dollar (US$)
WMD	weapons of mass destruction

Abstract

Economic sanctions are a popular tool of modern foreign policy. However, they may have a negative collateral damage to the political system of the target state. The leader shifts the costs of sanctions from his supporters to the population and uses the opportunity to centralize power. Furthermore, the external threats enable him to blame enemies abroad for his (economic) mismanagement. Though anecdotal and empirical evidence supports the basic argument, it is not clear under which circumstances sanctions have an autocratizing effect. Newer data on sanctions and regimes enable to test the most plausible hypotheses. Several variables try to explain the negative impact of economic sanctions on the level of democracy: the economic costs of sanctions, a democratic goal of sanctions (sanctions designed for improving democracy), a personalist regime, the level of regime legitimacy, the level of economic vulnerability, and the level of development. All sanctions by the UN, the EU and the U.S. that were imposed between 1990 and 2015 are used for the quantitative analysis. Surprisingly, none of the sanctions variables had a negative impact on the level of democracy. Both economic costs and democratic goal correlate with a higher level of democracy, as well as the level of development. The analysis contributes with several key findings to the debate: Sanctions with high economic costs do not cause autocratization. Aid sanctions and arms embargoes correlate with a higher level of democracy; the type of sanction is crucial for its side-effects. Sanctions are not a binary variable and should not be used as such in quantitative analyses. Sanctions have a de jure goal and a de facto goal; an evaluation of sanctions that is only based on the de jure goal is misleading. In summary, sanctions are not as bad – and perhaps not as useless – as many fear.

Keywords: Economic sanctions; Coercive diplomacy; Regime types; Autocracies; Democratization

Executive summary

Research puzzle

Anecdotal evidence suggests that economic sanctions have a negative impact on the political sphere. Several prominent cases in the last decades show how leaders of a state that is targeted by sanctions use those to their advantage. One example is Yugoslavia in the early 1990s. The UNSC imposed comprehensive economic sanctions on Yugoslavia to end Milosevic's involvement in the war in Bosnia-Herzegovina. However, the sanctions rents benefited mainly Milosevic and his clique. They boosted a black market that gave rise to a powerful criminal class with ties to the regime; and the disruption of trade benefited state-owned enterprises and the economic-political elite. Moreover, Milosevic could blame outsiders for his own economic mismanagement. The external threat created a pro-regime rally around the flag. These sanctions lead to a weakening of the opposition and democratic reform efforts.

Large-N evidence supports the claim that sanctions have an autocratizing effect. Scholars found that sanctions increase repression, cause protectionism, strengthen the leader, enhance economic transfers from the population to the leader's coalition, decrease the level of political freedoms and democracy in general. Though there is anecdotal and large-N evidence, it is still puzzling why sanctions have such a negative collateral damage. Especially in the last decades, sanctions were increasingly aimed at enhancing the level of democracy and designed in the respective way. New data and variables that combine insight from different strands of literature encourage to ask the question: Why do some economic sanctions have a negative impact on the level of democracy in the target state but others not?

Sanctions are defined as a set of rules that restrict a state. Economic sanctions are a set of economic rules that restrict a state. They are imposed by a state, a regional organization or an international organization, on another state or entities or individuals related to that state. By coercing, constraining or signaling, sanctions are imposed to achieve a non-economic policy goal. Sanctions can include non-economic measures (such as visa ban, diplomatic sanctions). Sanctions can include economic measures (trade ban, investment ban), then they are called economic sanctions. Usually, sanctions include non-economic and economic measures.

Literature review

Despite their long history, economic sanctions became target of an academic debate only in the last decades. Especially after the numbers of sanctions exploded in the 1990s, the debate got more aggressive. The overwhelming majority of scholars holds a very negative view about the success of sanctions. After the devastating impact of sanctions in Iraq was known, the focus of academics shifted from the question of success to the question of impact, and scholars published many analyses on the unintended side-effect of economic sanctions on mainly humanitarian issues like health, but also on human rights and democracy.

Recent articles analyze in large-N studies the impact of sanctions on the level of democracy: Using data between 1972 and 2000, Peksen et al. find that the effects of economic sanctions significantly reduce the level of democracy in the target state.[1] They argue that sanctions restrict the flow of goods to the targeted country, the remaining goods within the state are controlled by the regime which gets more powerful than before. Using newer data, Soest et al. conclude that sanctions with a democratic goal correlate with an increased level of democracy in the targeted state, thus suggesting that democratic sanctions are successful.[2]

Hypotheses

The dependent variable is the level of democracy. *Definition: A liberal-democratic state is a state with an overall high level of political rights, civil liberties, and state capacity.* Political rights include political participation and political pluralism; civil liberties include individual rights, checks and balances and restrictions of the executive; state capacity refers to governance and performance of the state. An autocratic state is a state with an overall low level of political rights, civil liberties, and state capacity. The low level of state capacity can be explained with the low level of public goods invested by the leader. He invests resources into his supporters to buy their loyalty, not into the state.

There is no universally accepted variable that can explain either democratization or autocratization. Consequently, a large number of explanatory variables can be found in democratization literature. Due to methodological reasons the number of variables is limited. Anecdotal and empirical evidence and current research suggest the use of explanatory variables from three different spheres: the

1 Peksen & Drury 2010.
2 Soest & Wahman 2015.

impact and design of sanctions, the political system of the targeted state, and economic characteristics of the target state.

Hypothesis 1: The higher the economic costs of the sanctions to the target state are, the more likely is a negative impact on the level of democracy in the target state. Economic costs of sanctions are the main argument in many articles. High economic costs make success and unintended side-effects more likely. In many cases, they hurt the opposition more than the government. Furthermore, the regime's monopoly on law gives members of the leader's coalition a huge advantage in conducting illegal (or somewhat legal) activities. Additionally, economic sanctions lead to protectionism and, in the long-term, to the rise of powerful interest groups that lobby for market protection. Definition: Economic costs of sanctions is the amount of wealth of the target state that gets lost due to sanctions.

Hypothesis 2: The less sanctions focus on democracy, the more likely is a negative impact on the level of democracy. Sanctions with a democratic goal correlate with an increased level of democracy, find Soest & Wahman.[3] They are designed in an effective way not to have a negative effect on the level of democracy. Definition: The democratic goal of sanctions is the explicitly stated aim of sanctions senders to increase the level of democracy by using these sanctions.

Hypothesis 3: The more personalized rule in the target country is, the more likely is a negative impact on the level of democracy. Sanctions literature suggests that the target's regime type is one of the most important factors of sanctions success. Based on Geddes,[4] Wright focuses on institutional differences among regimes and distinguishes personalist regimes from institutionalist regimes (military, dominant party, corporatist/monarchist).[5] Personalist leaders can more easily redistribute goods in times of economic crises such as sanctions. Furthermore, institutionalized regimes offer peaceful leadership change through succession rules, whereas a personalist regime will shift the economic costs away from his key supporters to other groups and the population. The book adds liberal democracies to institutionalist regimes to categorize the whole universe of regimes. Definition: A personalist regime is a regime in which power is institutionalized on a low level. Effective rule and leadership succession depend on one person or his personal network.

Hypothesis 4: The higher the level of legitimacy of the ruler in the target country is, the more likely is a negative impact on the level of democracy. A psychological

3 Soest & Wahman 2015, p. 957.
4 Geddes 1999, pp. 121–122.
5 Wright 2008, p. 323.

effect might strengthen the leader: A high level of legitimacy reduces the costs of loyalty for the leader. A recent large-N study finds that "sanctions strengthen authoritarian rule if the regime manages to incorporate their existence into its legitimation strategy."[6] Definition: Regime legitimacy is the acceptance of political authority.

Hypothesis 5: The higher the level of economic vulnerability of the target economy is, the more likely is a negative impact on the level of democracy. A country with a low level of economic interdependence is used to a non-trade situation and does not need to change its economic rules much. A country that is exposed to the world economy on a high level, needs to adapt to the sanctions regime. Independently from the real economic costs of sanctions, the country will adopt policies that protect crucial sectors of the economy. Protectionism strengthens the role of politics in business and the role of business in the economy, thus leading to clientelism and kleptocracy. Definition: Vulnerability is the ability to be influenced or hurt. The economic vulnerability of a country is an indicator for the degree how much a country may be affected by external economic shocks. It can be measured by the economy's dependence on export and import with the world.

Hypothesis 6: The less developed the target country is, the more likely is a negative impact of economic sanctions on the level of democracy. One of the most famous theories in comparative politics is that democratic and economic development are systematically interrelated. Lipset claimed that democracy was enabled by a process of modernization that includes industrialization, education, and more factors.[7] Definition: Development is a process of change and advance. The development level of a country is an indicator that measures how advanced a country is in important areas such as wealth, education and healthcare.

Mechanism

The theoretical model assumes three main players within a political system: the leader/leadership, his winning coalition, and the population.[8] The secret of leader survival lies in the careful balancing of repression and loyalty rewards (economic transfers or political power) and its constant re-adjustment. Political stability is understood as the equilibrium of these three elements (economic transfers,

---

6 Grauvogel & Soest 2014, p. 635.

7 Lipset 1959, p. 80.

8 The model is based on Wintrobe's view of a political system as marketplace; Wintrobe 1990.

political power, repression). External shocks such as economic sanctions can disrupt the system. Usually, sanctions decrease the leader's budget. As soon as he is no longer able to provide goods to his supporters or the population, his political survival is in danger. If the winning coalition is not satisfied, it might attempt a coup (vertical threat). If the population is not satisfied, it might protest and attempt a revolution (horizontal threat). It depends on many factors how the leader is going to react to crises. His tools are always the same: economic transfers, political rights, repression/civil liberties. They belong to different spheres of the state, and regime stability is based on an equilibrium of these tools. They mirror the tripartite definition of democracy and autocracy (state capacity, civil liberties, political rights). The factors that explain the leader's reaction and the following process are the variables (and their combination) mentioned in the previous section.

Before applying repression or redistributing political power, the leader will transfer economic goods, either to his winning coalition (private goods) or the population (public goods). In a personalist regime (variable 3), he has to increase goods to his coalition because the coalition supports him in exchange for monetary advantages. If the economic vulnerability of the country is low (variable 5), the leader might not need to change the mix of redistribution because the economy (and his budget) is not very much affected. The higher the economic costs of sanctions are (variable 1), the more difficult is the remix of goods. Very high economic costs can decrease the leader's budget substantially, and he might not have any goods, neither for the population nor for his coalition, and may rely on repression.

In contrast, a high level of development (variable 6) helps the population to decrease the information asymmetry and to overcome the collective action problem, which may lead to a revolutionary attempt. When the population, however, agrees on the leader's offer (more or less public goods), it can lead to stability and an equilibrium. This happens especially when the level of legitimacy of the leader is very high (variable 4), and when the leader succeeds in stimulating nationalist feelings. In such cases, sanctions have a so-called rally around the flag effect. Another threat to the leadership comes from his winning coalition: If the coalition does not accept the goods it got (or didn't get), it can stage a coup d'état (vertical threat). A coup is more likely if the sanctions target specific groups within the system as most democratic sanctions do (variable 2).

After facing the mentioned vertical and horizontal threats, the leader still has two tools: The first one is increased (or also decreased) repression of the population or a purge of his coalition. If repression is too expensive or not effective, he can rely on his second tool: (de-)centralization of his political power. He can centralize political power, or he can establish political institutions and co-opt oppositional forces or enfranchise larger parts of the population. His actions rely on the mix of variables.

Methodology

The unit of analysis is the country-year of countries that were targets of sanctions (n =1440). Due to data issues, only sanctions with the UN, the EU or the U.S. as sender are considered. Only sanctions that were imposed between 1990 and 2015 and were in place for more than one year are included (60 target countries). In addition to the known sanctions datasets HSEO, GIGA, TIES, and TSC, primary sources such as the UNSC resolutions and other legal texts are used. The dependent variable is the change of the level of democracy. In order to compensate for the flaws of both scores, a combined score of Freedom in the World and Polity IV is used.

Sanctions variables: Variable 1, economic costs of sanctions to the target state, proved to be most difficult to operationalize. If the measurement is only based on the design, the results will be misleading. The most comprehensive sanctions will have no impact, if the pre-sanctions trade level is close to zero (as North Korea post-1993 shows). If the measurement is based on absolute numbers such as the decline of GDP, it is impossible to distinguish the sanctions effects from other effects such as economic stagnation (cf. post-2014 sanctions against Russia). Therefore, most scholars simply estimate the economic damage done by sanctions. This book uses a combination of ex-ante threat (using GIGA) and ex-post damage (using TIES or HSEO). Variable 2, democratic goal of sanctions, is based on the GIGA sanctions dataset. Each sanction episode that explicitly focuses on democracy is coded as 1; otherwise, it is coded as 0 (dummy variable).

Regime variables: Variable 3, personalist regime, is a dummy variable based on Geddes et al.'s Autocratic Regimes dataset (GWF). In addition, liberal democracies are coded as non-personalist. Variable 4, regime legitimacy, is taken from the State Fragility Index and Matrix (SFIM).

Economic variables: Variable 5, economic vulnerability, measures the export dependency of the target state. The World Bank provides comprehensive data on the exports of goods and services in percent of the GDP. Variable 6, development, uses data from the Human Development Index (HDI), with the sub-indicators life expectancy at birth, expected years of schooling, mean years of schooling, and GNI per capita.

Control variables: One variable for natural resources controls for the resource curse hypothesis, using World Bank data. Another variable controls for civil war, using the dataset Major Episodes of Political Violence (MEPV).

The econometric model for the variables is:

$democracy=\alpha^1 costs+\alpha^2 goal+\alpha^3 personalism+\alpha^4 legitimacy+\alpha^5 vulnerability+\alpha^6 development+\beta^1 resources+\beta^2 war+\mu it$

Data type: panel data; regression analysis with two-step system GMM (SYSGMM); statistical software: Stata 14.

Findings

There is no correlation between any of the sanctions variables and an increased level of autocracy. Instead, some of the variables show a correlation between sanctions and an increased level of democracy, some are not significant at all.

Variable	*Hypothesis*	*Result*
IV 1: Economic costs	The higher the economic costs of the sanctions to the target state are, the more likely is a negative impact on the level of democracy in the target state.	Not confirmed, opposite correlation: The higher the economic costs of the sanctions to the target state are, the higher is the level of democracy.
IV 2: Democratic goal	The less sanctions focus on democracy, the more likely is a negative impact on the level of democracy.	Confirmed. Furthermore, sanctions with a democratic goal correlate with a higher level of democracy.
IV 3: Personalist regime	The more personalized rule in the target country is, the more likely is a negative impact on the level of democracy.	Not confirmed, no correlation.
IV 4: Regime legitimacy	The higher the level of legitimacy of the targeted regime is, the more likely is a negative impact on the level of democracy.	Not confirmed, no correlation.
IV 5: Economic vulnerability	The higher the level of economic vulnerability of the target economy is, the more likely is a negative impact on the level of democracy.	Confirmed, but weak and negligible impact.

(*continued on next page*)

Variable	*Hypothesis*	*Result*
IV 6: Development	The less developed the target country is, the more likely is a negative impact on the level of democracy.	Confirmed. Furthermore, the more developed the target country is, the more likely is a positive impact on the level of democracy.

Variable 1: Previous literature argued that sanctions have a negative impact on the level of democracy, especially when they are comprehensive. Economic theory suggests an even stronger political impact with higher economic costs. The present analysis, however, did not confirm that, and found a correlation with a higher degree of democracy instead. Economic sanctions do not cause autocratization, both variables do not even correlate. This does not necessarily mean that sanctions are a cause of democratization, but it shows that anecdotal evidence of cases of sanctions with a negative impact on the level of democracy cannot be generalized. The finding is in line with the most basic sanctions mechanism that was described as naïve: Sanctions with high economic costs disrupt the targeted political system and have transitional effects, perhaps in the context of a global, regional or temporal trend. External punishment legitimizes oppositional forces and may help the citizens to overcome their collective action problem.

Variable 2: Democratic sanctions (sanctions with the goal of improving democracy) correlate with a higher level of democracy. In these cases, sender states impose sanctions in a smart way to target specific groups within the political system of the targeted state. Sanctioning the right groups deprives the leader of crucial support and strengthens oppositional forces. This finding confirms Soest & Wahman.[9]

Variable 3: A personalist regime does not correlate with a higher or lower level of democracy. Many autocratic regimes are perhaps not consolidated enough to distinguish different mechanisms.

Variable 4: A high degree of legitimacy of the regime in the target state does not correlate with a lower or higher level of democracy.

Variable 5: In the main model, a high level of vulnerability (economic interdependency or interconnectedness) correlates with a lower level of democracy,

9 Soest & Wahman 2015.

but the coefficient is negligible and varies substantially in different robustness checks.

Variable 6: As theory and empirical evidence suggests, a higher level of development correlates with a higher level of democracy. The result confirms modernization theory that assumes a relation between economic and political development. A high level of development – education, income, health – decreases the information asymmetry of autocracies and helps the population to overcome the collective action problem.

Types of sanctions: A further analysis looks at the types of sanctions. Arms embargoes correlate with a higher level of democracy. Arms embargoes hurt a ruler's repressive capacity. This may force him to rely on other tools such as decentralizing political power and giving more civil rights. Aid sanctions – the cut of financial aid – also correlate with a higher level of democracy. Foreign aid is often aimed at state building and promoting rule of law and democracy but is also an external revenue source for the leader that helps him providing private goods to his supports, thus financing kleptocratic structures. Once these revenue streams disappear, the leader needs other means to keep the system stable such as providing more political rights. Improving the level of democracy is also the best way to make sure that foreign aid will re-appear in the future.

Implications

The findings have several implications at the metatheoretical and macrotheoretical level. The operationalization showed how difficult it is to operationalize sanctions and to measure their effects or even their "success." In everyday life, the question of success is not that relevant. Policymakers are not so much concerned about the usefulness of sanctions per se; they need to choose the best possible tool in a specific situation under specific circumstances.

Furthermore, sanctions do not exist in a vacuum: In the toolkit of foreign policy, the economy is only one sphere besides diplomacy, military and information.[10] When states apply sanctions against countries with which they have no pre-sanctions trade, sanctions are clearly signaling. The variable economic costs help to see whether sanctions are aimed as a signal. This book distinguishes between de jure and de facto goal: Whereas the *de jure goal* refers to the publicly stated goal, the *de facto goal* refers to Giumelli's taxonomy of coercing, constraining and signaling sanctions.[11] This categorization has the implication

10 Baldwin 1985, pp. 13–14.

11 Giumelli 2010, 2011, 2013, 2015.

that signaling sanctions cannot be evaluated as non-successful just because they did not reach their ambitious goal.

There are more methodological implications of the findings. Democratic sanctions after 2000 have a much stronger positive effect on the level of democracy than those before. This may indicate that the sanctions re-design around 2000 made the sanctions tool much more sophisticated. However, the basic problem of all quantitative sanction research is the quantification of sanctions. It is extremely difficult if not impossible to compare them with each other and to describe their effects. Large-N analyses have only limited validity.

Policy recommendations

Policymakers need to be aware of different mechanisms of sanctions. Some sanctions are coercing, others constraining, others signaling. The goal does not need to be communicated publicly – information asymmetry is an important good in international relations. However, policymakers need to be aware of different mechanisms of sanctions.

Policymakers should recognize so-called secondary sanctions as normal sanctions against their state. Secondary sanctions are not some sort of collateral damage of 'normal' sanctions. Instead, they directly target a state and its economy.

Policymakers should develop sanctions and counter-sanctions capabilities. Sanctions need to be implemented properly. Numbers suggest that the EU is under-developed regarding its sanctions capabilities, especially in comparison with the U.S. Recent so-called secondary sanctions by the U.S. made clear that the EU is not only sender but also target of sanctions.

Lessons learned

1. Sanctions with high economic costs do not cause autocratization. The findings of this book debunk the argument that economic sanctions with high economic costs are responsible for an autocratization of the targeted state as a myth. The analysis conducted in this book finds a significant correlation between sanctions with high economic costs and the level of democracy. Cases that suggest otherwise are not prototypical sanctions cases but infamous anomalies, particularly known for their "failure". In other cases, sanctions follow (not cause) autocratization, such as post-2014 sanctions against Russia. This book does not claim that economic sanctions with high economic costs cause democratization, but it claims that they do not cause

autocratization – there is no correlation, so the claimed causality cannot be true.

2. Aid sanctions and arms embargoes correlate with a higher level of democracy. The type of sanction is crucial for its side-effects. Arms embargoes hurt the repressive capacity in the targeted state. Aid sanctions are particularly harmful to an autocrat because they directly hurt his revenue streams. Once they disappear, he needs to rely on other tools to keep the system stable – such as granting political rights. This will also guarantee the lifting of sanctions. This finding should be an incentive for further research.
3. Sanctions are not a binary variable and should, therefore, not be used as such in quantitative analyses. Though this seems to be self-evident, many articles use sanctions as a dummy variable. Similarly, many scholars assume that comprehensive economic sanctions equal high economic costs of sanctions. This is wrong. High economic costs result from the affected trade linkage and the implementation of sanctions. Sanctions consist of a complex net of legal regulation and laws, from different bodies, and their goal, design, and scope need to be included in a quantitative analysis of sanctions. Using sanctions as a binary variable is misleading and may suggest wrong findings.
4. Sanctions have a de jure goal and a de facto goal; an evaluation of sanctions that is only based on the de jure goal is misleading. Whereas the de jure goal refers to a publicly stated purpose of sanctions, the de facto goal refers to the inherent mechanism (coercing, constraining, signaling). Many sanctions function as a signal; they should not be evaluated as non-successful just because they did not reach their de jure goal. An evaluation of sanctions needs to include the de facto goal, though it may be very difficult to establish in most cases.

In conclusion, sanctions are not as bad – and probably not as useless – as academic and non-academic debates suggest. When policymakers want to employ them, they should not forget that the economy is only one sphere in foreign policy. The right combination of tools is necessary to achieve a goal.

1 Sanctions: Useful toys of diplomacy or disastrous weapons of mass destruction?

1.1 Anecdotal evidence

1.1.1 Yugoslavia 1992–1995

> "The Security Council [decides] that all States shall prevent [the] import into their territories of all commodities and products originating in the Federal Republic of Yugoslavia (Serbia and Montenegro) exported therefrom after the date of the present resolution [...]."
>
> —*UNSC Resolution 757, 1992-05-30*

Belgrade, May 1992: The United Nations Security Council (UNSC) just had announced to impose the most comprehensive economic sanctions on the Federal Republic of Yugoslavia (FRY) it ever imposed. These sanctions should end Slobodan Milosevic's involvement in the war in Bosnia-Herzegovina. The ban includes import, export, financial transactions, and even academic and cultural cooperation and Yugoslavia's participation in international sports events.[12] These sanctions are described as "the most rigorous implementation effort ever attempted in the history of sanctions."[13]

Years later, scholars write that the sanctions significantly strengthened Milosevic and his clique, they increased his budget, his power and the overall level of repression,[14] and they "undercut democratic reform movements."[15] A powerful criminal class with ties to the regime emerged which could benefit from the black market. While the middle class impoverished and half of the population slipped below the poverty level, 5 percent of the population have become enormously rich.[16] Sanctions "reflect an effort to manipulate the vulnerabilities that come from economic interdependence, but sanctions can unintentionally foster clandestine forms of interdependence."[17] The literature on sanctions against Yugoslavia found three reasons for this surprising outcome:

---

12 Brooks 2002, p. 46.

13 Andreas 2005, p. 357.

14 Kaempfer, Lowenberg, & Mertens 2004, p. 46.

15 Cortright & Lopez 2000c, p. 75.

16 Brooks 2002, p. 47.

17 Andreas 2005, p. 357.

First of all, the sanctions unintentionally boosted a thriving black market, that gave rise to a powerful criminal class with ties to the regime. Smugglers controlled the trade in oil and other goods.[18] Milosevic's son even became the smuggling head in one border area.[19] Smuggling was seen as a patriotic duty by the regime and publicly praised. It led to a criminalizing of society which didn't end with the fall of Milosevic – the criminalized collateral damage of sanctions had a long-lasting, post-sanctions legacy.[20]

Second, the disruption of trade benefited state-owned enterprises, which could sell their products independently from their quality. The economic (-political) elite had an interest in maintaining the sanctions.[21] The regime was able to gain a large share of sanctions rents, not only through criminal activities but also through centralizing the distribution of goods. These sanctions rents "might be smaller than the earnings from legitimate pre-sanctions trade but they have the advantage of accruing directly to the regime and its immediate circle of supporters."[22] Furthermore, the regime systematically destroyed and appropriated properties by minorities and citizens that were not part of the winning coalition.[23]

And third, the sanctions enabled Milosevic to blame others for his economic mismanagement and to increase Serbian nationalism, which resulted in a pro-regime rally around the flag.[24] The Milosevic regime became "a mixture of communist heritage and a nationalist mafia that monopolized the still existing resources."[25]

What were the political results? The sanctions weakened the opposition forces: Middle-class liberals and students left the country. Sanctions on academic cooperation hurt intellectuals. Independent media were isolated. The sanctions strengthened the regime: The enemy abroad lead to hardline nationalism. The economic-political elite gained the sanctions rents. Powerful criminal gangs with ties to the apparatus rose with a long legacy.[26] The economic sanctions against

18 Brooks 2002, pp. 46–47.
19 Andreas 2005, p. 341.
20 Andreas 2005, p. 335.
21 Woodward 1995b, p. 294.
22 Kaempfer, Lowenberg, & Mertens 2004, p. 39.
23 Woodward 1995a; cf. Peksen 2017, p. 219.
24 Licht 1995.
25 Licht 1995, p. 158.
26 Woodward 1995b, p. 149; Cortright & Lopez 2000c, pp. 75–76.

Yugoslavia "strengthened the very power structures that it sought to challenge, and weakened or even destroyed the civil society and political opposition."[27]

1.1.2 Iran 2006–2016

> "Anytime you see a statement coming out of the government, just remember there's a rat's nest of people fighting underneath the surface."
>
> —*K. Harris on the Iranian leadership*[28]

In July 2015, the Joint Comprehensive Plan of Action was signed, an agreement aimed at ending the nuclear weapons program of the Islamic Republic of Iran. Also, it partly ended the economic sanctions imposed by the United Nations Security Council. Regarding this policy outcome, the sanctions against Iran can be evaluated as a success story, contradicting the pessimist narrative of ineffective sanctions.[29] However, the economic sanctions left their mark on Iranian politics and society: Sanctions enhanced a process of autocratization that started already before the imposition of sanctions. The ruling elite around president Ahmadinejad and his military clique used the absence of external actors to redistribute the resources and to accumulate wealth and power. The business portfolio which his clique grabbed ranged from oil fields to the monopoly of telecommunication. Iran was described as transforming from theocracy to military dictatorship.[30] How could that happen?

The sanctions were imposed in 2006. Iran's announcement of the nuclear program convinced the Security Council (UNSC) of the United Nations to apply economic sanctions, consisting of travel bans, an arms embargo, freezing of assets and commodity boycotts.[31] Both the U.S. and the EU executed additional unilateral sanctions in various fields, especially in the energy (oil and gas), transportation, and financial sector (exclusion from SWIFT), which came close to a full-trade embargo.[32] Four key factors indicated a high impact of economic sanctions in Iran: a significant pre-sanction trade linkage, limited substitution possibilities for sanctioned goods, unexpected sanctions scale, and unexpected SWIFT sanctions.[33]

---

27 Licht 1995, p. 159.

28 Qtd. in Filkins 2013.

29 For a general overview, cf. Nephew 2018.

30 Alfoneh 2013.

31 Giumelli & Ivan 2013, p. 13.

32 Patterson 2013, p. 135.

33 Bergeijk 2015, p. 51.

In the last decades, the overly complex and therefore weak constitutional design with a multipolar distribution of power – which is prone to fights for power – enabled several groups in Iran to accumulate wealth and power. The Islamic Revolutionary Guard Corps (IRGC), a military elite group with strong ideological claims, emerged as most powerful group. Under the presidency of Ahmadinejad almost all members of the cabinet were members of the IRGC, including the president himself.[34] The IRGC cemented not only their political influence but also their economic power, especially in the branches of finance, construction, telecommunication (monopoly on the internet), heroin production[35] and in the oil industry (president Ahmadinejad gave the IRGC the control over an oilfield – before that, the National Iranian Oil Company had the monopoly on the oil and gas sector.[36] Legal and illegal dummy companies at home and abroad and the weak legal system enabled the IRGC to benefit from economic sanctions: Foreign companies had to leave the country – the Supreme Leader announced a "resistance economy."[37] The IRGC closed the gap and strengthened its economic and political standing at home.[38]

Whereas the liberal urban middle class suffered most from the sanctions, the elite-loyal upper-middle class had the most opportunities in circumventing the sanctions and in taking advantage of the vast opportunities the new black market offered. Especially Dubai-based companies and dummy companies of Iranian businessmen and influential actors such as the IRGC were active in illegal oil exports and money laundering.[39] These domestic winners of the economic sanctions also opposed the nuclear deal of president Rouhani. In contrast to the case of Yugoslavia, sanctions didn't cause a rally around the flag, still, they enabled the ruling elite to accumulate a massive amount of wealth and to further centralize power.[40]

1.2 The analytical puzzle

In both the Federal Republic of Yugoslavia and the Islamic Republic of Iran, economic sanctions helped the regime to consolidate its power. The regime

34 Alfoneh 2013, p. 30; Ehteshami 2009, p. 14.
35 Qtd. in Kálnoky 2011.
36 Alfoneh 2013, p. 165.
37 Bazoobandi 2015, p. 64.
38 Alfoneh 2013, pp. 165–191.
39 Bazoobandi 2015, pp. 61–62.
40 Bergeijk 2015, pp. 53, 56; Dizaji & Bergeijk 2013, p. 734.

centralized the distribution of goods and benefited from the sanction rents. The sanctions unwillingly created the opportunity for members of the elite to accumulate even more resources in political and economic terms (power and wealth). In Yugoslavia, disrupted trade led to benefits for the local political, economic, and criminal elite and weakened middle class and opposition. In Iran, we observe since the mid-2000s a shift of power from a so-called theocracy to a military dictatorship. The sanctions helped the new political elite to strengthen its power by offering opportunities in business. The sanctions disadvantaged the middle class and strengthened those in power. In both cases, economic sanctions had a remarkable spill-over effect on the political sphere of the target country. Economic causes and psychological factors explain the process.

The evaluation of sanctions by media was devastating: "Sanctions have seemed only to empower dictators," writes The New York Times in regard to the cases of North Korea, Iraq, Cuba and others,[41] and another journalist describes sanctions as "a policy that helps dictators."[42] Not only media, but also scholars observe similar dynamics to the ones described in the previous chapter in a number of countries that were subject to sanctions, e.g., in Ian Smith's Rhodesia in the 1960s,[43] in Haiti in the early 1990s,[44] in Saddam's Iraq in the 1990s,[45] and in contemporary Russia: Some think that U.S. and EU economic sanctions against Russia led Putin "to consolidate his authoritarian rule."[46] By import substitution policies, "the Russian leadership has been able to reallocate resources to its allies within the elite and also to key economic constituencies across Russia."[47] Also, sanctions enabled the Kremlin to blame the West for the poor performance of the economy and could thus generate a pro-regime rally around the flag.[48]

Besides anecdotal evidence, scholars found empirical evidence that sanctions encourage leaders to increase repression,[49] reduce the level of political freedom in the target country,[50] decrease the level of democracy,[51] they cause protectionism

---

41 The New York Times, 2003-11-08, qtd. in Marinov 2005, p. 575.
42 Weisberg 2006.
43 Rowe 2000.
44 Gibbons & Garfield 1999.
45 Peksen & Drury 2009, p. 401.
46 Feaver & Lorber 2015.
47 Connolly 2015, pp. 37–38.
48 Connolly 2015, p. 38.
49 Wood 2008, p. 489.
50 Peksen & Drury 2009, p. 393.
51 Peksen & Drury 2010.

benefitting the elite,[52] enhance economic transfers from the population to the elite,[53] and they stabilize autocratic rulers with strong claims to legitimacy.[54] With pressure from all sides, a very popular tool of modern foreign relations comes under scrutiny.

Though we have anecdotal and empirical evidence for the described effect, it is puzzling why some (or so many) sanctions increase the level of autocracy. In many cases, sanctions should increase the level of democracy, not decrease them. This book does not analyze the effectiveness of economic coercion but its collateral damage to democracy and its spill-over effect on the internal power structure. Why do some sanctions have an autocratizing impact? The proposed mechanisms are not fully convincing. An analytical gap between case studies, (game) theoretical analysis, and large-N studies urges to specifically ask for the reasons of the deeply disturbing correlation. New data and a combination of autocracy theory and empirical evidence shall help with answering the research question: Why do some economic sanctions have a negative impact on the level of democracy in the target state but others not?

1.3 Relevance and novelty

Research on economic dynamics within the system and their impact on regime stability and breakdown is essential not only because of the autocratic resilience in the last decade. The changing political and ideological landscape, with increased economic protectionism and political nationalism, also leads to the question whether economic sanctions are more damaging than useful in the foreign policy toolbox. To know which circumstances are responsible for an autocratizing effect of sanctions is vital for political decision-making. This study wants to contribute by conducting a comprehensive analysis. Reviewing the existing literature, several issues justify a thorough evaluation of the sanctions-autocracy hypothesis.

Ideological bias: Economic sanctions and their effects are heavily debated in politics, media, and academic scholarship. Some see them as a hawkish demonstration of power, others as a peaceful tool of conflict resolution. The prevailing wisdom in scholarship is that economic sanctions have a negative impact on democracy and human rights and are therefore counterproductive. However, the debate about sanctions and their impact on democracy is shaped by proponents

52 Pond 2017, pp. 1074–1075.

53 Peksen 2017, p. 221.

54 Grauvogel & Soest 2014, cf. Grauvogel, Licht, & Soest 2017.

and opponents and seems to be ideologically biased. There are reasons to suspect that this mirrors the ideological cleavage between realists and liberals in political theory and practice: "[R]ealists tend to denigrate the utility of economic statecraft […], neoliberals believe that economic interdependence can affect the behavior of nation-states for the better."[55] This (quantitative) analysis does not seek to confirm or disconfirm a specific position in the debate and may be helpful in clarifying the facts.

Data bias: Most scholars see economic sanctions as inefficient and even counterproductive, with an (unintended) negative impact on humanitarian issues and democracy. Most of the mentioned studies have a scope of around 1960 to the early 2000s when the standard dataset by Hufbauer et al. was re-introduced.[56] Examples: Peksen claims that sanctions lead to increasing repression, using cases between 1982 and 2000.[57] Peksen and Drury, using cases from 1972 to 2000, write that sanctions reduce the level of political rights and civil liberties.[58] However, sanctions changed a lot since the late 1990s, especially after the experience of the devastating humanitarian impact of sanctions in Iraq. Since then, economic sanctions are mostly combined with measures targeting the elite. Is the collateral damage of economic sanctions still present if we control for the new design of sanctions, and if we consider this issue when selecting the time frame? This study includes cases both before and after 2000.

Economic crises mechanism: Scholars of economic sanctions argue that economic sanctions are causal variables of democratic backsliding: They strengthen the incumbent elite. Comprehensive economic sanctions can have dynamics comparable to those of economic crises. However, many scholars of economic crises think that crises are a causal variable of democratization. They create windows of opportunities in autocratic regimes and catalyze regime change.[59] This contradiction is puzzling and was indicated multiple times as a research desideratum: "scholars should focus on how and under which conditions an economic crisis can be turned into a political crisis that will ultimately endanger a democratic regime."[60] Differing views on the same subject ask for a combination of insights of both study areas. Whereas previous non-anecdotal research on the political side-effects of economic sanctions does not provide a credible

55 Drezner 1999a, p. 8; cf. Portela 2010, p. 10.
56 Hufbauer, Schott, Elliott, & Oegg 2007.
57 Peksen 2009, p. 75.
58 Peksen & Drury 2010.
59 Teorell 2010, p. 75.
60 Erdmann 2011, pp. 27–28.

explanation of the underlying mechanism, economic crisis literature suggests valuable explanations on how a leader can turn an economic crisis into a political opportunity. The theoretical mechanism proposed in this book assumes three players (the leader, his winning coalition, the population), and three goods (repression, economic transfers, political power), with political stability understood as an equilibrium of these goods.

Regime categorization: Previous research suggests that the political constitution of the target state is crucial for the outcome of economic sanctions. So far, studies in this debate didn't distinguish various types of regimes. Scholars recommended to "pay greater attention to the burgeoning work on politics in authoritarian countries,"[61] and to disaggregate different autocratic regime types in future analyses.[62] Among the many possibilities, this book bases its regime categorization on Geddes[63] (personalist, military, single-party, monarchy) and Wright[64] (personalist versus institutionalist), including liberal democracies to categorize the whole universe of regimes.

Sanctions categorization: The main problem of previous sanctions research is the image of sanctions as a binary variable (dummy), which is more than problematic – it is simply wrong. Sanctions consist of a variety of legal texts; in some cases, they are nothing more than a symbol. Most debate contributions distinguish, at maximum, only between "comprehensive" and "targeted" sanctions, which is no satisfying distinction. This book tries to distinguish sanctions according to their economic impact and their goal (and, in a second step, by their design). The reference articles for the present research question do not include this critical factor which is strongly suggested by the sanctions debate, neo-classical trade theory, and economic crises theory.

61 Drezner 2011, p. 104.

62 Soest & Wahman 2012, p. 30

63 Geddes 1999, pp. 121–122.

64 Wright 2008, p. 323.

1.4 Defining and conceptualizing sanctions

> "The term 'economic sanctions' is used in so many different ways that there is much to be said for avoiding it altogether. Unfortunately, the term is so deeply embedded in the literature of economic statecraft that ignoring it is impossible."[65]

There is no consensus in the literature regarding a standard definition of economic sanctions. Instead, several synonyms seem to describe a similar phenomenon: economic coercion, economic statecraft, economic warfare, embargo, boycott, positive and negative sanctions, comprehensive sanctions, targeted sanctions... The naming is often confusing. Several scholars use these terms interchangeably; others offer a more precise and differentiating approach.

Following Russell's fourfold division of forms of power (wealth, armaments, civil authority, influence on opinion)[66] and Lasswell's fourfold division of policy instruments (words, deals, goods, weapons),[67] Baldwin develops the following taxonomy of techniques of *statecraft*: diplomacy (negotiation), military statecraft (use of force), economic statecraft, propaganda (manipulation of information). These four are the tools of statecraft in the international arena (cf. Fig. 1). Policymakers usually use a combination of them.[68] (For Hufbauer et al., however, are sanctions

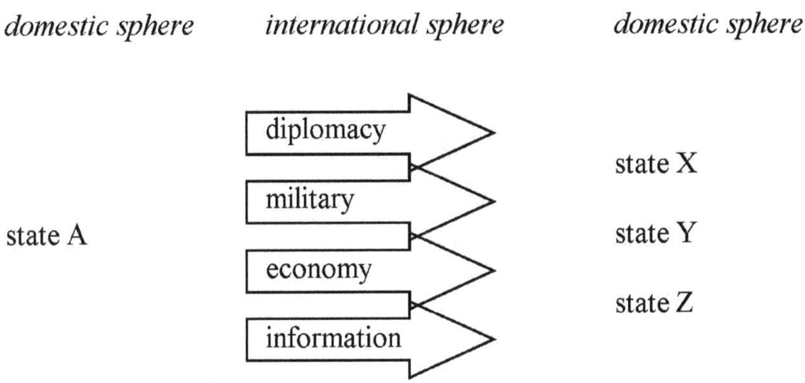

Fig. 1: Techniques of statecraft, based on Russell/Lasswell/Baldwin

65 Baldwin 1985, p. 36.
66 Russell 2004 [1938], p. 4.
67 Lasswell 1958.
68 Baldwin 1985, pp. 13–14.

just a "part and parcel of international diplomacy".[69]) Baldwin says to study statecraft is "to consider the instruments used by policy makers in their attempts to exercise power, i.e., to get other to do what they would not otherwise do."[70]

Among the different forms of statecraft, Baldwin defines *economic statecraft* as "the use of economic means to pursue foreign policy goals,"[71] without clarifying the foreign policy goal. Pape argues for a narrow definition and distinguishes economic sanctions from *trade wars* which refer to economic means (increasing tariffs in a sector, stop oil production) for an economic goal (decrease tariffs in another sector, increasing oil price).[72] Most scholars exclude the pursuit of economic goals from a definition of economic sanctions.

Many academics build their definition of *economic sanctions* on the seminal book by Hufbauer et al.: "We define economic sanctions to mean the deliberate, government-inspired withdrawal, or threat of withdrawal, of customary trade or financial relations."[73] Peksen defines economic sanctions as "deliberate, government-led restrictions of export, import and the flow of finance."[74] Some scholars see boycotts and embargos as synonyms or subtypes of economic sanctions. According to Daoudi et al., a boycott implies no use of (legal or military) force, whereas an embargo is a prohibition of trade by government order; thus it is connected with the force of law.[75] A standard definition of economic sanctions usually contains two central elements, economic means and a political aim: "the coercive measure needs to be economic in nature and its aim needs to be political."[76] More recently, the imposition of sanctions was defined as "creating a set of systematic, overarching rules of behavior."[77]

Baldwin distinguishes further between *positive and negative sanctions*: Whereas negative sanctions are punishments, positive sanctions are rewards.[78] He emphasizes the power of positive sanctions and criticizes political science for excluding them from their concept of power.[79] Other scholars classify the stopping of foreign aid as part of positive sanctions.[80] Bergeijk, using a traditional

69 Hufbauer, Schott, Elliott, & Oegg 2007, p. 5.
70 Baldwin 1985, p. 9.
71 Baldwin 1985, p. 9.
72 Pape 1997, pp. 93–94.
73 Hufbauer, Schott, Elliott, & Oegg 2007, p. 3.
74 Peksen 2014, p. 486.
75 Daoudi & Dajani 1983, pp. 4–5.
76 Portela 2010, p. 1.
77 Nephew 2018, p. 8.
78 Baldwin 2011, p. 706.
79 Baldwin 1971, p. 19.
80 Morrison 2014.

neo-classical trade model, compares a non-sanction situation with economic interdependence and a sanctions situation with autarky.[81]

It is crucial to include the *goal* of sanctions into the definition of sanctions. The success of sanctions is usually assessed based on the goal and on the target's compliance with the goal. A typical categorization of goals, based on official documents, is provided by the sanctions dataset by Portela et al.:[82] democratization, support human rights, fight against narcotics, stop biological and chemical weapons of mass destruction, end nuclear proliferation, termination of bellicosities and/or establishment of peace agreement, fight terrorism (including releasing of hostages).

Economic sanctions can be further categorized with dichotomous typologies like punishing or coercing, substantive or symbolic, expressive or instrumental, or coercive or symbolic. Whereas most scholars, like Hufbauer et al., base the categorization of sanctions goals on policy changes within the target country,[83] few also mention symbolic goals such as punishment, appeasing the audience in the sender state, trying to appear active in the international arena,[84] and trying to influence the behavior of third countries, e.g., deterring and preventing the development of nuclear weapons. Did sanctions against North Korea prevent South Korea and Japan from developing their own nuclear weapons? Sanctions "move freely – even simultaneously – between the world of preventive diplomacy and the world of coercive diplomacy."[85]

Lindsay argues that economic sanctions have a high impact as international or domestic symbols and deterring states, though they likely fail when the goal is compliance.[86] Symbolic sanctions can be aimed at reputation and be applied to areas of culture, education, or sports: "Images matter."[87] If sanctions are symbolic/expressive and show disapproval, they can hardly succeed according to their intended goal, though scholars evaluate them as "non-successful." The fact that states pursue multiple objectives is an explanation why state leaders like sanctions so much despite the opposition from mainstream academia: "To the extent that sanctions impose an injury on the wrongdoer, international sanctions cannot but 'work.' "[88]

Giumelli distinguishes between *coercing*, *constraining* and *signaling* sanctions. Coercing sanctions seek a behavioral change of the target regime. Constraining

81 Bergeijk 2009, pp. 119–120.
82 Portela & Soest 2012 (GIGA sanctions dataset).
83 Hufbauer, Schott, Elliott, & Oegg 2007, pp. 52–53.
84 Drury 2001, p. 486; Nossal 1989.
85 Cortright & Lopez 1995, p. 202.
86 Lindsay 1986.
87 Baldwin 1985, p. 372.
88 Nossal 1989, p. 322.

sanctions aim at undermining the capabilities of the target regime to achieve policy objectives (zero-sum game). Signaling sanctions do not try to reach a certain effect through material damage because they would be ineffective in such cases; instead, they aim at the domestic and the international audience, they stigmatize non-compliance with a norm.[89]

The challenge for scholars (and for the targets of sanctions) is to see the real goal of sanctions, to know what the sanctions are intended for. Information asymmetry can be part of the sender's strategy. Sanctions are not always intended to succeed in their ostensible goal.[90] "Targets and goals are usually multiple," writes Baldwin;[91] Kaempfer et al. distinguish between real and stated goal.[92] In addition to Giumelli's taxonomy, this book adds a distinction between *de jure goal* and *de facto goal*. Whereas the de jure goal refers to the official goal stated in the legal text, for example in the respective resolution of the UN Security Council, the de facto goal refers to the mechanism, what Giumelli describes as coercing, constraining or signaling. This categorization of sanctions has implications for the success debate: Often, sanctions pursue "high policy" goals (security or political issue).[93] It is highly unlikely that a dictator will agree on retiring. Such sanctions are often intended as a signal. An evaluation of sanctions, based on the de jure goal, is, therefore, misinterpreting the very nature of sanctions.

There are different players in the sanctions game. The *sender* is the executive institution of a state (government), a regional organization (European Commission in the EU) or the UN (Security Council). The *de jure target* is related to another state or a state-like entity (such as state-like terror groups: ISIS/Daesh, Al Shaabab, Al Qaeda). The target can be further distinguished on the macro level (whole state or whole economy), the meso level (specific sectors or entities), or the micro level (individuals). Scholars mention further *de facto targets*: Barber distinguishes primary (target-related), secondary (sender-related) and tertiary (international system related) objectives.[94] Sender or system-related goals are often justified with a target-related issue.[95] Hufbauer et al. see a triple signal of sanctions: to the sender, to allies, to domestic audience.[96]

89 Giumelli 2010, 2011, 2013, 2015.
90 Dashti-Gibson, Davis, & Radcliff 1997, p. 616.
91 Baldwin 1985, p. 371.
92 Kaempfer & Lowenberg 1988, p. 792.
93 Drezner 2003, p. 650.
94 Barber 1979.
95 Jones & Portela 2014, p. 15.
96 Hufbauer, Schott, Elliott, & Oegg 2007, p. 7.

Finally, sanctions can be distinguished according to their *type*. The sanctions dataset by Portela et al. provides a useful categorization of types of sanctions:[97] arms embargo, freezing of financial assets held by individuals, aid sanctions, commodity embargo (import or export of selected commodities such as natural resources), comprehensive trade embargo (complete ban of trade and financial relations), diplomatic sanctions (also includes suspension of membership in international organizations), flight ban (prohibition of operating flights), financial sanctions (investment ban, ban on financial transactions), interruption of military cooperation, visa ban (includes travel ban).

Furthermore, sanctions can target soft power issues (such as cultural and academic cooperation or participation in sports events). Portela et al. add another category for sanctions imposed to enforce sanctioning. This type of sanctions, also called secondary sanctions, is similar to the other types of sanctions, they just refer to a new target. The mechanism (economic means, political goal) is the same.

In this book, sanctions are defined as a set of rules that restrict a state. Economic sanctions are a set of economic rules that restrict a state. They are imposed by a state, a regional organization or an international organization, on another state or entities or individuals related to that state. By coercing, constraining or signaling, sanctions are imposed to achieve a non-economic policy goal. Sanctions can include non-economic measures (such as arms embargo, visa ban, diplomatic sanctions). Sanctions can include economic measures (trade ban, investment ban), then they are called economic sanctions. In most cases, both economic and non-economic measures are applied together; therefore, the terms sanctions and economic sanctions are usually used interchangeably. In this book, the term economic sanctions refers to economic or mixed measures, whereas the term sanctions refers to non-economic measures.

1.5 Outline of the book

This book is structured in three parts, each consisting of two chapters. The first part reviews the debates in research on economic sanctions and on autocratic regimes, and presents the main variables mentioned in these debates. The second part provides an analytical framework for the impact of economic sanctions on political regimes. The third part tries to reply to the original research question.

The first part of the book, consisting of Chapter 2 and Chapter 3, searches in the literature for the most relevant factors for the research question. Chapter 2

97 Portela & Soest 2012 (GIGA sanctions dataset).

starts with a historical overview on the development of economic sanctions and presents the debates that shaped sanctions research in the past decades: first, the debate about the unintended impact of sanctions on state and society, second, the debate about the effectiveness of sanctions. The last part is particularly important because similar variables might be relevant for the present research question. Among those variables are design-related variables (such as economic costs to the target, duration, targeted measures, threats, symbolic use) and state-related variables (such as institutions in the sender and target state, international institutions, multilateral versus unilateral sanctions, allies, issue). The chapter ends with a look at the autocratization debate, and at potential reasons of the alleged democratic backlash in the last decade.

Chapter 3 builds hypotheses. It extracts from the previous literature review the most likely variables which may explain why some economic sanctions have a negative impact on the level of democracy in the target state but others not. Some of these variables refer to the design of sanctions, some to the political system of the target state, and others to economic characteristics of the target state. After each variable, a hypothesis is formulated. The chapter also includes a detailed definition of the dependent variable democracy, based on a continuous scale. The chapter combines literature, examples, and debates.

The second part of the book is the analytical core and provides the theoretical and analytical tools for the last part. Chapter 4 introduces the causal mechanism which connects international economic sanctions and domestic autocratization. First, it presents the players – leadership, winning coalition, population – then, it presents the "market of political survival." According to the market analogy, political life can be seen as a market in which goods are exchanged. The chapter includes the variables identified in the previous chapter and ends with modeling the game of survival. After establishing a sound theoretical model, Chapter 5 selects and quantifies the cases, operationalizes all variables, gives information on the limitations of the study and ends with the econometric model.

The third part of the book evaluates the results. Chapter 6 presents the findings. It starts with the main model, includes extensive robustness checks, and interprets the findings in line with the hypotheses established in Chapter 3. Chapter 7 presents metatheoretical implications for the academic sanctions debate (ontological, methodological, epistemological), provides research recommendations (related to sanctions research and regime research) and policy recommendations, reflects the use of economic statecraft, and concludes with a list of lessons learned.

The appendix includes an overview of the cases of economic sanctions in the last decades that was used for the database, a list of types and goals of sanctions, and the code and results of the quantitative analysis.

Part I Reviewing

"Apply this economic, peaceful, silent deadly remedy and there will be no need for force. The boycott is what is substituted for war."

—U.S. president Woodrow Wilson, 1919[98]

"[E]conomic sanctions [...] may have contributed to more deaths during the post-Cold War era than all weapons of mass destruction throughout history."[99]

98 Qtd. in J. Gordon 1999, p. 123.
99 Mueller & Mueller 1999, p. 43.

2 The collateral damage of sanctions

Part I of this book reviews the literature and develops hypotheses. This chapter reviews the literature on economic sanctions and autocracies. It starts with a brief overview over the historical development of sanctions, looks at the impact of economic sanctions on the state and its political system, summarizes the determinants of sanctions success, and finally looks at the so-called autocratic reversal and variables mentioned in the autocratization debate.

2.1 Economic sanctions in an age of interdependence

2.1.1 Pre-modern era

Economic statecraft existed a long time before our modern Westphalian state system came into existence, and was already advised by Sunzi, Thucydides, and Machiavelli to policymakers.[100] An early example of classical economic sanctions was applied in 432 BCE in Ancient Greece, the Megarian decree.[101] Some authors see the ancient and medieval siege of cities – such as the Roman siege of Jerusalem in 72 CE and the Mongolian siege of Baghdad in 1257[102] – as the forerunner of modern sanctions: The close-off of a walled city starves the whole population into submission.[103] The attackers seek a policy change through pressuring the whole society and thereby harming non-combatants.[104] Furthermore, medieval states and state-like entities used multilateral coercion – during the crusades, the papacy banned the sale of war material to the Saracens, and the Hanseatic League regularly employed collective trade boycotts against its enemies.[105]

The modern Westphalian territorial state led to a centralization of power in favor of the "sovereign" ruler and enabled thereby a new dynamic between the political and the economic sphere. The American colonies boycotted British goods in the 1760s; during the Napoleonic Wars (1793–1815), France and Britain engaged in economic warfare; and in the American Civil War (1861–1865), the Northern states cut off the Southern Confederates from foreign imports. Since

100 Peksen & Drury 2009, p. 393.
101 Baldwin 1985, pp. 150–154; Hufbauer, Schott, Elliott, & Oegg 2007, p. 9.
102 Askari, Forrer, Teegen, & Yang 2003, pp. 7–13.
103 Allen 2005, p. 120.
104 J. Gordon 1999, pp. 125–126.
105 Farrall 2007.

then, there was no decade without economic sanctions.[106] However, most of these cases included the use or threat of military force, which influences the political effect. Economic sanctions were mostly used as a tool of warfare, not merely as a tool of foreign policy.

The industry-based economy of the new territorial states and the massive population growth since the 19th century in Europe led to growing international interdependence and a growing interest in economic statecraft. Scientific discovery and technological progress changed the character of both war and economic life.[107] The peace movement around 1900 placed great hope in non-violent conflict resolution such as economic measures. Economic warfare in its modern form has been developed during World War I, with an effectiveness not known before; the Allied blockade was even described as a major factor for Germany's defeat.[108]

2.1.2 League of Nations

In the aftermath of the horrors of World War I, U.S. President Wilson advocated the use of economic sanctions as a substitute for war.[109] A new type of economic sanctions, multilateral sanctions, was then at the heart of the peace-enforcement process of the new-established League of Nations:[110] A member of the league who resorted to war was to be subjected to immediate trade and financial sanctions.[111] In total, the League of Nations is associated with eight sanction episodes. The sanctions targeting smaller states like Yugoslavia, Turkey and Bulgaria were successful; others failed when they targeted more powerful states. The League of Nations failed to sanction Japan for its invasion of China

106 Askari, Forrer, Teegen, & Yang 2003, pp. 7–13; Hufbauer, Schott, Elliott, & Oegg 2007, pp. 39–41.
107 Doxey 1980, p. 11.
108 Doxey 1980, p. 12.
109 J. Gordon 1999, p. 123.
110 Taubenfeld & Taubenfeld 1964, p. 183.
111 The Covenant of the League of Nations 1924, Article 16: "Should any Member of the League resort to war in disregard of its covenants under Articles 12, 13 or 15, it shall ipso facto be deemed to have committed an act of war against all other Members of the League, which hereby undertake immediately to subject it to the severance of all trade or financial relations, the prohibition of all intercourse between their nationals and the nationals of the covenant-breaking State, and the prevention of all financial, commercial or personal intercourse between the nationals of the covenant-breaking State and the nationals of any other State, whether a Member of the League or not. [...]"

in 1931, which would have been a clear case of sanctions according to the legal framework of the League of Nations. The sanctions against fascist Italy after its invasion of Ethiopia failed so miserably – also because they were not supported by states like Germany and the U.S. – that they were removed, and the League of Nations was soon demised.[112]

2.1.3 United Nations

The successor of the League of Nations, the United Nations, should have guaranteed peace and prosperity following the horrors of World War II. However, the Cold War soon disabled the new institutions. During the Cold War, the Security Council of the United Nations (UNSC) applied economic sanctions only one time (in 1965 against Southern Rhodesia). The sanctions against South Africa (starting in 1962) were imposed by the General Assembly and were, therefore, not binding.[113] However, the UNSC applied non-economic measures such as arms embargoes[114] and diplomatic sanctions[115] several times. The end of the Cold War antagonism brought new attention to the UNSC which got the opportunity to shape inter-state relations on a global level actively. One of its favorite tools was the enforcement of economic sanctions, which led to nicknaming the 1990s as "the sanctions decade."[116] The comprehensive sanctions against Iraq, Yugoslavia, and Haiti were considered as failures and followed by military action. Another reason for the dramatic increase in the number of sanctions was the "ever increasing global economic, political, technological, communicative and social linkage."[117] The increasing economic interdependence also created new opportunities in trade strategies and therefore incentives for sanctions.[118] The increasing globalization of crime and the proliferation of weapons of mass destruction (WMD) was another reason for the desire of an effective UNSC which was capable of acting fast and thoroughly. Whereas the UNSC imposed

---

112 Wallensteen 2000, p. 1, p. 16; see also Simons 1999; Askari, Forrer, Teegen, & Yang 2003.
113 Luck 2006.
114 Knight 2004.
115 Doxey 1996.
116 Cortright & Lopez 2000b.
117 Soest & Wahman 2012, p. 6.
118 Bergeijk 1995, p. 445.

sanctions against only one country between 1945 and 1990, it imposed sanctions against 14 countries between 1990 and 2000.[119]

2.1.4 Re-design: Targeted sanctions

A major trend shaped the use of sanctions in the last two decades: The combination of comprehensive economic sanctions with so-called targeted sanctions. Mainly thee arguments caused this re-design of economic sanctions: the first one was the question of success. The general optimism of the 1990s in International Relations theory and practice was quickly overshadowed by the genocides in the Western Balkans and Rwanda. Economic sanctions successfully contributed to the end of Apartheid in South Africa, but they apparently failed in many other cases, most notably in the case of Haiti and Iraq. Though Iraq lost half of its GNP in lost trade,[120] Saddam refused to back down, and military force was necessary to restore the independence of Kuwait.

Secondly, the Iraqi case had devastating humanitarian consequences: During the comprehensive sanctions of the UNSC against Iraq, 500,000 children died, and the and the country's child mortality rate almost doubled.[121] Mueller et al. write: "economic sanctions may well have been a necessary cause of the deaths of more people in Iraq than have been slain by all so-called weapons of mass destruction throughout history."[122] Media, scholars, and politicians blamed the sanctions for these dead, and a transnational network of activists, NGOs and IGOs campaigned against sanctions.[123] The Economist wrote in 1999: "Economic sanctions are a blunt policy tool, liable to give anybody but their intended target a bloody nose."[124] Comprehensive economic sanctions, so this second argument, lead to suffering of the weak and innocent population, whereas the elite finds ways to circumvent the sanctions.

The third argument was that economic sanctions were not only ineffective and had a terrifying humanitarian impact, but they were even counterproductive

---

119 Target countries (year of imposition): Iraq (1990), the former Yugoslavia (1991, 1992 and 1998), Libya (1992), Liberia (1992), Somalia (1992), parts of Cambodia (1992), Haiti (1993), parts of Angola (1993, 1997 and 1998), Rwanda (1994), Sudan (1996), Sierra Leone (1997 and 2000), Afghanistan (1999) and Ethiopia and Eritrea (2000). Source: Cortright & Lopez 2000a.

120 Drezner 1998, p. 709.

121 Surveys quoted in Dyson & Cetorelli 2017, p. 1.

122 Mueller & Mueller 1999, p. 51.

123 Hawkins & Lloyd 2003.

124 Qtd. in Slavov 2007, p. 1701.

and strengthened the regimes they should hurt. In Haiti, the military junta used the flourishing black market for accumulating wealth, in Iraq, Saddam stabilized his hard regime.[125]

Already in 1992, the UN High Commissioner for Refugees, Sadako Agata, stated that sanctions should operate "without making the disadvantaged even more disadvantaged."[126] In January 1995, UN Secretary-General Boutros-Ghali said that the imposition of sanctions raises "the ethical question of whether suffering inflicted on vulnerable groups in the target country is a legitimate means of exerting pressure on political leaders whose behavior is unlikely to be affected by the plight of their subjects."[127] He didn't reject the use of sanctions in general but called for reforms in their design. In 2000, Secretary-General Kofi Annan called sanctions a "blunt instrument which hurt large numbers of people who are not their primary targets."[128]

The intensive discussions in media, scholarship and on (inter)state-level led in the 1990s to a re-evaluation of traditional economic sanctions, and eventually to a process in which many states agreed on a re-design. Instead of simply cutting off a country from the international or bilateral market and hurting the country as a whole, "smart" sanctions should target the elite with travel restrictions, asset freezes and other measures: "their logic is to maximize the impact on the responsible individuals […], while minimizing humanitarian consequences for the innocent population."[129] The Swiss-sponsored Interlaken meetings (1998–1999) resulted in a handbook on the implementation of targeted financial measures; the German-sponsored Bonn-Berlin meetings (1999–2000) focused on travel bans and arms embargoes; and the Swedish-sponsored Stockholm meetings (2001) improved the sanctions machinery at the UNSC.[130] The evaluation and re-design of sanctions is considered as a "rare success story of fruitful collaboration between scholars, policymakers, and diplomats."[131] However, even targeted

125 Giumelli 2015, p. 1352.

126 Qtd. in Lopez & Cortright 1997, p. 7.

127 Qtd. in Gordon 2011, p. 317.

128 Qtd. in Allen & Lektzian 2013, p. 121.

129 Giumelli 2015, p. 1352.

130 The official final reports for the Interlaken process: Biersteker, Eckert, Romaniuk, Halegua, & Reid 2001; for the Bonn-Berlin: Brzoska 2001a; Brzoska 2001b; for the Stockholm process: Wallensteen, Staibano, & Eriksson 2003. The United Nations report (the "Fowler report"): Fowler 2000. Cf. Dos Reis Stefanopoulos & Lopez 2014, pp. 49–50; Drezner 2011, pp. 100–101.

131 Drezner 2011, p. 96.

sanctions with the UN as sender have unintended consequences in 91 percent of the cases.[132]

A second trend in the last decades which got not much academic attention is the regionalization of economic sanctions. Besides the UNSC, many regional organizations discovered economic sanctions as a handy tool against members and non-members: the EU, the British Commonwealth, and especially organizations in the Southern hemisphere such as the Organization of American States, the African Union (AU), OPEC, or the Economic Community of West African States (ECOWAS).[133] Unilateral or regional sanctions precede 78 percent of UNSC sanctions.[134] The failed integration of states into a world economy (Doha process), and the further integration of states into regional economic blocs give latter more political power. Whereas the UNSC applies more targeted sanctions and less comprehensive sanctions, regional organization tend to use rather comprehensive economic sanctions.[135]

2.2 Impact on democracy

The main articles dealing with the impact of economic sanctions on the political system were published within the last decade. Some articles deal with the (game) theoretical mechanism, others analyze large-N evidence. Before looking at the theoretical approach underlying most academic contributions and at the mechanism in detail, the next pages introduce the reference articles with a similar research question.

In a series of articles, Peksen & Drury argue that comprehensive economic sanctions have a negative impact on democracy. Sanctions "are more harmful than helpful in the promotion of democratic freedoms and human rights." Economic sanctions, so their argument, reduce the level of political freedoms in the target state. They "enhance the regime's coercive capacity and create incentives for the regime's leadership to commit political repression."[136] Sanctions restrict the flow of goods to the targeted country; the remaining goods within the state are controlled by the leadership. Regime-supporting groups will be more dependent on the regime than before the imposition of sanctions. Analyzing cases between 1970 and 2000, they find a decrease in democracy of 30 percent and a decrease

132 Biersteker, Eckert, Tourinho, & Hudáková 2013, p. 17.
133 Lopez & Cortright 2011, p. 534.
134 Brzoska 2015, p. 1341.
135 Cortright, Gerber, & Loper 2005.
136 Peksen & Drury 2009, pp. 393–398.

of human rights of 70 percent after ten years of sanctions. In an article published one year later and using data from 1972 to 2000, Peksen et al. argue that comprehensive and longer sanctions have a more significant negative impact on the level of democracy (political rights and civil liberties) than limited sanctions. The regime "can use the economic disruption [...] as a strategic tool to manipulate access to and redistribute resources made scarce by sanctions to enhance its authority and subsequently to weaken opposition groups."[137] Analyzing cases between 1960 to 2005, Peksen finds that sanctions with high economic costs push the regime to "pursue predatory policies" and to "selective expropriation and politically motivated redistribution of private property." This policy of predation compensates the regime and its coalition "for the decline in tax base, export earnings, and foreign assistance caused by the sanctions."[138]

Soest & Wahman come to a less depressing conclusion: Using cases between 1990 and 2010, they observe a significant correlation between democratic sanctions and an increased level of democracy in targeted authoritarian countries.[139] They criticize that most studies do not take the explicit goal of sanctions into account. The authors agree with Peksen that autocratic leaders "tend to survive with a mixed strategy of repression and co-optation." However, "repression is generally a less efficient tool for regime survival in the long term than co-optation" which does not cause dissent.[140] From this perspective, economic instability can indeed lead to regime accommodation or regime collapse, especially when a regime relies on a small winning coalition.[141] The costs of democratic sanctions are particularly high for an autocratic regime because "means such as vote rigging, interfering with the media and repressing the opposition are regularly necessary to stay in office."[142] The results of their quantitative analysis support recent democratization research which emphasizes the importance of economic decline for short-term democratization. The authors suggest disaggregating different autocratic regime types in future analyses.[143] The authors use mainly variables related to the democratization literature, but not related to the design of sanctions.

Analyzing cases between 1976 and 2001, Wood finds that comprehensive economic sanctions by the UN and U.S. increase the level of repression. This is the best

137 Peksen & Drury 2010, p. 243.
138 Peksen 2017, p. 218.
139 Soest & Wahman 2012, 2015.
140 Soest & Wahman 2015, p. 960.
141 Bueno de Mesquita & Smith 2010.
142 Soest & Wahman 2012, p. 29.
143 Soest & Wahman 2012, p. 30.

way for the leader to stabilize the regime, protect supporters, decrease the threat posed by oppositional elite members, and decrease popular unrest.[144] Grauvogel et al. find that sanctions can strengthen an authoritarian regime if it "manages to incorporate their existence into its legitimation strategy."[145] This occurs when the target regime has strong claims of legitimacy and only limited (social or economic) linkages to the sender which makes it easier to discredit sanctions. Strong claims to legitimacy enhance the cohesion of the ruling elite and allow regimes to delegitimize any criticism.

The mentioned articles present large-N evidence and give an impression of the main arguments in the debate. Before explaining the economic and psychological mechanisms in detail, it is necessary to briefly point to the theoretical fundament on which most articles are built. Wintrobe, Kaempfer & Lowenberg, and Kirshner apply a public choice approach to economic sanctions. They do not ask whether economic sanctions bring a policy change in the target country but look for the impact of economic sanctions on different interest groups in the target country. Not states, but individuals and groups are the units of analysis.

Wintrobe develops first models that explain how sanctions push autocrats to redistribute goods from the mass citizenry to supporters.[146] His book "The Political Economy of Dictatorship" provides the basis for many analyses dealing with sanctions.[147] Interest groups in the target state fight for political power and economic wealth. The actions of different influential groups within the state are crucial. Autocrats have two ways to survive, repressing opponents and rewarding the loyalty of supporters: "The dictator who wishes to remain in office therefore faces a trade-off between these two alternatives."[148] The size of the support coalition depends on rents and the opposition. Natural resources (in rentier states) lengthen the duration of authoritarian regimes.[149]

Kaempfer and Lowenberg anticipate and prepare with their research more targeted sanctions since the late 1990s: Sanctions can have the desired impact if they are "designed to selectively affect the appropriate interest groups."[150] The relevant task, therefore, is to identify the relevant pressure groups within the target country and to model the impact of economic hardship on these groups

144 Wood 2008, p. 489.
145 Grauvogel & Soest 2014, p. 635.
146 Wintrobe 1990.
147 Wintrobe 1998.
148 Wintrobe 1998, p. 46.
149 Ulfelder 2007.
150 Kaempfer & Lowenberg 1988, p. 786; cf. Kaempfer & Lowenberg 1988, 1992, 1999, 2000, 2007.

and the regime's ability to reward supporters and suppress opposition.[151] The ruling elite is the group which can most easily gain then rents accruing from sanctions-induced changes in terms of trade.[152] The leader's budget increases and his position is strengthened. Building on Wintrobe, Kaempfer et al. write that an autocrat builds his power on legitimation and repression.[153] Repression means the elimination of opposition; loyalty means awarding rents to supporting groups. Therefore, the leader needs a re-allocation of resources. Autocrats can easily allocate scarce resources to their support groups to strengthen elite cohesion, and "redistribute resources to important socio-economic constituencies that will ensure popular, as well as elite, support for the regime."[154]

In a similar approach, Kirshner writes that the pure effectiveness itself ("if they work") is less relevant for policy makers than the question "how they function."[155] His microfoundations approach looks at how groups "within the target state are affected differentially." This is the "key to maximizing the chances that sanctions will be successful."[156] Economic pressure on the central government and the supporting core groups can have different results: The government yields because of a cost-benefit-analysis, or the population or the core group overthrow the regime.

Wood summarizes that economic sanctions encourage the leader of the target state to increase repression of human rights. Economic sanctions deprive a leader of the resources to pay their supporting coalition. Whereas institutional constraints hinder democratic leaders to redistribute costs (and to repress human rights), autocrats can transfer the sanctions costs easier to opposition groups or the population.[157] Costs are redistributed downward. If the leader succeeds in blaming external forces for the economic instability, he might profit from a rally around the flag; otherwise, he will face increasing dissent among the population and opposition groups and will see himself to be forced to increase repression.

2.3 Redistribution of wealth

Conventional wisdom is presented in the statement that sanctions "seemed not only to be ineffective in changing regimes, but even to entrench in power the

151 Cf. Bergeijk 2015, p. 52.
152 Kaempfer, Lowenberg, & Mertens 2004, p. 48.
153 Kaempfer, Lowenberg, & Mertens 2004.
154 Connolly 2015, p. 37.
155 Kirshner 1997, p. 32.
156 Kirshner 1997, p. 42.
157 Wood 2008, p. 494.

groups they were intended to undermine."[158] Through an economic mechanism, economic sanctions influence the political system of the target state. Already Galtung criticizes the "naive theory" which claims that value-deprivation leads to political disintegration because it "disregards the simple principle of adaption."[159] The target economy will simply adapt to the new circumstances and loses its dependence on the sender.[160]

An unintended consequence is that sanctions may hurt the opposition groups they should help, by "strengthening the regime, triggering large-scale emigration, and retarding the emergence of a middle class and civil society."[161] In authoritarian states, comprehensive economic sanctions might redistribute the wealth to the elite and "cripple the middle class." Sanctions have "the perverse effects of enriching the targeted elites, while simultaneously causing even greater impoverishment of civilian populations."[162] Economic sanctions increase the budget of the leader of an autocratic target state and strengthen his rule only if he can gain the profits made possible by the changes in the trade sector.[163]

Another consequence of economic sanctions is the deterioration of the economic security and private property rights of citizens in target countries. The regime "manipulate[s] the domestic economic conditions through arbitrary confiscation and redistribution of private property and wealth."[164] This may include expropriation of private property, seizure of foreign exchange reserves from companies and banks, nationalization of industries, and heavy taxation. These predatory policies shall firstly compensate for the economic damage caused by sanctions and monopolize the economic resources of society, and secondly "weaken the material capabilities of the opposition to mobilize citizens against the regime."[165]

The black market provides more opportunities: In Yugoslavia/Serbia, a powerful criminal class with ties to the Milosevic regime emerged in the 1990s which could benefit from the black market. While the middle class impoverished and half of the population slipped below the poverty level, 5 percent of the population have become enormously wealthy.[166] Sanctions contributed to a symbiosis between

158 Giumelli 2015, p. 1352.
159 Galtung 1967, pp. 388–389.
160 Wallensteen 2000.
161 Haass 1998, p. 202.
162 Damrosch 1994, p. 74.
163 Mertens 2000, pp. 29–30.
164 Peksen 2017, p. 221.
165 Peksen 2017, p. 219.
166 Brooks 2002, p. 47.

political leaders, organized crime, and transnational smuggling networks, which could "persist beyond the lifting of sanctions, contributing to corruption and crime and undermining the rule of law."[167]

2.4 Rally around the flag

Besides the presented economic mechanism, scholars mention psychological factors as triggers of autocratization during times of economic sanctions. Already in the 1960s, Galtung assumes "hidden forces" strengthening the target society after the application of economic sanctions.[168] The result is not only a failure of the goals of sanctions but even the opposite. Not political disintegration, but even integration can be the effect of value-deprivation. This concept applies especially when the "attack from the outside is seen as an attack on the group as a whole," and when the population of the target state cannot identify with the sender of sanctions. Galtung describes hereby a so-called rally around the flag. The regime portrays itself and the whole state as a victim of evil forces abroad. This may lead to increasing political cohesion: "The imposition of sanctions enables targeted leaders to pinpoint a clear external threat, which can be used as a focal point for a leader to unify the state."

Many scholars since Galtung mention and elaborate on this rally-effect. Olson writes that regime legitimacy and domestic coercive capability are the main factors that explain the positive or negative political effects of sanctions.[169] Even Cortright & Lopez – they tend to be sanctions-optimists – lament that sanctions hit disaffected opposition groups, whereas they provide autocrats "with leverage to create a 'rally around the flag effect' as a means of suppressing domestic opposition."[170] Sanctions enable autocratic leaders to demonize them as an "external threat to sovereignty and economic well-being"[171] and to blame them for the failure of their own economic policy.[172] Current examples are the latest sanctions on Iran and Russia. In case of religious or quasi-religious ideologies, sanctions "increase the magnitude and the persistence of religious ideology" and strengthen the theocratic regime. The material loss caused by sanctions can be replaced with religion or ideology.[173]

167 Andreas 2005, p. 335; cf. Selden 1999.
168 Galtung 1967.
169 Olson 1979, p. 493.
170 Cortright & Lopez 2000a.
171 Choi & Luo 2013, p. 218.
172 Connolly 2015, pp. 37–38.
173 Naghavi & Pignataro 2015, p. 9.

2.5 Repression

A crucial condition for the success of democratic sanctions is a potentially successful opposition group.[174] However, if oppositional groups are being hurt, it will have "perverse" consequences because an "impoverished citizenry will have fewer resources with which to oppose the regime and would therefore be cheaper to police."[175] Sanctions cause higher poverty rates which lead to unemployment and violence. They worsen government respect for physical integrity rights (freedom from disappearances, extra-judicial killings, torture, political imprisonment).[176] Other scholars even found that economic sanctions lead to a rise in the rate of domestic terrorism. Primary victims of comprehensive economic sanctions are not the elite and its supporters but the poorest segments of the population, which are more likely "to support or engage in terrorist activity" out of a sense of despair.[177] Affected by sanctions are all those groups outside the support base of the regime. In states with cleavages along ethnic lines, this leads to discriminatory economic and political practices, which may lead to a rise in violence and instability.[178] A "foreign aggression" such as sanctions also gives the regime an excuse for increasing the level of repression.[179]

Another explanation for the increase of repression is that the threat or application of sanctions has as a signal an encouraging effect on opposition groups and increases anti-government protests.[180] Economic shocks cause an uproar and may force the regime to apply repressive measures.[181] Sanctions lead to an increase in the prices of loyalty and repression because members of the support coalition may support a challenger, and opposition groups may be strengthened.[182] Since loyalty is harder to buy in short-term, autocrats tend to rely on repression,[183] especially when they lack legitimacy.[184] Gershenson et al. argue that the optimal way for an autocratic elite to respond to foreign pressure is to increase both repression and co-optation.[185]

---

174 Kaempfer & Lowenberg 1999, p. 51.
175 Kaempfer, Lowenberg, & Mertens 2004, p. 41.
176 Peksen 2009.
177 Choi & Luo 2013, p. 219; cf. Choi 2014.
178 Peksen 2014.
179 Nixon 2012.
180 Grauvogel, Licht, & Soest 2014.
181 Nixon 2012.
182 Kaempfer & Lowenberg 1992; Wood 2008.
183 Wintrobe 1998, p. 47.
184 Merkel 1999, p. 67.
185 Gershenson & Grossman 2001.

Escribà-Folch confirms that an autocratic ruler tends to increase spending in those sectors that benefit mainly his key constituencies when the budget is not severely affected by economic sanctions. Is the effect of sanctions on the budget higher, than the autocrat relies more on repression.[186] But not all leaders are able to use repression effectively. Especially in mixed regimes, leaders lack the legitimacy and ability to repress the opposition.[187] Sanctions might have an impact on third countries, too: Sanctions with the focus on human rights can improve the level of protection of human rights in countries that were not targeted.[188] They trigger a proactive behavior in non-sanctioned neighboring states.[189]

2.6 Destabilizing

Independently from the question how exactly sanctions are benefitting the regime, there seems to be a consensus that sanctions can destabilize the regime. With their game-theoretical selectorate model, Bueno de Mesquita & Smith show that leaders need to increase both public and private goods in times of economic shocks such as sanctions. However, revenue shocks "diminish the resources available for rewards" and threaten the leader directly. For democratic leaders are such economic shocks much more dangerous than for autocratic leaders because democratic leaders cannot match the offers of rivals and are easily deposed. Autocratic leaders need to compensate fewer supporters, and they are less constrained in budget re-arrangements. Whereas autocratic leaders fear revolutions and coups, democratic leaders fear budget shocks.[190]

Marinov concludes that leaders in target states are more likely to be replaced, especially in democratic countries and in mixed regimes. He adds that "the alleged ineffectiveness of economic pressure may, in part, be due to faulty analysis."[191] Studies of sanctions heretofore looked only within sanctions cases – which is "appropriate only if the question to be answered is why are some cases of coercion more successful than others. If the question is 'Does coercion work?,' we need to compare cases in which pressure was applied, to those in which it was not." He describes the often-discussed cases of Cuba, Iraq, and North Korea as "atypical outliers," and writes that "sanctions may be more effective than both their proponents and critics maintain."

186 Escribà-Folch 2012.

187 Allen 2008a.

188 Carneiro & Elden 2009.

189 Peterson 2014.

190 Bueno de Mesquita & Smith 2017.

191 Marinov 2005, pp. 565–575.

Escribà-Folch et al. write that sanctions destabilize autocratic regimes. The result of this destabilization depends on the type of authoritarian regime:[192] Single-party and military regimes increase spending to the benefit of their support groups; personalist regimes reduce spending and increase repression. Personalist dictators are more vulnerable to economic pressure because they often rely on external rents and trade taxes. Sanctions de-stabilize personalist ruler, which may be deposed. However, that does not mean liberalization or democratization: instead, sanctions "just increase the likelihood of an autocratic transition."[193] A personalist ruler may be followed by another one or a failed state.

2.7 Determinants of sanctions effectiveness

Before looking at the determinants of autocratization and defining the variables, it may be useful to look at the variables in the debate about the effectiveness and success of sanctions. The crucial question for policymakers is, what makes economic sanctions successful? Policy-analysts struggled long time with solving that puzzle. Striking is the fact that in the last two decades, the academic debate about sanctions was shaped by opponents of economic sanctions on one side ('sanctions pessimists' or 'traditionalists'[194]) and proponents on the other side ('sanctions optimists' or 'revisionists'[195]). Traditionalists see sanctions as largely ineffective and criticize the idea that economic pressure can induce policy change.

The overwhelming majority of scholars holds a very negative view about the success of sanctions:[196] "The general picture is that economic sanctions have been unsuccessful as a means of influence in the international system."[197] Scholars that evaluated the effectiveness of sanctions come to a highly pessimistic conclusion and estimate the percentage of success between 34 percent[198] and 3 percent.[199] Sanction-bashing became mainstream in scholarly literature: One scholar said in 2002: "sanction success is no longer an interesting question because sanctions

192 Escribà-Folch & Wright 2010; classification based on Geddes 1999, pp. 121–123.
193 Escribà-Folch & Wright 2015, p. 151.
194 E.g., Doxey 1996; Lektzian & Souva 2003; Pape 1997; Peksen 2009.
195 E.g., Cortright 2007; Cortright & Lopez 2000b; Hufbauer, Schott, & Elliott 1990.
196 Askari, Forrer, Teegen, & Yang 2003; Barber 1979; Galtung 1967; Haass 1997; Nincic & Wallensteen 1983; R. S. Olson 1979; Pape 1997, 1998; Tostensen & Bull 2002; Wallensteen 1968, 2000.
197 Wallensteen 1968, p. 262.
198 Hufbauer, Schott, Elliott, & Oegg 2007.
199 Pape 1997, p. 110.

simply do not work."[200] These so-called traditionalists see economic sanctions either as ineffective or even as counter-productive: "the deterrent and coercive force of sanctions is weak on almost every count."[201]

In recent years, a small academic opposition attacked conventional wisdom and criticized definition and measurement of success, selection bias, and methodological insufficiencies. Some scholars suggested to differentiate sanctions according to goals and offered various categorizations. Revisionists point to problems with the definition of success and different goals of sanctions.[202]

After decades of case studies, the dataset of a team of economists led by Hufbauer (HSEO) enabled a first wave of large-N studies.[203] It was the first large-N analysis of all sanction episodes since World War I and laid the foundation for most quantitative studies.[204] For HSEO, the most important variables for sanctions success are an achievable goal, high economic pain, military threat or force following the sanctions, no crosscutting interests of the sender allies.[205] In a meta-evaluation of other articles, Biersteker et al. mention the following factors: high trade volume, a psychological factor (expectations), a democratic target, strong multilateral political commitment, narrowly defined goals, multiple policy instruments.[206]

All of the variables mentioned in this chapter are also potential variables for the research question of this book. The following table reviews the most quoted variables mentioned by both empirical and theoretical contributions to the debate about the success and impact of economic sanctions. It is based on Kaempfer et al. (1990–2003)[207] and extended by the author.

---

200 Qtd. in Drury 2005, p. 175.

201 Doxey 1972, p. 547; cf. Doxey 1971, 1980, 1996.

202 The distinction in 'traditionalist' and 'revisionist' debate participants originally comes from Jentleson 2000. Portela 2010, p. 10, writes about sanctions proponents and opponents.

203 Hufbauer & Schott 1985; Hufbauer, Schott, & Elliott 1990; Hufbauer, Schott, Elliott, & Oegg 2007.

204 Their empirical assessment of economic sanctions was not only highly influential in scholarship: The authors testified in December 1990 before the U.S. Congress that "economic sanctions would likely compel Saddam Hussein to retreat from Kuwait." Pape 1997, p. 92.

205 Hufbauer, Schott, Elliott, & Oegg 2007, p. 178.

206 Biersteker & Bergeijk 2015.

207 Kaempfer & Lowenberg 2007, pp. 896, 903.

	Democratic (not autocratic) target	High costs to target	Trade linkage sender/ target	Cordial pre-sanctions ties/ allies	Issue salience (sender)/ ambitiousness	(Long) duration of sanctions
TOTAL	20+ 2–	9+	8+	8+ 1–	6+ 2–	6–1+
Bergeijk 1989			+			–
Hufbauer et al. 1990	+	+		+		–
Lam 1990		+		+		
Deheja & Wood 1992		+				
Damrosch 1993	+					
Bergeijk 1994			+			–
Fearon 1994	+					
Bergeijk & Marrewijk 1995						+
Smith 1996		+		+		
Dashti-Gibson et al. 1997		+			–	–
Kirshner 1997	+					
Pape 1997	+		+		+	
Bonnetti 1998				+		
Drury 1998		+				
Drezner 1999a				+		
Kaempfer & Lowenberg 1999						
Nossal 1999	+					
Drezner 2000						
Hart 2000		+				
Bolks & Al-Sowayel 2000	+					–
Cortright & Lopez 2001	+					
Brooks 2002	+					
Miers & Morgan 2002	+	+		–		
Nooruddin 2002	+			–		
Drezner 2003					+	
Jing et al. 2003				+		

Political instability of target	Economic weakness of target	Unilat. more successful than multilat.	Third party assistance to target	Targeted better than comprehensive	Democratic (not autocratic) sender	Multilat. cooperation among senders	Others
5+	4+	3+ 3–	3–	3+ 1–	3+	1+ 2–	
+							
+	+	+	–			–	–a
+	+						–b
+	+						
					+		
							+b
							+c
							+d
			–				
			–			–	–a
		+					
		–					
					+		
		+				–	
+	+						–e

	Democratic (not autocratic) target	High costs to target	Trade linkage sender/ target	Cordial pre-sanctions ties/ allies	Issue salience (sender)/ ambitiousness	(Long) duration of sanctions
Lektzian & Souva 2003	–					
Lacy & Niou 2004						
Allen 2005	+			+		
Hovi et al. 2005						
Marinov 2005	+					
Drury & Li 2006					+	
Ang & Peksen 2007					+	
Lektzian & Souva 2007	+					
Shagabut-dinova & Berejikian 2007						
Allen 2008a	+					
Allen 2008b	+					
Brzoska 2008						
Bapat & Morgan 2009						
Carneiro & Elden 2009	+					
Krustev 2010						
McLean & Whang 2010			+			
Whang 2010	+		+	+	+	
Drezner 2011						
Early 2011						
Wallensteen & Grusell 2012						
Lopez 2012						
Major 2012	+					
Bapat et al. 2013	–	+	+		–	
Whang et al. 2013			+			
Bapat & Kwon 2015						

Political instability of target	Economic weakness of target	Unilat. more successful than multilat.	Third party assistance to target	Targeted better than comprehensive	Democratic (not autocratic) sender	Multilat. cooperation among senders	Others
							+f
							+g
				+			
		–					
		–					
							+f
				–			
							–h
				+			
				+			
					+		+i
							+j

	Democratic (not autocratic) target	High costs to target	Trade linkage sender/ target	Cordial pre-sanctions ties/ allies	Issue salience (sender)/ ambitiousness	(Long) duration of sanctions
Beladi & Oladi 2015						
Biersteker & Bergeijk 2015	+		+		+	–
Spaniel & Smith 2015						

+ significantly positive effect of IV on DV (sanctions success)
– significantly negative effect of IV on DV (sanctions success)
Other independent variables:
a trade (not financial) sanctions
b small cost to the sender
c sender is a frequent sender
d uneven income distribution
e size of sender relative to the target
f sanctions as a threat
g information asymmetry
h sanctions buster
i involvement of international institutions; multiple issues
j sender's firm have a moderate share of target's market
k target's elasticity of substitution
l psychological factor (expectations); initial years of implementation; narrowly defined goal

The most quoted variables are the political constitution of the target state (20 articles), high economic costs of sanctions to the target (9), the trade linkage between sender and target (8), allies (8), achievable goal (6), duration of sanctions (6), political instability of the target (5), economic weakness of the target (4).

To summarize the literature review on sanctions: Despite their long history, economic sanctions became only in the last decades target of an academic debate. Especially since the numbers of sanctions exploded in the 1990s, the debate got livelier and more aggressive. This debate was mainly not a debate within the academic ivory tower, but between policy-analysts on one side and policymakers on the other side. Most scholars are convinced that economic sanctions are a highly if not completely ineffective tool. Politicians, however, increased the number of sanctions dramatically despite all academic warning. Some scholars argue that policymakers do not care about the long-term success of economic sanctions because they are mainly interested in securing the next elections; some few scholars replied that the question of success is not a binary question.

Political instability of target	**Economic weakness of target**	**Unilat. more successful than multilat.**	**Third party assistance to target**	**Targeted better than comprehensive**	**Democratic (not autocratic) sender**	**Multilat. cooperation among senders**	**Others**
							+k
						+	+l
							−g

After policymakers agreed on a re-design of sanctions in the late 1990s, the focus of academics shifted from the question of success to the question of impact. They analyzed the unintended side-effect of economic sanctions on mainly humanitarian issues like health, but also on human rights questions and democracy, especially since the wave of democratization in the 1990s and the autocratic backlash. Interestingly, scholars came – using partly the same datasets and similar variables – to very different conclusions. Scholars accused each other of being "fools,"[208] some suggested that pro-sanctions scholars contribute to and are responsible for humanitarian catastrophes worse than war,[209] and they accused each other on a methodological level for selecting the cases on the dependent variable[210] or selecting outlier cases.[211] Very striking is the observation that the main actors of the debate are not single, debate-changing academic texts, but the academics themselves: The most quoted participants of the debate seem either to attack or to defend the use of economic sanctions, most of their (positivist-quantitative) contributions always come to a similar conclusion.

Academia gives no satisfying answer to the question whether sanctions are useful, and if they are useful, under which circumstances they are useful. Some variables are quite convincing meanwhile: economic costs of sanctions (trade linkage, comprehensiveness), duration, targeted measures, institutions in the target state. Social scientists can help to design and to improve economic sanctions, which is very important. In the political decision-making process, however, the role of area studies is not less important. Knowledge of the dynamics within the target country is crucial for success and unintended impact of economic sanctions.

2.8 Determinants of autocratization

This book searches for those variables that explain why some sanctions have a negative impact on the level of democracy. Besides the sanction literature, democratization and autocracy research provides a number of variables. This sub-chapter briefly looks at the recent debate on an alleged autocratic reversal.

A well-known assumption is that "it is autocracy, not democracy, that has been the norm in human history."[212] Non-democracy, however, is not simply a

208 Morgan & Schwebach 1997.
209 Mueller & Mueller 1999.
210 Smith 1996.
211 Marinov 2005.
212 Kagan 2015, p. 30.

caesaropapist dictatorship. Instead, history confronts us with a wide variety of forms of polity: In ancient times, some of the most successful Mediterranean city states were organized as republics with institutions of somewhat collective decision-making (Athens, Carthago, Rome). Germanic entities in Northern Europe were organized in regular meetings for making decisions.[213] Many medieval and early modern city-states in Central and Eastern Europe were ruled by merchants and had some kind of electoral institutions.[214] Most of these cities and small territorial states have been conquered by aggressively expanding territorial monarchic states.[215] Historical evidence of well-functioning collective decision-making bodies challenges the narrative of modern (democratic) institutions that newly developed in the 19th century based on Greek ideas.

A remarkable development in the last 150 years is the expansion of government in Western democracies.[216] Industrialization and mass society led to the Bismarckian welfare state, expanded bureaucracy, and professionalization of politics with more planning. The central authority accumulated more power in all policy areas, not only in traditional core policy areas such as security and contract enforcement. Once the government extended its activities, it created a new bureaucracy after each crisis.[217] Some scholars see Bismarckian centralized welfare state as a precursor of both totalitarianism[218] and Keynesian interventionism.[219]

The last two centuries witnessed three waves of democratization: the first democratic wave in the 19th century, the second one after World War II, and the third one after the end of the Cold War.[220] According to Freedom House, by 1993, for the first time in human history, there were more democratic governments in the world than authoritarian ones.[221] The first democratic wave, however, was

213 Such institutions are considered as the oldest parliaments today: In Iceland, the Althing is active since the 10th century, similar the Tynwald on the Isle of Man and the Faroese Løgting.

214 Such as Florence, Bern, Frankfurt; maritime republics Venice, Pisa, Genova, Ragusa; Hanseatic League cities such as Hamburg, Lübeck, Danzig; Novgorod, Pskov; the Dutch Republic.

215 Such as the Napoleonic Empire (early 1800s), the newly created Kingdom of Italy (1861) and the newly created, Prussian-dominated German Empire (1871). The only surviving republican city-state in Europe is San Marino.

216 Becker 1985.

217 Zakaria 2003, p. 239.

218 Gentile 2011, p. 2629.

219 Merkel 2014, p. 112.

220 Huntington 1991.

221 Cf. Ulfelder 2012, p. 149.

followed by an autocratic wave (fascist and communist regimes from Portugal to Japan), and the second wave – at the beginning Cold War and decolonization – was followed by the establishment of a number of military dictatorships especially in Africa and Latin America. Also, the third wave of democracy was followed by developments which pessimists saw as a counter-movement.

2.8.1 Democracy in retreat

Many post-Cold War transitions ended in hybrid regimes[222] which are also labeled competitive authoritarian regimes,[223] illiberal democracies,[224] semi-authoritarian,[225] electoral authoritarian.[226] Many scholars see this in line with Huntington's concept of waves. Since the late 2000s, quantitative analyses employ a "democracy-in-retreat" narrative, and pessimism about the success of democracy became dominant in Political Science: With colorful words, scholars describe what they see as a democratic recession:[227] democratic breakdown,[228] rollback, erosion,[229] decline, deconsolidation,[230] failure, collapse,[231] transition from democracy,[232] and authoritarian reversal,[233] backsliding,[234] pushback,[235] and undertow, even "the beginning of the end for democracy" and the "resurgence of the predatory state."[236]

At the same time, public-opinion surveys found a decline in trust in core democratic institutions.[237] Freedom House speaks of a "freedom recession;"[238] and Puddington asks: "Is the tide turning?"[239] Diamond diagnosed a reverse wave

222 Diamond 2002.
223 Levitsky & Way 2010.
224 Zakaria 1997, 2003.
225 Ottaway 2003.
226 Schedler 2002, 2009.
227 Diamond 2015.
228 Diamond 2011; Erdmann 2011; Linz 1978; Maeda 2010.
229 Puddington 2010.
230 Foa & Mounk 2016, 2017.
231 Diskin, Diskin, & Hazan 2005.
232 Ulfelder & Lustik 2007.
233 Svolik 2008.
234 Alemán & Yang 2011; Dresden & Howard 2016; Shirah 2012.
235 Puddington 2007.
236 Cf. Diamond 2008; Levitsky & Way 2015, p. 45.
237 Schmitter 2015, p. 33.
238 Freedom House 2009.
239 Puddington 2008; cf. Puddington 2009.

which is especially relevant in a number of swing states (Russia): "[C]elebrations of democracy's triumph are premature. In a few short years, the democratic wave has been slowed by a powerful authoritarian undertow, and the world has slipped into a democratic recession."[240] Silitski warns of the emergence of an "authoritarian international."[241]

The assumed existence of a reverse wave is subject of an acrimonious debate among scholars. Plattner describes recent developments as stagnation, not as Huntington's "reverse wave."[242] Merkel strongly disagrees with Diamond's pessimistic diagnosis and the conventional wisdom of a "reverse wave" or a "democratic rollback". The number of autocratic regimes will neither increase nor decrease: "The global systemic competition is, for the time being, frozen."[243]

Levitsky et al. see almost no evidence for a democratic decline, and prefer to speak about autocratic consolidation after an "unprecedented authoritarian crisis" in the 1990s. Around 2000, most autocracies stabilized and adapted to the post-cold war environment: "the real story of the last decade is not democracy's 'meltdown,' but rather its resilience in the face of a darkening geopolitical landscape."[244] For Olson, the existence of autocracy and the process of autocratization are not a real puzzle, because it is the normal case in history, whereas democratic transition and consolidation are a puzzle indeed.[245] Kagan finds the stability of modern liberal democracies area surprising too: It is in the nature of rule that it is unstable, and each regime has to stabilize itself all the time.[246]

There are competing explanations for the reasons why some countries adopt a particular form of government, some follow the path of democratic transition and democratic consolidation while others not: socio-economic factors (modernization, inequality), elite-centered approaches (agency), institutions, political culture[247] or cultural-religious explanations.[248]

---

240 Diamond 2008.

241 Silitski 2010.

242 Plattner 2015, p. 7.

243 Merkel 2010, p. 29.

244 Levitsky & Way 2015, pp. 49, 57.

245 Olson 1993, pp. 569–575.

246 Kagan 2015, p. 30.

247 Almond & Verba 1963; cf. Lipset 1994, pp. 3–5.

248 Some scholars argue – partly based on Weber's "Protestant Ethic and the Spirit of Capitalism" (2010 [1905]) – that Protestant countries are more likely to modernize and democratize, whereas a Catholic, Orthodox, Muslim or Confucian tradition hinders democratic development. (Grigoriadis 2016; Huntington 1991; Lipset 1994) Putnam 1993 defines latter traditions as prone to "vertical structures"; Grigoriadis 2016 defines

2.8.2 Autocratization

Erdmann complains that there is almost no research on the transition from democracy to non-democratic regimes,[249] though such processes touch "nearly every continent and a majority of new democracies."[250] Levitsky et al. warn of a "democratizing bias" in the democratization literature, for example when characterizing mixed regimes as partial democratic or "as undergoing prolonged transitions to democracy."[251] This implies that the transition to democracy is a somewhat natural process. Few scholars, such as Alemán et al., focus on the occurrence of "autocratizing transitions" in regimes of all types.[252]

By traditional transitologists, transition is defined as "the interval between one political regime and another."[253] Competing concepts are transformation, regime change, system change; often, such terms are related to democratization and imply a transition from autocracy to democracy. Transitologists distinguish three subsequent phases of democratization: liberalization, democratization (institutionalization), consolidation.[254] After consolidation, autocratic reversal is practically eliminated.[255] Both "transition" and "transformation" are used mainly in one direction: the shift from autocracy to democracy, also called democratization. Few scholars criticize this democratization bias among transitologists and describe the transition paradigm, which means that "toppling dictators leads to democracy," as "myth."[256] In fact, since World War II, autocratic regime breakdown resulted in more than half of all cases in some type of new autocracy.[257]

The term autocratization is not widely used. Though "autocratization" seems to be the most logical one to describe a process in analogy to democratization, it is almost non-existent in academia. It is used by Lindberg,[258] Bueno de Mesquita et al.,[259]

---

them as "collectivist". Woodberry 2012 claims that Protestant missions are associated with democracy. Some of such culturalist studies simply ignore hidden variables.

249 Erdmann 2011.

250 Shirah 2012, p. 4.

251 Levitsky & Way 2002, pp. 51–52.

252 Alemán & Yang 2011.

253 O'Donnell & Schmitter 1986, p. 6.

254 Merkel 2011, p. 2622; Schneider & Schmitter 2004.

255 Svolik 2008, p. 153.

256 Escribà-Folch & Wright 2015, p. 257.

257 Geddes, Wright, & Frantz 2014.

258 Lindberg 2009, p. 317.

259 Bueno de Mesquita & Smith 2009, p. 193.

and by Dresden et al.[260] The few scholars dealing with autocratization or related concepts define it according to their definition of autocracy and democracy. They use a mainly procedural definition of democracy (elections) as the basis. For Dresden et al., authoritarian backsliding is "a decrease in the competitiveness of the electoral playing field, which results from an increase in the incumbent executive's concentration of power."[261] Based on Levitsky et al.,[262] the authors include: manipulating elections, violating civil liberties, creating an uneven playing field for the opposition, and reducing the institutional constraints on executive power. This happens mostly not in liberal democracies but in hybrid regimes where there is already an "uneven playing field."[263] Shirah rightly mentions that autocratization can occur "with or without a complete return to [autocratic] rule." Based on Freedom House, he defines this process as "any significant decrease in the political rights or civil liberties enjoyed by citizens in a new democracy."[264] However, autocratization does not necessarily mean a full transformation of the regime; it also refers to a partial regress of freedom.

2.8.3 Triggers of autocratization

What are the reasons for or triggers of autocratization? The most often mentioned variables mirror the democratization debate. In analogy to modernization theory, which is the major research paradigm in the democratization debate, scholars mention variables related to the economy: economic development,[265] lower economic growth,[266] low level of income,[267] poverty,[268] a malfunctioning economy,[269] inequality.[270] Economic crises affect the timing of democratic deconsolidation.[271] They are seen as the primary trigger for regime breakdown and autocratization.

260 Dresden & Howard 2016, p. 1122.
261 Dresden & Howard 2016, p. 1124.
262 Levitsky & Way 2010, pp. 365–368.
263 Dresden & Howard 2016, p. 1122.
264 Shirah 2012.
265 Svolik 2008; Maeda 2010.
266 Maeda 2010.
267 Alemán & Yang 2011.
268 Kapstein & Converse 2008.
269 Diskin, Diskin, & Hazan 2005.
270 Kapstein & Converse 2008.
271 Svolik 2008.

The world economic crisis of the late 1920s is seen as a major reason for the rise of autocratic regimes in Europe.[272]

Some scholars focus on institutions and find presidentialism more vulnerable to democratic breakdown than parliamentarian democracy.[273] Others find that it is rather a military legacy,[274] a military authoritarian past,[275] or the presence of a massive security apparatus.[276] Furthermore, unfavorable history,[277] ethnic fragmentation,[278] cleavages,[279] and mass political conflict[280] may explain autocratization. Another argument is related to governmental instability[281] and to state capacity. New regimes tend to overburden themselves by "plac[ing] all unsolved problems [...] on their agenda simultaneously, presumably to maximize support, without realizing that in doing so they also maximize the number of persons likely to be affected negatively by their reforms."[282] Though most variables are related to economic development and the political regime, scholars emphasized that no outstanding variable is responsible for defects in democracy,[283] autocratic backsliding[284] or "capable of predicting democratic collapse."[285]

272 Linz 1978.
273 Svolik 2008; cf. Boix 2003, pp. 150–155.
274 Cheibub 2007, p. 140.
275 Svolik 2008.
276 Alemán & Yang 2011.
277 Diskin, Diskin, & Hazan 2005.
278 Kapstein & Converse 2008.
279 Diskin, Diskin, & Hazan 2005.
280 Alemán & Yang 2011.
281 Diskin, Diskin, & Hazan 2005.
282 Linz 1978, p. 41.
283 Merkel 2004, p. 62.
284 Shirah 2012.
285 Diskin, Diskin, & Hazan 2005.

3 Explanatory factors

Why do some economic sanctions have a negative impact on the level of democracy in the target state but others not? Literature and anecdotal and empirical evidence in the previous chapters suggest using different explanations: Some are related to the design of sanctions; some are related to the target state, especially to political and economic characteristics. Based on the literature review in the previous chapter, examples, and debates, this chapter builds hypothesis that try to explain why some sanctions have a high collateral damage to the political system of the target state. Before that, it needs to be clarified and defined what exactly needs to be explained: democracy.

3.1 A multidimensional definition of democracy and autocracy

> "All happy families resemble one another; each unhappy family is unhappy in its own way."
>
> —*Leo Tolstoy, Anna Karenina*[286]

Today, around half of all states have a liberal-democratic constitution with a very similar set of institutions. As mentioned in the previous chapter, history knows a vast variety of different types of rule: desert clans, oligarchies, military dictatorship, electoral pseudo-democracy, and so on. It is hardly possible to find one standard definition for all these types of rule that do not match the definition of liberal democracy. However, scholars agreed on using one term for all of them: autocracy.

Autocracy is not a specific type or category of government that can be described and defined. Rather, this term developed as the dystopian antonym to what most would describe as a "good government." Loewenstein distinguishes autocracy from constitutionalism.[287] Kelsen and most academics describe all non-democratic regimes as autocratic.[288] Autocracy is an umbrella term for all types of rules which do not fit the definition of (liberal) democracy. Then, what is a liberal democracy? Unlike natural sciences, social science knows no standardized concept which could be the starting point for all theories and hypotheses of

286 Tolstoy 2014 [1878], p. 3.
287 Loewenstein 1969, qtd. in Sandschneider 1995, p. 9.
288 Kelsen 1925; Sandschneider 1995, p. 9.

human interaction.[289] The absence of an established paradigm leads, for example, to contradicting definitions, classifications, and theories of regimes.[290] There is no recognized definition of power, government, or democracy. For Gallie, democracy is one of the "essentially contested concepts,"[291] and Lijphart calls it a "concept which virtually denies definition."[292]

Reviewing the whole literature on regime types, it is not clear whether it is better to see democracies and autocracies in distinct categories or on one scale. In real-life, "no two political systems are identical."[293] Each system has its own dynamics, and we would need one category for each. Therefore, each categorization is an abstraction. The question whether we see all those regimes on a scale or in pigeonholes depends not only on the worldview but also on the question what we need this virtual classification for.

The first method of classifying regimes is a categorization according to types: Classical theories on non-democratic regimes from the 1930s on worked mainly with a distinction between democratic, authoritarian and totalitarian systems, especially since Linz.[294] Since then, scholars enrich the scale and add various categories and sub-categories, such as post-totalitarianism and sultanism,[295] hybrid regimes,[296] competitive authoritarianism,[297] and electoral authoritarianism.[298] Fig. 2 shows a meta-classification that combines different approaches.

In the course of the 19th and 20th century, the distinction of democracies from autocracies was an easy one, few states before 1945 could be defined as liberal-democratic. The implosion of the Soviet Union was followed by the rise (or consolidation) of so-called hybrid regimes that are in a somewhat grey zone between democracy and autocracy. States adopted democratic institutions but used them more or less as façade. More regimes than ever before adopted electoral elements but failed any substantive test.[299] This led scholars of regimes to introduce

289 Cf. Ray & Russett 1996.
290 Gilbert & Mohseni 2011, p. 272; Munck 2001.
291 Gallie 1956, p. 184.
292 Lijphart 1977, p. 4.
293 Bueno de Mesquita, Smith, Siverson, & Morrow 2003, p. 42.
294 Linz 1975.
295 Linz & Stepan 1996.
296 Diamond 2002.
297 Levitsky & Way 2002.
298 Schedler 2002.
299 Diamond 2002, p. 22.

<table>
<tr><td colspan="5">*Linz 1975:*</td></tr>
<tr><td>Totalitarianism</td><td colspan="3">Authoritarianism</td><td>Democracy</td></tr>
<tr><td colspan="5">*Diamond 2002:*</td></tr>
<tr><td>Closed Authoritarian</td><td>Hegemonic Electoral Authoritarian</td><td>Competitive Authoritarian</td><td>Electoral Democracy</td><td>Liberal Democracy</td></tr>
<tr><td></td><td colspan="2">*Schedler 2002:*
Electoral Authoritarian
Ottaway 2003:
Semi-Authoritarian</td><td></td><td></td></tr>
<tr><td></td><td></td><td colspan="2">*Diamond, Linz & Lipset 1995:*
Semi-Democracy</td><td></td></tr>
</table>

Fig. 2: Categorization of regime types, based on Gilbert & Mohseni[300]

new categories of democracies and autocracies with adjectives, so-called hybrid regimes.[301] Democracies have been described as illiberal,[302] defective,[303] authoritarian, flawed, partial, hybrid, pseudo, façade, stalled, low-intensity, delegative.[304] Autocracies have been described as electoral,[305] competitive,[306] liberalized.[307] Such hybrid regimes are not necessarily transitional regimes, as previously assumed.[308] Instead, they consolidated or re-consolidated in a non-democratic fashion.[309]

Due to the debate over the problem of the blurred boundaries between democracy and autocracy, the conceptualization of democracy with well-defined characteristics was "overshadowed by the conceptualization of regimes on a single continuum spanning from liberal democracy to closed authoritarianism."[310] There is no qualitative distinction between different regime types; instead, it measures different characteristics on a scale. The linear continuum connects two opposite poles, often employed together with thresholds.[311] Whereas a

300 Gilbert & Mohseni 2011, p. 275.

301 Karl 1995.

302 Zakaria 1997.

303 Merkel 2004.

304 Qtd. in Schmitter 2015, p. 37.

305 Schedler 2006.

306 Levitsky & Way 2002.

307 Brumberg 2002.

308 Merkel 2004.

309 Burnell 2010, p. 2.

310 Gilbert & Mohseni 2011, p. 282.

311 Brownlee 2009; Diamond 1999, 2002; Epstein, Bates, Goldstone, Kristensen, & O'Halloran 2006; Howard & Roessler 2006; Schedler 2002, 2006.

categorization allows us to control for distinct mechanisms, a continuous scale enables us to check the degree and intensity of a regime form. On a continuous scale, democratization and autocratization can be defined as antonyms. Both classifications, therefore, can be helpful in a different context. The research question determines the classification.

The current puzzle asks about "more" and "less" democracy; a scale is better for measuring such a shift. Instead of drawing a simple linear continuum from democracy to autocracy, the following multidimensional approach covers what is defined as the main features of liberal democracies. A modern liberal democracy combines already in its name three fundamental characteristics: state capacity (power, authority), political rights (participation and accountability), and civil liberties (constitutionalism, rule of law, institutions).[312] The combination of the liberal element (constitutionalism, Rechtsstaat) and the democratic element (political participation of all citizens) goes back to the era of enlightenment, the combination with the "modern" state is rooted in the territorial state and the mass society.

3.1.1 State capacity

The most essential pre-condition of a liberal democracy is the state itself: "no state, no Rechtsstaat, no democracy."[313] Without "stateness" – a capable state – no modern democracy is possible.[314] Fukuyama defines governance as "a government's ability to make and enforce rules, and to deliver services."[315] State capacity can be equaled with output-oriented performance. Citizens cannot enjoy political rights and civil liberties very much if the state is not capable of enforcing the rules and deliver basic services. The state needs to invest in public service. State capacity is much more difficult to establish than political rights or civil liberties.[316] Examples of such state-building failure are post-2003 Iraq and post-2001 Afghanistan. Fukuyama points at the sequence of these three legs: "Many states with relatively high-performing governments – China, Japan, Germany, France, and Denmark, for example – created modern Weberian bureaucracies under authoritarian conditions; those that subsequently went on to become democracies inherited meritocratic state apparatuses that simply

312 Møller & Skaaning 2011, p. 86; Fukuyama 2015, p. 12.
313 Linz 1997, p. 118.
314 Linz & Stepan 1996, p. 17.
315 Fukuyama 2013, p. 350.
316 Fukuyama 2015, p. 12.

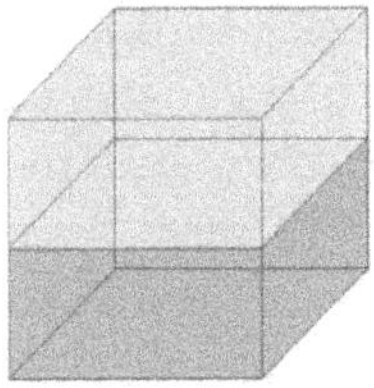

Fig. 3: The first dimension: state capacity

survived the transition."[317] Building on Shefter,[318] Fukuyama argues that "the sequence by which democracy [...] and state modernity were established has determined the long-term quality of government."[319] A modern state bureaucracy can survive the democratic extension of the franchise, latter before state reforms leads to clientelism. The primary motive for creating a modern state was not "grassroots pressure from informed and mobilized citizens, but rather elite pressure, often for reasons of national security," as the belligerent history of early modern Europe shows, as well as China during the Spring and Autumn and Warring States periods. Fukuyama emphasizes the conflict between state-building (starting with creating of police and military forces) and democracy promotion (starting with restrictions of power, decentralization, rule of law).[320] The measurement of executive branch quality (or state capacity) is one of the main tasks of contemporary political science. Fukuyama suggests using bureaucratic autonomy and capacity (taxation; professionalization of the bureaucracy) as a measure.[321] Fig. 3 shows the dimension state capacity.

3.1.2 Political rights

At the core of most classical democracy definitions is the electoral element: Schumpeter sees democracy as a government not by the people, but as a government legitimized by the people (through elections).[322] Przeworski

---

317 Fukuyama 2015, p. 16.
318 Shefter 1994.
319 Fukuyama 2015, p. 17.
320 Fukuyama 2005.
321 Fukuyama 2013.
322 "The democratic method is that institutional arrangement for arriving at political decisions in which individuals acquire the power to decide by means of a competitive struggle for the people's vote." Schumpeter 1976 [1942], p. 269.

defines democracy as "a system in which parties lose elections" and as "organized uncertainty."[323] Dahl writes that "a key characteristic of a democracy is the continuing responsiveness of the government to the preferences of its citizens, considered as political equals."[324] Alvarez defines democracy as a regime "in which some governmental offices are filled as a consequence of contested elections."[325] Linz sees democracy as government pro tempore.[326] Dahrendorf thinks that democracy is a system that makes it possible to get rid of a government without spilling blood.[327] Huntington writes elections might not solve other problems, but at least they solve the problem of tyranny.[328] For Merkel too, the electoral regime is at the core of his concept of embedded democracy, and he adds four other features: political rights, civil liberties, horizontal accountability, effective power to rule.[329] Freedom House uses three arguments as indicators for political rights in their annual Freedom in the World report: an electoral process at the core (free and fair elections of executive and legislative, fair electoral laws), political participation and pluralism (political competition of parties, access to competition, non-interference of others).[330] These political rights are here used as the second axis in the multi-dimension matrix of democracy. Unlike Gilbert et al. but similar to the academic mainstream,[331] this axis is here seen as a continuum connected to two opposite poles. Fig. 4 shows the dimension political rights.

323 Przeworski 1991, pp. 10–13.
324 Dahl 1971, p. 1.
325 Alvarez, Cheibub, Limongi, & Przeworski 1996, p. 5.
326 Linz 1994.
327 Dahrendorf 2003.
328 Huntington 1991, p. 263.
329 Merkel 2004, p. 42.
330 Freedom House 2018 (Methodology).
331 Diamond 2002; Epstein, Bates, Goldstone, Kristensen, & O'Halloran 2006; Schedler 2002, 2006.

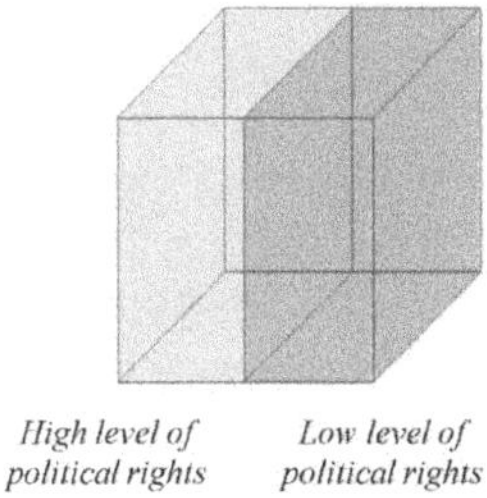

Fig. 4: The second dimension: political rights

3.1.3 Civil liberties

> "If they are powerful enough, let them come and demolish it."
> —*Recep Tayyip Erdogan, then Prime Minister of Turkey, in 2014 after the Supreme Administrative Court ruled that the construction of the presidential palace in a protected forest was illegal*[332]

The third characteristic of modern liberal democracies is institutionalized rule that protects the citizens from the authority. Rule of law is defined as a set of rules "that are binding not just on citizens, but also on the elites who wield coercive power,"[333] and therefore protect individual rights.[334] A lack of institutionalized power is for many scholars a typical feature of autocracies: "[A]utocratic power by definition implies that there cannot be any judges or other sources of power in the society that the autocrat cannot overrule."[335] A term which is often used for this liberal element of modern states is constitutionalism because constitutions are the central characteristic of modern states which guarantee the protection of the interests and liberties of the citizens against the majority and the central authority.[336]

This argumentation is in the tradition of liberal political ideas, such as habeas corpus, property rights, protection against torture by authorities, fair trial, freedoms of movement, of speech, etc.[337] John Locke and Adam Smith emphasized the non-political sphere of society beyond the political sphere. This civil society

332 Qtd. in The Telegraph, 2014-11-05.
333 Fukuyama 2005, p. 12.
334 For a general overview, cf. Maravall & Przeworski 2003.
335 Olson 1993, p. 571.
336 S. Gordon 1999, p. 4.
337 Schneider & Schmitter 2004, p. 61.

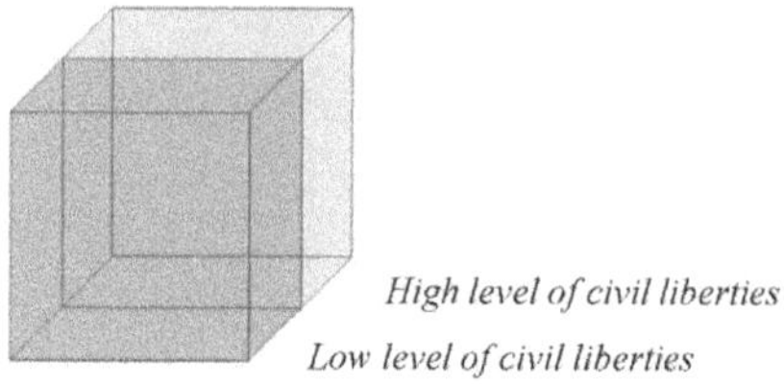

Fig. 5: The third dimension: civil liberties

should protect the natural rights of the citizens, their self-determination, and self-ownership. This definition of freedom is a negative one: It means freedom from state intervention. Montesquieu imagined checks and balances which would constrain the central authority.[338] The liberal tradition developed in opposition to unchecked state authority; however, key elements and institutions of liberal democracies (parliaments, rule of law) existed already before the formulation of liberal theories, e.g., in ancient Mediterranean city republics and late-medieval merchant states. Surprisingly, it was Machiavelli who preferred a liberal republic over a corrupt principality, because only a republic could promote freedom and stability. He called for a system in which liberty and law could co-exist "in such a manner that no one from within or without could venture upon an attempt to master them."[339]

Freedom House uses as indicators for civil liberties freedom of expression and belief, associational and organizational rights, rule of law, personal autonomy and individual rights. This basically describes what we know as First-Amendment Rights (1791): freedom of expression, freedom of assembly and association, freedom of religion, freedom of movement.[340] Fig. 5 shows the dimension civil liberties.

3.1.4 Sequence of rights

Whereas everyone seems to agree that state capacity is the base for political rights and civil liberties, scholars argue heavily about which of the latter ones comes first. In central Europe, "the constitutional infrastructure captured by the German phrase of the Rechtsstaat was in place before the franchise was extended in the nineteenth and twentieth century."[341] According to Marshall's model of evolution of rights,

338 Montesquieu 1995 [1748]; cf. for Locke and Smith: Merkel 2004, pp. 45–46.
339 Machiavelli 1950 [1531], p. 256 (Discourses I, chapter 55); qtd. in Bueno de Mesquita et al. 2003, pp. 3–4.
340 Cf. Møller & Skaaning 2013, pp. 84–85.
341 Møller & Skaaning 2013, p. 86.

civil rights developed in the 18th century, political rights in the 19th century, and social rights (the welfare state) in the 20th century.[342] First came rule of law, then came democracy. Sartori writes: "From liberty we are free to go on to equality; from equality we are not free to get back to liberty. The itinerary is non-reversible."[343]

The question is whether the constitutional and the democratic element support each other[344] or contradict each other.[345] For Kelsen and Hayek, the constitutional state and democracy are different concepts with different aims.[346] Both Hayek and Friedman see a liberal autocracy as a suboptimal short-term alternative on the way to a liberal democracy.[347] Huntington too emphasizes the advantages of one party regimes for low-income countries: Autocratic regimes are not bound by electoral cycles and policy consultation and can focus on long-term plans for economic development.[348] Other scholars, however, argue that it is unlikely that autocrats may embrace constitutional liberalism in the absence of elections to hold their powers in check, and they describe the "law-abiding autocrat" as an oxymoron.[349] An illiberal democracy is still better than an illiberal non-democracy: It is better to have Ahmadinejad as "president" and not as a pure dictator.

3.1.5 A multi-dimensional model

In the previous pages, three elements which constitute a modern liberal democracy were found: The first element, here defined as state capacity, refers to the performance of the state and its ability to provide service. The second element, political rights, refers to the political sphere and to the ability of citizens to participate in the political process, political pluralism and democratic accountability of the leadership. The third element, civil liberties, restrains the state and protects the personal sphere of the individual citizen. It protects minorities from state authority (first element) and a democratic or non-democratic majority (second element). A high level of these three elements accounts for stability and prosperity. Together, they form a multi-dimensional cube as shown in Fig. 6.

This cube shows examples and displays all dimensions as binary variables. For state capacity (X), a satisfying measurement does not exist yet. Most scholars use

342 Marshall 1950.
343 Sartori 1987, p. 389.
344 E.g., Habermas 1996, p. 300; Lauth 2004, p. 166.
345 E.g., Zakaria 1997; 2003.
346 Kelsen 1963 [1929]; Hayek 1971, p. 126.
347 Cf. Knutsen 2016, p. 376.
348 Huntington 1968.
349 Carothers 2007; Lindberg 2006; Møller & Skaaning 2011, p. 81.

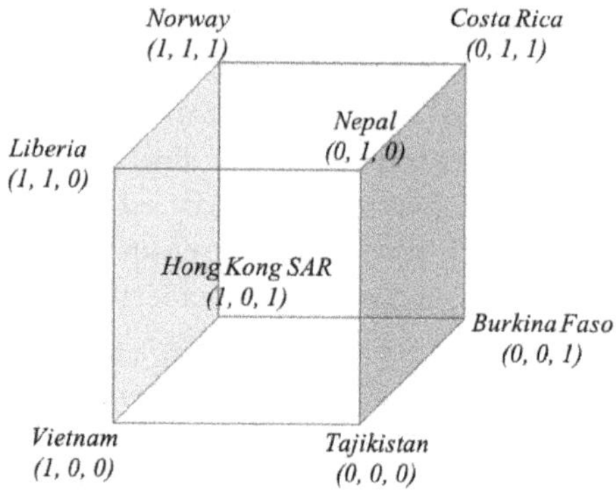

Fig. 6: A multi-dimensional model of regimes
X: state capacity, Y: political rights, Z: civil liberties
1 = high level; 0 = low level[350]

indicators related to the state's capability to collect taxes for the measurement of state capacity,[351] in this case, the indicator integrity of the taxpayer base.[352] For political rights (Y) and civil liberties (Z), the data is taken from the respective scores of the Freedom in the World Index.[353]

To summarize: Democracy is an "essentially contested concept."[354] Each definition has ideological implications. Defining it through the electoral procedure alone will lead to the accusation that the scholar plays down the danger of electoral autocracies. Based on the research question, the previous modeling and on

350 The visualization is based on a different theoretical model by Gilbert & Mohseni 2011, p. 293.

351 Fukuyama 2013, p. 353.

352 Source: database Indicators of the Strength of Public Management Systems (ISPMS), published by World Bank in 2014. Used sub-indicator: "the extent to which taxpayers are registered in a complete database system with comprehensive direct linkages to other relevant government registration systems and financial sector regulations," data from different years, last available data used. Data for this index exist for few countries only, which restricts the case selection and explains the use of small countries. Coding: A and B = 1, C and D = 0. World Bank's ISMPS provides no data on Hong Kong SAR, China; however, the indicators of Index of Economic Freedom (Heritage Foundation 2017) strongly suggest a coding of 1 (sub-indicators for indicator "regulatory efficiency" between 83 and 95 percent, which is among the highest rates worldwide).

353 Freedom House 2018; coding: 1–3 = 1; 4–7 = 0.

354 Gallie 1956, p. 168.

a feasible measurement, a three-dimensional definition is the best solution for the definition of a liberal-democratic state:

Definition: A liberal-democratic state is a state with an overall high level of political rights, civil liberties, and state capacity.

Political rights include political participation and political pluralism; civil liberties include individual rights, checks and balances and restrictions of the executive; state capacity refers to governance and performance of the state. The current definition enables a measurement on a continuous scale, which is relevant for the research puzzle. The opposite of a liberal democracy is described as an autocracy. Due to the vast universe of very different regime types that do not qualify as liberal-democratic states, the definition of autocracy is a negative one:

Definition: An autocratic state is a state with an overall low level of political rights, civil liberties, and state capacity.

The low level of state capacity can be explained with the low level of public goods invested by the leader. He needs to provide private goods to his supporters to buy their loyalty. Of course, not all autocratic states have a low level of state capacity. In general, however, autocratic leaders prefer to invest resources in their supporters, not simple citizens. The smaller the group of supporters is, the less people profit from the goods. Students of autocracies must be aware of the fact that "autocracy" is a virtual concept and only an auxiliary term: It will be difficult to find similar dynamics within the system. More helpful are analyses of different regime types, though most of such studies tend to over-classify.

The above definition of democracy and autocracy has three advantages: It is the best way to deal with the enlargement of the "grey zone" since the 1990s, the hybridization of regimes with increasingly blurry classic characteristics of democracies. Also, it fits the theoretical mechanism proposed in the next chapter. Finally, it is measurable on a continuous scale which is important for the research question.

No universal variable explains either democratization[355] or autocratization. The research question, empirical evidence and the critique of current research in the first chapter suggest using explanatory variables that are connected to the impact and design of sanctions and variables that are connected to political and economic characteristics of the target state of sanctions. The chapter builds on the previous literature review and partly summarizes the main arguments.

355 Huntington 1991.

3.2 Sanctions variables: Economic costs and democratic goal

Marinov writes that the unintended political impact of sanctions depends on the type of sanctions, the regime and on the target country's economic health and resources.[356] The most important variables are related to the design and imposition of sanctions. Bergeijk suggests using impact variables and additional public choice variables (the target's political system) for an econometric analysis of the impact of sanctions.[357]

3.2.1 Economic costs of sanctions to the target

The economic impact of sanctions is the main argument in many articles: The higher the costs of sanctions as a percentage of the target's GNP is, the higher is the chance of success.[358] The larger the pre-sanctions target's dependence on the sender is, the higher is the impact on its economy. According to the explanation that was ridiculed as a "naive theory"[359] and as "donkey psychology of economic diplomacy,"[360] economic punishment of the target state leads to a policy change. The sender states pressure through economic sanctions the whole economy of the target state. This external pressure forces the targeted government to change specific policies: "the more value-deprivation, the more political disintegration."[361] Peksen et al. argue that comprehensive economic sanctions have a greater negative impact on the level of democracy than limited sanctions.[362]

Economic sanctions include comprehensive trade embargoes (import and export), commodity embargoes related to specific sectors of export-dependent economies (e.g., coffee sanctions against Idi Amin's Uganda[363]) and aid sanctions (reduction of aid). These types of sanctions affect the target country's macroeconomy. Sanctions that entirely isolate the target state do not exist anymore. According to the Targeted Sanctions Dataset, the last comprehensive sanctions were implemented in 1994, and all sanctions since are more or less "targeted."[364]

---

356 Marinov 2005, p. 572.

357 Bergeijk 2009, pp. 126–130.

358 Hufbauer, Schott, Elliott, & Oegg 2007.

359 Galtung 1967, p. 388.

360 Bergeijk 2009, p. 115.

361 Galtung 1967, p. 388; cf. Dashti-Gibson, Davis, & Radcliff 1997; Kaempfer, Lowenber, & Mertens 2004.

362 Peksen & Drury 2010.

363 Cf. Escribà-Folch & Wright 2015, p. 147.

364 Biersteker, Eckert, Tourinho, & Hudáková 2013.

Targeted does not necessarily mean elite-targeted, it also refers to sector-targeted sanctions. The most comprehensive sanction regime today, targeting North Korea, does not include a full embargo. Instead it consists of a variety of sector-targeted sanctions, such as financial sanctions and commodities embargo (coal, iron, etc.). Additionally, there are elite-targeted sanctions (travel ban, asset freeze) and security-related measures (arms embargo, technology, aviation fuel).

Leaders manipulate the national economic policy to counterbalance the economic pressure, for example via tax incentives for foreign investors, or help by regional economic blocs (50 percent of today's world trade is conducted within regional organizations).[365] Shin et al. explain the low success rate of sanctions with the low impact of comprehensive economic sanctions on the target economy. If the trade linkage is too low, no damage can be done. Bergeijk proves a positive relationship between the success rate of economic sanctions and proportional trade linkage. Sanctions critics mostly overlook the fact that non-sufficient trade linkage leads to sanction failure: "The numerical predominance of failures per se, however, hardly provides evidence for the ineffectiveness of [sanctions]. More specifically, a sanction should fail if the – theoretical – conditions for a success are not being met."[366]

Many scholars confuse the comprehensiveness of sanctions with economic costs of sanctions or use the comprehensiveness of sanctions as main indicator for the economic pain experienced by the target state. One example is the current sanctions regime on North Korea (DPRK), which is by policymakers, scholarship, and media often considered as paradigmatic proof of non-effectiveness of economic sanctions. North Korea seems to have adapted to the sanctions regime and be insensitive to sanctions.[367] Applying the argument of trade linkage, the pre-2016 sanctions regime can hardly be effective because the trade linkage between the main senders and the target was too low. Comprehensive sanctions did not automatically translate into high economic costs of sanctions to the target.

Among the three major economic blocks worldwide – the U.S., the EU and China – only the U.S. and the EU applied sanctions in a comprehensive way. The U.S. imposed sanctions in 1950, in 1993, lifted them partly in 1995, and

365 Shin, Choi, & Luo 2016.

366 Bergeijk 2009, p. 119.

367 Haggard & Noland 2017; cf. Wolfgang Nowak, former Head of Planning at the German Federal Chancellery, who still deals with the North Korea issue, in an interview by ZDF, 2017-09-04.

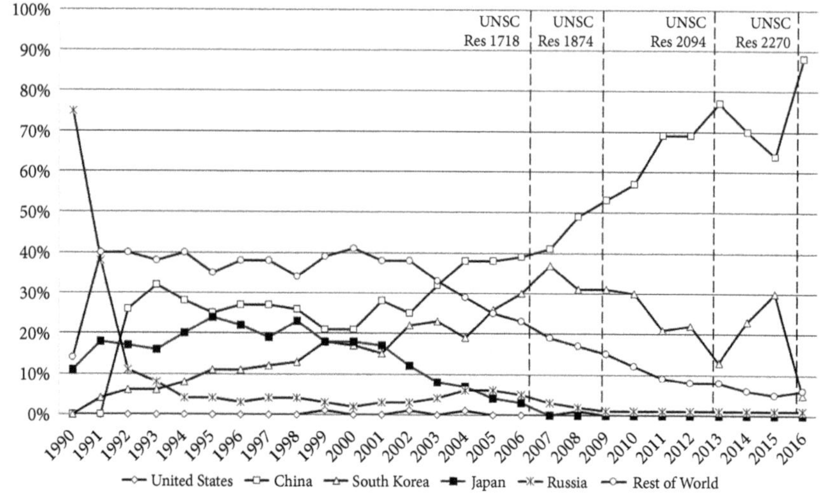

Fig. 7: North Korea's total trade, 1990–2016[368] (adjusted, share of total)

Major UNSC resolutions targeting North Korea:

RES/1718 (2006) arms embargo, assets freeze
RES/1874 (2009) arms embargo
RES/2094 (2013) financial sanctions, luxury goods
RES/2270 (2016) commodity embargo (coal, minerals, fuel)
RES/2397 (2017) commodity embargo (iron, steel, machinery)

imposed sanctions again together with the UNSC in 2006. The trade linkage between North Korea and the U.S. was near zero even before the imposition of "comprehensive" sanctions.

Fig. 7 shows that North Korea relied in 2016 with 90 percent on the Chinese market. The leverage of the PR China is, obviously, higher than that of the EU or the U.S.

Furthermore, many states did not apply economic sanctions on the DRPK in a proper way or not at all. The DPRK case says more about non-compliance to international agreements than about an alleged non-effectiveness of

368 I am indebted to Stephan Haggard and Kent Boydston for sharing the raw data with me. For a similar diagram with fewer years and countries, cf. Haggard & Noland 2017, p. 73. Data sources: South Korea's Ministry of Unification, UN comtrade database, estimates by Haggard & Noland 2017; cf. Haggard 2016.

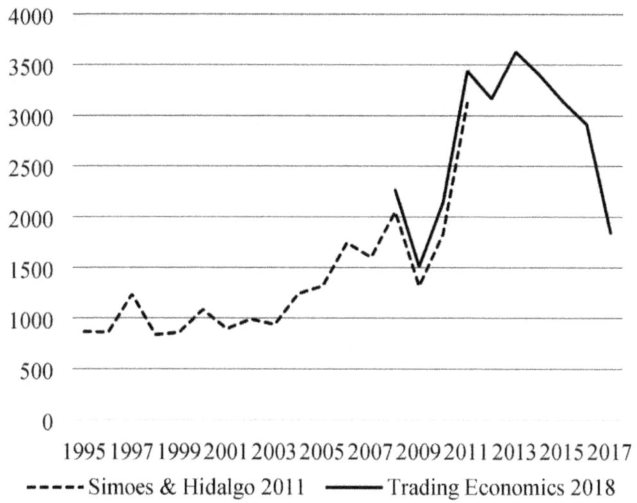

Fig. 8: North Korean exports in M. USD, 1995–2017[369]

economic sanctions. One year after the new resolution 2270 passed the UNSC (banning North Korean export of rare minerals and import of aviation fuel) in 2016, the responsible Panel of Experts complained that 116 (!) states yet had to submit, among them five members of the European Union and five members of the GCC.[370] In March 2018, the Panel of Experts complained once again about the international network of accomplices that helps the DPRK to keep pace in evading the sanctions regime. Whereas some countries are not aware of the details of the sanction regime, other ignore or resist it: The DRPK "continued to export almost all the commodities prohibited in the resolutions, generating nearly 200 million [USD] in revenue between January and September 2017." And: The 2017 "expansion of the [sanctions] regime is yet to be matched by the requisite political will […] necessary to

369 Data from Simoes & Hidalgo 2011; Trading Economics 2018.

370 EU member states: Croatia, Estonia, Portugal, Slovakia, Slovenia; GCC member states: Bahrain, Kuwait, Oman, Qatar, Saudi Arabia. UNSC Panel of Experts 2017, p. 100.

drive effective implementation."[371] Under the pre-2016 conditions, sanctions on the DPRK are unlikely to be effective. The DRPK case is not an example of ineffectiveness of sanctions, but an example of failed implementation especially by those states the DPRK depends upon. A look at absolute export numbers shows how North Korean export increased constantly during the sanction regime, despite so-called comprehensive sanctions – until UNSC resolutions 2094 and 2270.

Fig. 8 shows the drop of North Korean exports in 2016 and 2017. In these years, the UNSC expanded the sanctions regime (RES 2270) and the DPRK's biggest economic partner China started to comply with it. Soon later, the DPRK announced to end the nuclear tests. The North Korea case is no proof of sanctions success, as it is difficult to determine what "sanctions success" is and which tools of statecraft caused the North Korean announcement; furthermore, it is simply too early to evaluate the situation. However, long-term compliance of the DPRK with the demands of the UNSC would prove economic sanctions to be a highly effective tool, given the extremely short time sanctions were applied properly. Scholars need to clearly distinguish the design-related comprehensiveness from the real economic costs of sanctions.

How can high costs of economic sanctions lead to a decrease of the overall level of democracy? First, high economic costs can hurt the opposition more than the government: If the state has the monopoly on specific resources, sanctions deprive the opposition of organizing resources abroad. Comprehensive sanctions decrease the national income but do not decrease the leadership's budget. The citizens lose resources, and, perhaps, the leadership gains resources. Especially autocratic leaders are "relatively immune from sanctions because they can extract rents from restricted trade and financial flows, turning sanctions into opportunities to increase control over the levers of power."[372] In Yugoslavia, the sanctions deprived opposition forces of resources including information.[373] Sanctions increased the opposition's collective action problem.

Second, the regime's monopoly on law gives members of the leader's coalition a considerable advantage in conducting illegal or somewhat legal activities such as smuggling or money laundering abroad, as happened in Iran: The Islamic Revolutionary Guard Corps (the military organization behind Ahmadinejad's government) was very successful in using the sanctions period for conducting

371 UNSC Panel of Experts 2018, pp. 4–5.

372 Escribà-Folch & Wright 2015, p. 130; cf. Rowe 2000; Kaempfer, Lowenberg, & Mertens 2004; Lektzian & Souva 2007; Peksen & Drury 2010.

373 Peksen 2010, p. 452.

illegal business abroad and along the Iranian border. The end of sanctions, thus, may decrease the income for such groups. Similarly, allies of the Milosevic regime started smuggling oil and other scarce goods. They established bank accounts on Cyprus for facilitating smuggling activities.[374]

The leader tries to shift economic costs away from his own supporters to minimize the effects of sanctions on his capacity to rule.[375] Supporters of the leader become more dependent on him. The harder the sanctions are, the more the supporter's leader rely on close ties to him.[376] The stronger the leader and his coalition become, the weaker the opposition will be: The flow of resources to the leader's supporters disadvantages potential opposition groups.

Definition: Economic costs of sanctions is the amount of wealth of the target state that gets lost due to sanctions.

Hypothesis 1: The higher the economic costs of the sanctions to the target state are, the more likely is a negative impact on the level of democracy in the target state.

3.2.2 Democratic goal of sanctions

Soest & Wahman argue that sanctions aiming at the promotion of democracy correlate indeed with an increased level of democracy.[377] The application of repression is often counter-productive: It sends a signal to the population and the opposition and may result in regime collapse.

Another explanation for the effect of democratic sanctions is the increased imposition of such sanctions in the recent decades when sanctions designers followed a public choice approach. Instead of targeting the macro-economy and hoping that the leader's budget will decrease, these new "smart" sanctions target influential persons and groups within the target state, such as the leader or his key supporters. They are intended to harm those responsible for the targeted policy and to raise the costs of non-compliance "while avoiding the collateral damage that comes with comprehensive trade embargoes."[378] This has a signaling effect to the opposition and rival factions within the winning coalition.[379] Such sanctions, especially when aimed at democracy and human rights, are smart

374 Andreas 2005, p. 342; Escribà-Folch & Wright 2015, p. 127.
375 Marinov 2005, p. 566.
376 Peksen 2010, p. 245.
377 Soest & Wahman 2015, p. 957.
378 Drezner 2011, p. 100.
379 Escribà-Folch & Wright 2015, p. 130.

enough to avoid an autocratization of the system by systematically targeting the leader's coalition.

In the classic academic debate on sanctions success, only a few articles focus on the success of so-called smart sanctions. Though there is room for improving smart sanctions, no alternative technique is more effective to humanitarian concerns, summarizes Lopez.[380] Shagabutdinova et al. find that smart sanctions are not only more humanitarian but even more effective.[381] Heine-Ellison finds no evidence that targeted sanctions are more effective than comprehensive sanctions.[382] Major et al. explain the lack of success with the difficulty of imposing such sanctions in practice.[383] Biersteker et al. conclude that targeted sanctions are effective in coercing about 10 percent of the time, in constraining 28 percent, and in signaling 27 percent.[384]

Many articles use comprehensive sanctions as one variable and targeted sanctions as another. This book, however, cares more about the inherent mechanisms and distinguishes design-related elements according to their effect. Therefore, the first variable refers to the economic costs to the target state, and the second variable refers to the goal democracy and to the measures that are specifically designed at reaching that goal. Democratic goal is an important variable because it allows not only to control for unintended side-effects but also to measure the success.

Definition: The democratic goal of sanctions is the explicitly stated aim of sanctions senders to increase the level of democracy by using these sanctions.

Hypothesis 2: The less sanctions focus on democracy, the more likely is a negative impact on the level of democracy.

3.3 Regime variables: Personalism and legitimacy

Besides sanctions-related variables, variables related to the political system of the target state are most relevant. One variable focuses on categories of political regimes, another one on the degree of legitimacy of the leadership.

3.3.1 Personalist regime

Sanctions literature suggests that the target's regime type is one of the most important factors of sanctions success.[385] There is strong evidence that the

380 Lopez 2012, p. 145.
381 Shagabutdinova & Berejikian 2007.
382 Heine-Ellison 2001.
383 Major & McGann 2005.
384 Biersteker, Eckert, Tourinho, & Hudáková 2013.
385 E.g., Nooruddin 2002.

regime type affects the way targets respond to economic sanctions.[386] Several scholars recommended to "pay greater attention to the burgeoning work on politics in authoritarian countries,"[387] and they suggest disaggregating different autocratic regime types.[388] "Beware autocratic regimes," write Hufbauer et al.[389] Sanctions against democracies are more likely to succeed than sanctions against non-democracies because democracies are more susceptible to economic coercion.[390] It has various reasons: Democratic leaders are more constrained by institutions in their response to the imposition of sanctions. Electorally vulnerable democratic leaders have larger audience costs than their autocratic rivals.[391] Also, democracies are more transparent and open; they send more reliable information about their likely behavior. The "response of mixed and authoritarian systems are more difficult to predict."[392]

In autocratic states, political and economic elites are often connected, and it is easier for the regime to shift the sanctions costs to the opposition and to keep the sanctions rents for themselves.[393] The allocation of scarce goods is easier for strong leaders; they can shield their supporting coalition from the economic hardship caused by sanctions. Control of scarce resources gives those powerful elite members leverage over their rivals. Also, it's much easier for the elite to engage in black-market activities.[394]

But – are autocracies all alike? Scholars found that some autocratic regime types are more stable than others.[395] Also, economic susceptibility varies among regimes types.[396] The regime type determines changes in the regime leadership; different systems have different dynamics.[397] Geddes bases her categorization of regime types on the question who rules. She distinguishes personalist, military, single-party

386 Allen 2005, 2008a, 2008b.

387 Drezner 2011, p. 104.

388 Soest and Wahman 2012, p. 30

389 Hufbauer, Schott, Elliott, & Oegg 2007, p. 166.

390 Allen 2005, 2008a, 2008b; Bolks & Al-Sowayel 2000; Brooks 2002; Carneiro & Elden 2009; Kirshner 1997; Lektzian & Souva 2007; Marinov 2005; Nooruddin 2002.

391 Fearon 1994; Smith 1998.

392 Allen 2008a, p. 255.

393 Allen 2008a, 2008b.

394 Allen 2008b, p. 925.

395 Geddes 1999; Hadenius and Teorell 2007; Brownlee 2009.

396 Wright 2008.

397 Escribà-Folch 2013, p. 178.

regimes, amalgams (later, she adds monarchies).[398] She hypothesizes that regimes types differ in elite cohesion, which makes single-party regimes more stable than military regimes. In a personalist regime, the leader "usually came to power as an officer in a military coup or as the leader of a single-party government." He has "consolidated control over policy and recruitment in his own hands, in the process marginalizing other officers' influence and/or reducing the influence and functions of the party." A personalist leader is a strongman who can often rule independently from institutional restrictions (such as elections or courts). In a single-party regime, the party controls access to political power, and in a military regime, the leader is an officer who has the "support of the military establishment" which can influence policy choice and appointment.[399] Comparing cases of regime failures, Escribà-Folch finds that 36 percent of personalist regimes, 62 percent of military regimes, and 40 percent of party-based regimes end in democracy.[400]

Hadenius et al. develop a similar categorization, based on the mode of maintaining power: monarchies (hereditary succession); military regimes (use/threat of military force); electoral regimes (democracies, single-party, limited multi-party and no-party based regimes).[401] Similarly, Magaloni et al. distinguish military, monarchic, single-party, and dominant-party autocratic regimes.[402] Based on Geddes, Wright focuses on institutional differences among regimes and distinguishes personalist regimes from institutionalist regimes (military, single-party, corporatist).[403] Mousseau distinguishes states with (contract-poor) personalist economy from states with contract-intensive economy, and argues that latter – not democracy or interdependence – may account for democratic peace.[404]

This book, based on Wright and Geddes, distinguishes personalist and institutionalist regimes, latter including military regimes (Thailand), dominant party regimes (Vietnam) and monarchical regimes (the Gulf states). In personalist regimes, the leader is ruling through personal networks, and he comes to power through elections (Putin, Erdogan), coups (el-Sisi), or a revolution (Khomeini). Unlike Geddes, there is no residual category for amalgams. However, this book includes another type: democracies. Due to a change in the constitutional

398 Geddes 1999.
399 Geddes 1999, p. 20.
400 Escribà-Folch 2013, p. 178.
401 Hadenius & Teorell 2007.
402 Magaloni & Kricheli 2010.
403 Wright 2008, p. 323.
404 Mousseau 2013.

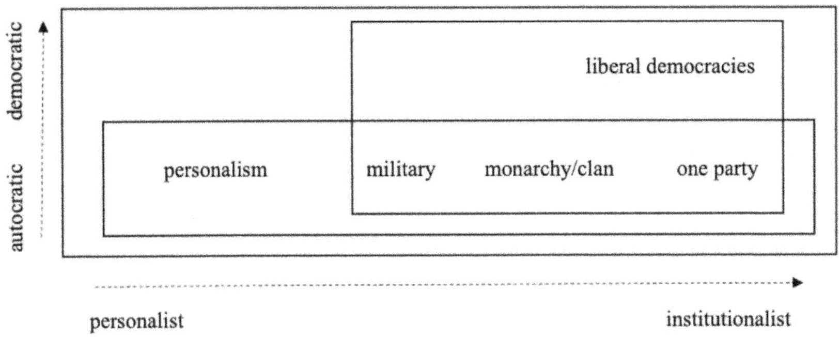

Fig. 9: DAPI regime matrix (Democratic Autocratic Personalist Institutionalist)

culture in last decades worldwide – everyone claims to be a democracy and holds some kind of elections – the central cleavage is not necessarily between elections and non-elections. The institutionalization of power could be one feature that helps to distinguish the many regimes in the grey zone. The distinction in institutionalist and personalist rule can be applied to democracies too, with liberal democracies clearly in the institutionalist sphere. But what about electoral democracies and all those hybrid regimes? Applying Occam's razor, there is no place for hybrids. The bar for liberal democracy can be raised high enough so that all hybrids fall into one of the autocratic categories. Most electoral democracies will probably fall into the personalist class. Combining these different ideas and models, we get a full classification of regimes, called DAPI regime matrix (Democratic Autocratic Personalist Institutionalist). By using both a horizontal and a vertical continuum, this model has the advantage of categorizing the whole universe of regimes. Fig. 9 shows the DAPI regime matrix.

Institutions are defined as rules. In institutionalized systems, political power is rule oriented. The leader needs to follow rules, his succession will follow rules. In personalist regimes, however, the leader is above such rules. He makes the rules, not follows them. Reviewing the extensive literature on regime types and the sanctions debate, it seems that sanctions destabilize personalist regimes more than others.[405] Economic sanctions decrease state revenues. Personalist leaders usually depend on patronage to keep the elite loyal; thus, they are much more hit by sanctions than other leaders. Furthermore, institutionalized regimes offer peaceful leadership change through succession rules. Regimes with personalist

405 Escribà-Folch & Wright 2015, p. 137.

rulers cannot credibly commit to power-sharing through institutions. Since both economic transfers and the distribution of political power are not available, a personalist ruler will turn to increased repression.[406]

Definition: A personalist regime is a regime in which power is institutionalized on a low level. Effective rule and leadership succession depend on one person or his personal network.

Hypothesis 3: The more personalized rule in the target country is, the more likely is a negative impact on the level of democracy.

3.3.2 Regime legitimacy

Economic sanctions strengthen a regime through mobilizing support: "By strategically stoking nationalist sentiment the incumbent may successfully shift blame to the sender."[407] Facing an external enemy, a leader may turn to nationalism to increase loyalty to the regime.[408] Sanctions, thus, may help legitimize autocratic rule,[409] as happened with the Castro regime in Cuba.[410] Another example is contemporary Venezuela where political mismanagement caused an economic crisis. The regime claims to be the victim, not the cause of economic hardship and blames "external enemies" instead. Sanctions, independently from their design and scope, support that narrative and legitimize the actions of the incumbent regime. With an overall low level of legitimacy, however, an economic shock might help citizens to overcome their collective action problem and increase the mobilization capacity of oppositional forces.[411] Depending on the level of legitimacy, sanctions can signal domestic groups either to back the leader or the opposition.[412]

A high level of legitimacy reduces the costs of loyalty for the leader. According to Wintrobe, loyalty and repression are the major goods in the political market.[413] Sanctions reduce the leader's power "as long as the positive effect of economic

---

406 Escribà-Folch 2012, p. 683; Escribà-Folch & Wright 2015, p. 141; Escribà-Folch & Wright 2010; Escribà-Folch & Wright 2016, p. 12.

407 Wood 2008, p. 495.

408 Escribà-Folch & Wright 2015, pp. 126–127; cf. Grauvogel & Soest 2014; Kaempfer, Lowenberg, & Mertens 2004.

409 Galtung 1967.

410 Burgsdorff 2009, p. 46.

411 Escribà-Folch & Wright 2015, pp. 125–126.

412 Cf. Kaempfer & Lowenberg 1992; Escribà-Folch & Wright 2015.

413 Wintrobe 1990, 1998.

suffering on the price of loyalty is greater than the negative effect on the price of repression, so that on net the price of power increases."[414] Only when the leader attains his legitimacy from economic success and the state engagement in the economy is high, economic crises might lead to regime instability and democratization.

Both loyalty and legitimacy are abstract concepts and can hardly be measured in real-life. Tanneberg et al. declare themselves "sympathetic" with Weber, Arendt, Friedrich & Brzezinski, Linz, who all emphasize ideological or normative support for political systems; however, "in lack of valid and reliable quantitative data this intuition falls into the domain of small-N comparisons."[415] Grauvogel et al. conduct an expert survey to find out the degree of legitimacy of regimes.[416] They find that "sanctions strengthen authoritarian rule if the regime manages to incorporate their existence into its legitimation strategy."[417] The variable legitimacy is crucial because it accounts for the psychological mechanism of economic sanctions.

Definition: Regime legitimacy is the acceptance of political authority by the population.

Hypothesis 4: The higher the level of legitimacy of the ruler in the target country is, the more likely is a negative impact on the level of democracy.

3.4 Economic variables: Vulnerability and development

A third main factor next to the design of sanctions and the political regime is the economic constitution of the target state. Among the many economic variables, two seem to be more important than others: first, the economic vulnerability (openness) of the target state, and second, the level of economic and overall development.

3.4.1 Vulnerability

Economic openness tells us how well a country is integrated into the world economy. Economic openness promotes economic wealth and promotes communicative linkages which can strengthen oppositional forces. At the same time, it is more vulnerable to external threats.[418] The traditional neo-classical trade

414 Kaempfer, Lowenberg, & Mertens 2004, p. 45.
415 Tanneberg, Stefes, & Merkel 2013, p. 127.
416 Grauvogel & Soest 2014, p. 641.
417 Grauvogel & Soest 2014, p. 635.
418 Briguglio, Cordina, Farrugia, & Vella 2009; United Nations Development Programme 2011.

model allows us to see economic sanctions as "mirror images of the movement from the no-trade situation of autarky to a state of the world in which free trade prevails and all countries benefit from international specialisation according to their respective comparative advantage."[419] Economic sanctions are in opposition to free trade; a sanctioned state is similar to an autarkic state. Bergeijk writes that economic sanctions further reverse economic interdependence, and are, therefore, probably more successful in inter-state relationships with a higher degree of economic interdependence.[420]

According to a neo-classical model of trade with two goods and three countries, sanctions benefit a third country if it exports and imports the same types of goods as the target country, or if it engages in sanctions-busting activities.[421] Some groups in the target state can benefit from economic isolation.[422] To substitute for lost imports, a regime establishes policies comparable to a classical import substitution industrialization. If the goods of country A cannot be consumed in country B anymore, the good X (produced by country B) will become more competitive (though it is not better than its competitors) and on long-term more expensive and worse in its quality. The owner and the employees of the company benefit while the consumers suffer. Thus, arms embargoes will dramatically support the domestic arms industry and benefit a military-industrial complex eventually.[423] By increasing market protection in both the short and long run, economic sanctions stimulate the development of domestic industries in the target country: "Sanctions create a powerful domestic interest group in the target country who benefits from market protection and has the economic resources and political clout to secure that protection."[424]

The effect of trade sanctions can be compared to that of tariffs: "they raise domestic prices and protect domestic producers who would otherwise be unable to compete with foreign producers."[425] This import substitution industry could not compete once the sanctions are lifted; therefore, producers lobby for privileged access to the domestic market long-term. Thus, sanctions undermine international trade liberalization, as they create political incentives for increased market protection in the target states. Furthermore, the state supports specific

419 Bergeijk 2009, pp. 119–120.
420 Bergeijk 2009, p. 120.
421 Slavov 2007.
422 Pond 2015, 2017.
423 Brooks 2002, p. 10.
424 Pond 2017, p. 1075.
425 Pond 2017, p. 1074.

industries via subsidies. Companies have no incentives to lobby for liberalization but for getting a bigger share of the sanctions rents.[426] Powerful interest groups lobby for market protection,[427] as happened in Yugoslavia[428] and South Rhodesia.[429] Economic sanctions can be path-dependent because they create in long-term, unintentionally, a mercantilist economy.[430]

Domestic producers, who would be unable to compete with foreign producers under normal circumstances, are protected by the state at the expenses of the macro-economy and the consumers. Sanctions usually target groups that are politically influential. However, these groups are probably also influential enough to convince the leadership to keep privileged access to the market even after the end the sanctions. Pond, therefore, argues, that sanctions have a long-term impact on the economic structure of the target state: They create a powerful domestic interest group that uses its rents to pressure the leadership to protect their market rents also in future.[431] Post-2014 financial sanctions against Russia cut off Bank Rossiya from payments via Visa and MasterCard. The Russian president Putin announced to develop a Russian credit card system and close the market for foreign competitors.[432]

This argument explains the rise of a military-bureaucratic authoritarian regimes in Latin America and elsewhere in the 1960s: This industrialization strategy brought together industrialists and working class, both benefitting from protectionism against foreign competitors by import quotas, tariffs and foreign exchange regulations. However, the benefits proved to be only short-term: Once the limits of domestic growth were reached, industry proved to be non-competitive internationally, followed by foreign exchange shortages, negative growth rates, and mass unemployment. The economic crisis led to increased political polarization and, eventually, to military coups in face of Cuban-style coup threats.[433]

---

426 Kaempfer & Lowenberg 1999, pp. 53–54.
427 Pond 2017.
428 Andreas 2005.
429 Peksen 2010, p. 244.
430 Interest groups within the sender countries have protectionist interests too, as the anti-Apartheid sanctions against South Africa show. Kaempfer & Lowenberg 1999, pp. 53–54; cf. Kaempfer & Lowenberg 1988.
431 Pond 2017, p. 1074.
432 Pond 2017, p. 1074.
433 Özbudun 2011.

A country with a low level of interdependence is used to a non-trade situation and does not need to change its economic rules much. The more a country is integrated into the global economy, the more it needs to adapt to the sanctions regime. It adopts policies that protects core sectors of the economy. The costs of protectionism are born by the aggregate economy and the consumers who are forced to buy cars from the heretofore non-competitive company. The winners are the workers and the owners of that company.[434] Protectionism strengthens the role of politics in business and the role of business in the economy. Independently from the economic costs, sanctions lead to a clientelist alliance of business community and political groups that will do its best to collect the fruits of the no-trade situation. They exchange political protection for economic benefits. A patron-client network including political, economic, and military elites is not only a characteristic of autocracies[435] but also a step towards it. Protectionism leads to autocracy, summarizes Friedman, because it develops its own dynamics. Once a state imposes a measure such as direct control on foreign exchange, this leads inevitably to import substitution and to further steps "in a never-ending spiral."[436]

Definition: Vulnerability is the ability to be influenced or hurt. The economic vulnerability of a country is an indicator for the degree how much a country may be affected by external economic shocks. It can be measured by the economy's dependence on export and import with the world.

Hypothesis 5: The higher the level of economic vulnerability of the target economy is, the more likely is a negative impact on the level of democracy.

3.4.2 Development

One of the best-known assumptions in comparative politics is that democratic and economic development are systematically interrelated. Since the 19th century, scholars – including Marxists, liberal economists, and monarchists – observe a relationship between market and (parliamentary) democracy.[437] The dominant research program in the democratization debate became the modernization theory as formulated by Lipset. He claimed that democracy was enabled and consolidated by a process of *modernization*: "the factors of industrialization, urbanization, wealth, and education are so closely interrelated as to form one common factor.

434 Brooks 2002, pp. 34, 49.
435 Bueno de Mesquita, Smith, Siverson, & Morrow 2003; Wintrobe 1998.
436 Friedman 2002 [1962], p. 57.
437 Glassman 1991, p. 65.

And the factors subsumed under economic development carry with it the political correlate of democracy."[438] Economic growth develops a middle class which wants to secure its economic welfare through political participation. Economic prosperity affects democracy positively by disrupting traditional social structures (clan, class, caste) and by increasing mobility, education.[439] The emerging middle class pushes for political participation.

The statistical correlation between economic development and democracy is strongly positive; rich countries tend to be more democratic. The exact causes, however, are still unclear. It is "maddeningly difficult"[440] to find out which sub-variables of modernization are causes of democracy and which are effects. Most scholars interpret sub-variables of economic development as causal variables for democracy: higher income per capita,[441] GDP per capita,[442] economic growth,[443] market institutions,[444] resource distribution,[445] equality,[446] economic freedom,[447] low inequality,[448] high inequality.[449]

For Moore Jr., it is the middle class which pushes for democratization;[450] for Rueschemeyer et al. it is the working class;[451] for Albertus et al. it is the economic elite: Economic elites suffer more from political elites in autocracies than in democracies, and they prefer democratization especially when they can participate in "constitutional engineering."[452] For Weingast, democracy is a "self-enforcing equilibrium" which results from all actors who simply maximize their own welfare.[453]

---

438 Lipset 1959, p. 80.
439 Huntington 1968, pp. 49–50.
440 Coppedge 1997.
441 Boix 2011; Dahl 1971; Huntington 1991; Wu & Davis 1999.
442 Svolik 2008.
443 Jeitschko, Linz, Noguera, & Semykina 2014.
444 Boudreaux & Holcombe 2017.
445 Vanhanen 2003, p. 183.
446 Benhabib & Przeworski 2006, p. 271.
447 Friedman 2002 [1962], p. 9; confirmed by Wu & Davis 1999; Lawson & Clark 2010, p. 231; cf. cf. Sartori 1987; Schumpeter 1976 [1942].
448 Boix 2003.
449 Acemoglu & Robinson 2000b.
450 Moore Jr. 1966.
451 Rueschemeyer, Stephens, & Stephens 1992.
452 Albertus & Menaldo 2014.
453 Weingast 1997.

Other scholars doubt the causality often associated with modernization hypothesis.[454] Instead, they interpret both variables as covariates and find alternative explanations in history (critical junctures), or in a temporally[455] or spatially[456] clustered democratization. Despite the many alternative explanations on the correlation between economic and political development, the modernization hypothesis is still the most convincing explanation for democratization, and, thus, needs to be included in a quantitative analysis of the economic impact on the political system.

Definition: Development is a process of change and advance. The development level of a country is an indicator that measures how advanced a country is in important areas such as wealth, education and healthcare.

Hypothesis 6: The less developed the target country is, the more likely is a negative impact of economic sanctions on the level of democracy.

3.5 Control variables: Natural resources and war

Additional variables are necessary to control for the effect independent factors might have, though they are not directly related to the research question. This analysis includes natural resources and civil war as control variables. Both are typically used in academic papers dealing with the side-effect of economic sanctions.

3.5.1 Natural resources

Building on the resource curse and rentier state hypothesis, the model includes resources as a control variable. Natural resources help stabilize autocratic regimes that are targeted by sanctions.[457] Research on the effects of natural resources like oil, gas, and minerals states that they hinder democratic development. Ross was the first one who claimed that natural resources hinder democratic transition and consolidation.[458] Resources provide the autocrat with the one thing he needs most: money. Therefore, he is more independent from the overall economic performance.

Governments use resource revenues to "relieve social pressures that might otherwise lead to demands for greater accountability" (rentier effect).[459] The leader can distribute goods and is independent of taxation of his citizens and

454 E.g., Acemoglu, Johnson, Robinson, & Yared 2008, 2009.
455 Boix 2011; Gunitsky 2014; cf. Cf. Levitsky & Way 2010.
456 Bader, Grävingholt, & Kästner 2010; Brinks & Coppedge 2006; Gleditsch & Ward 2006; cf. Gunitsky 2014, p. 592.
457 Escribà-Folch & Wright 2015, p. 141.
458 Ross 2001.
459 Ross 2001, p. 332.

their claim for political representation (no representation without taxation). He can buy off potential competitors and opponents, which leads to corruption and clientelism: "Kleptocratic policies are more likely when foreign aid and rents from natural resources provide rulers with substantial resources to buy off opponents."[460] Wright et al. find that resource wealth lowers the risk of coups.[461]

Furthermore, the government can spend much more money on internal security and repression, thus suppressing opposition (repression effect).[462] Hard repression can stabilize the country, however, it can also increase tensions: Wenar argues that resource dependent countries are more prone to civil conflict.[463] Also, if resource wealth does not lead to higher education and greater occupational specialization, it does not lead to democracy either.

Ross sees a correlation between resource dependency and higher rates of child malnutrition, lower life expectancy, lower healthcare and education budgets, higher illiteracy rates, and higher poverty rates.[464] Thus, resources increase the consolidation and durability of regimes,[465] especially when targeted by economic sanctions.[466] A 1 percent increase in natural resource dependence can increase the likelihood of an autocratic regime by nearly 8 percent.[467]

The overwhelming majority agrees with the basic hypothesis.[468] Few scholars disagree and point to third variables:[469] Arab region, a Muslim majority population, weak state capacity,[470] bad governance, autocracy already before the discovery of resources, a low level of industrialization.[471] Haber et al. argue that weak state capacity jointly determines autocracy and high levels of resource reliance, and the "resource curse" is, in fact, a "resource blessing" because it helps the state to modernize.[472]

460 Acemoglu, Robinson, & Verdier 2004, p. 162.
461 Wright, Frantz, & Geddes 2015.
462 Ross 2001, p. 332.
463 Wenar 2008.
464 Ross 2001.
465 Cf. Smith 2004; Ulfelder 2007.
466 Escribà-Folch & Wright 2015, p. 141.
467 Wantchekon 2002.
468 E.g., Ulfelder 2007; Wantchekon 2002.
469 E.g., Herb 2005.
470 Haber & Menaldo 2011.
471 Humphreys 2005.
472 Haber & Menaldo 2011.

Definition: Resources are valuable possessions of a country; natural resources are valuable possessions provided by nature.

3.5.2 Civil war

Previous research showed that violent conflicts harm political development. The more people protest against the regime, the more the regime might feel to be forced to apply violent means to keep control.[473] The database Major Episodes of Political Violence (MEPV) distinguishes inter-state conflicts from societal conflicts, latter including civil conflicts and ethnic conflicts. Once inter-state conflicts have an impact on the society, they also can be defined as civil war.

Definition: Civil war is an armed conflict within a country.

3.6 Summary

Among the many variables mentioned both in the sanctions and the democratization literature, the most convincing ones have been selected. Two variables are related to the design of sanctions: economic costs and democratic goal. The variable economic costs measures the economic impact of sanctions. The variable democratic goal of sanctions is crucial because it allows not only to control for unintended side-effects but also to measure the success. Two variables are related to the political sphere of the target country: The variable personalist regime, defined as opposite of an institutionalist regime, controls for the type of regime. Previous literature found that the regime type is one of the main factors of sanctions outcome. Legitimacy, a second variable, controls for the psychological mechanism that sanctions could initiate: If the state leader has strong claims to legitimacy, external threats tend to increase support for him, whereas leaders with weak claims to legitimacy might face instability and potential overthrow. Two variables come from the economic sphere: The economic vulnerability of the targeted regime is important for the leader's ability to counter economic shocks. The more the country depends on the world economy, the more its economy may potentially be affected by economic sanctions. The variable development comes from classic modernization theory that sees some correlation between economic and political development. One control variable controls for the effect of natural resources (resource curse hypothesis), another one for the effect of armed conflict.

473 Peksen & Drury 2010, p. 252.

Due to methodological reasons, the number of variables is limited. The most important design-related, state-related, and economy-related variables were chosen. Many other variables from democratization literature and sanctions literature cannot be included in the quantitative analysis. The most important variable that was not included is the threat of sanctions. Several scholars argued that sanctions can have an impact or even be successful already at the threat stage because the targets might adjust their policies in anticipation of potential costs,[474] so no economic costs for the target economy can be measured. Drezner writes that the most successful cases of economic coercion end at the threat stage, which may understate the success rate of economic sanctions.[475] Lacy et al. agree and point out that sanctions are only imposed when the threat was not successful.[476] The reason why this book excludes sanction threats is the problematic measurement of threats and their impact. Usually, there are no explicit announcements or even legal texts providing details on the threatened sanctions. This book mainly focuses on an economic mechanism; the signaling effect of threats is difficult to measure.

The following chapter explains the mechanisms underlying the variables and combines sanctions literature, economic crises literature, and an agency approach based on autocracy research.

474 Smith 1996; Bergeijk 2009, p. 126; Krustev 2010; Lacy & Niou 2004.

475 Drezner 2003.

476 Lacy & Niuo 2004.

Part II Designing

"What is important here is cash. [A] leader needs money, gold and diamonds to run his hundred castles, feed his thousand women, buy cars for the millions of boot-lickers under his heels, reinforce the loyal military forces and still have enough change left to deposit into his numbered Swiss accounts."

—Mobutu Sese Seko, President of Zaire 1965–1997, attr.[477]

"It was just too expensive."

—Pik Botha, South African Minister of Foreign Affairs 1977–1994, on his government's decision to abandon apartheid[478]

477 Qtd. in Bueno de Mesquita & Smith 2011, introduction.
478 Qtd. in Wintrobe 1998, p. 163.

4 The market of political survival

At least since Machiavelli, modern political strategists and scholars think about the best strategies of a leader to retain power. Only in the last decades, the role of the agency was put into the focus of democratization literature too.[479] A famous analogy is the market of political survival, with different players and goods or tools. Threat to leadership survival can come from within the system (competing elite groups, example: Egypt 2013), from within the state (mass uprising, example: Russia 1917, Venezuela 2017), or from outside the state (exogenous, example: Iraq 2003).

The current chapter provides a theoretical mechanism on the political effects of economic sanctions. First, it looks at the players in the game and sees how economic crises can disrupt a stable political system. Then, it looks at tools – or "goods," following the market analogy – and thinks about what a leader can do to keep the system stable. Finally, it integrates the variables of this book together with goods and players into one model.

Partly, this chapter will repeat the factors presented in the previous chapters. It is crucial to embed hypotheses into a sound theoretical model and to look at them from different perspectives. Some contributions to the debate provide spectacular findings: "[S]anctions are likely to exacerbate women's rights."[480] "[S]anctions prompt the government to pursue ethnic-based discriminatory [...] political practices."[481] "[E]conomic sanctions will likely inflict significant damage on media independence."[482] The theoretical explanation, however, is sometimes weak. Therefore, it is important to search in existing literature for the main arguments (Chapter 2), establish hypotheses (Chapter 3), and integrate them into a theoretical model to look at them in a larger context (current Chapter 4).

---

479 E.g., Tullock 1987; Wintrobe 1998.

480 Drury & Peksen 2014, p. 463.

481 Peksen 2014, p. 480.

482 Peksen 2010, p. 462.

4.1 Players: Horizontal and vertical threats

"Democracies can be made (or unmade) in the act of making them."[483]

After Rustow observed that democracy is a result of elite choice,[484] a new strand of scholarship shifted the focus from socio-economic (structural) preconditions to a "world driven by human agency."[485] Teorell writes that democracy is "promoted by long-term structural forces such as economic prosperity, but also by peaceful popular uprisings and the institutional setup of authoritarian regimes." Short term, however, "elite actors may play a key role, particularly through the importance of intra-regime splits."[486]

In this new strand of autocracy research, which exists mainly since the early 1990s and thus coincides with the third wave of democratization, political elites are the main actors and the crucial elements of any political transition. The autocratic leader is a rational actor who is maximizing his power and also his economic benefits.[487] His learning and adjustment capability is an argument against modernization theory.[488] Recent contributions combine structuralist theories such as the old assumption that inequality is the driving force in democratization,[489] with agency-based tools of game theory.[490] Bueno de Mesquita et al. argue that leaders with a small winning coalition survive economic crises best. Their so-called selectorate model does not distinguish between democratic or autocratic institutions; instead, it analyzes any political system according to the size of its actors: the population, the selectorate (the group that selects the leader), the winning coalition, and the incumbent leader or leadership.[491] Relevant is not the institutional design of the political system but the variation of the size of the winning coalition relative to the selectorate.

In contrast to the more sophisticated selectorate model, this book distinguishes only between three players within a political system: leadership, winning

483 Di Palma 1990, p. 8.

484 Rustow 1970.

485 Ulfelder 2012, pp. 149–150.

486 Teorell 2010, abstract.

487 Geddes 1999; Olson 1993; Tullock 1987; Wintrobe 1990.

488 Bueno de Mesquita & Downs 2005.

489 Lipset 1960; Moore Jr. 1966.

490 Whereas Acemoglu & Robinson 2006 describe the horizontal threat of revolution, Bueno de Mesquita & Smith 2017 focus mainly on the vertical threat of coups.

491 Bueno de Mesquita, Downs, Smith, & Cherif 2005; Bueno de Mesquita & Smith 2009, 2010, 2011, 2017; Bueno de Mesquita, Smith, Siverson, & Morrow 2003.

coalition, and population. The leadership can be just one person in dictatorships, the whole government in liberal democracies, or the politburo or its standing committee in one-party regimes.

The leader needs a winning coalition to stay in power; it is "made up of those residents whose support is essential for sustaining the incumbent in office."[492] In states with a close relationship between political and economic elite, this can include a business community, in other states, it can be a political party or the military. Tang et al. define the winning coalition as business elite (and the leadership as the political elite).[493] The threat to the leadership from the winning coalition – a coup d'état – is defined as vertical threat. The leader has to take care of his winning coalition and redistribute enough goods to it. According to O'Donnell & Schmitter, there is "no transition whose beginning is not the consequence – direct or indirect – of important divisions within the authoritarian regime."[494]

The third important player is the population. The revolutionary threat from the population is defined as the horizontal threat. If the leader has not enough public goods to redistribute to them, he can rely on political rights, enfranchisement, a further institutionalization of power, or a higher level of civil liberties. In Iran, kleptocratic behavior by members of the winning coalition increased significantly over the last two decades, at the same time, civil liberties increased slightly, thus distracting from the first issue.

In most cases, sanctions are in some way aimed at decreasing the leader's budget. Whereas comprehensive economic sanctions aim to decrease it through targeting the macro-economy, sanctions on a smaller scale can target the leadership and the winning coalition directly. In recent years, scholars argue that economic decline – caused by economic shocks, recession or sanctions – can be a crucial short-term factor for political transition. An economic crisis disrupts the balance of power and provides an opportunity for political change.[495] It deprives the leader of what he needs most: money. Especially the stability of autocratic regimes relies on the distribution of wealth: "Economic crises [...] create a basis for a series of unexpected, unpredictable events."[496] Such unpredictable threats change the game, and all players need to adapt their strategies.

An economic crisis can be or exogenous, caused by worldwide recession or by economic sanctions, or endogenous to domestic politics, as the Chavezian regime in Venezuela shows in an exemplary fashion. Similar to the relation

492 Bueno de Mesquita & Smith 2009, p. 171.

493 Tang, Huhe, & Zhou 2017, p. 76.

494 O'Donnell & Schmitter 1986, p. 19.

495 E.g., Teorell 2010; Boix & Svolik 2013.

496 Desai, Olofsgård, & Yousef 2009, p. 96; cf. O'Donnell & Schmitter 1986.

between economic development and political transition, the one between economic crises and political transition is rather unclear too. A number of studies see economic crises as a major source of regime (and democratic) failure.[497] Economic crises are "usually seen as the most important single reason for regime breakdown,"[498] as powerful autocracies (Louis XVI, Soviet Union) and liberal democracies (Weimar Republic) show.

Economic crises pose a substantial threat to a leader: Economic crises can reduce the leader's budget who might not be able to buy loyalty and lead to elite defection and coup attempts,[499] mobilize popular protest,[500] and split the elite over the question of how to respond best to the economic crises.[501] The leader must appease both the elite and the population.[502] The unrests in Venezuela in 2017 are an example of how difficult that is. The economic crisis triggered popular unrest and elite defections because elite members were displeased with the lowered rents during times of crisis. As soon as a leader is no longer able to provide resources to his supporters, his political survival is in danger,[503] and he needs to rely on other tools. The vertical threat (elite) is more dangerous than the horizontal one (population): 68 percent of all autocrats between 1945 and 2002 were deposed by a coup.[504] The leadership can also use the horizontal threat against the vertical one. One of the major problems for the leader is that horizontal and vertical threats are often mutually reinforcing: "Elite splits will embolden opposition activists as much as mass uprisings encourage elites to leave the seemingly sinking ship, thereby making their perception of immanent regime breakdown a self-fulfilling prophecy."[505] Fig. 10 shows the players.

Economic crises – to which economic sanctions belong – disrupt the careful balance of what makes a political system stable. The leader has to re-adjust the whole system; if he succeeds, he can stay on as leader, if he fails, he has to leave his office and another leader will follow him, in some cases even democratization or autocratization may take place.

---

497 Burke & Leigh 2010; Gasiorowski 1995; Haggard & Kaufman 2016; Przeworski, Alvarez, Cheibub, & Limongi 2000; Svolik 2008.
498 Geddes 2004, p. 26.
499 Haggard & Kaufman 1997.
500 Bratton & van de Walle 1997.
501 O'Donnell & Schmitter 1986.
502 Geddes 2004; O'Donnell & Schmitter 1986; Przeworski 1991.
503 Bueno de Mesquita, Smith, Siverson, & Morrow 2003, pp. 26–27.
504 Svolik 2009.
505 Tanneberg, Stefes, & Merkel 2013, p. 117.

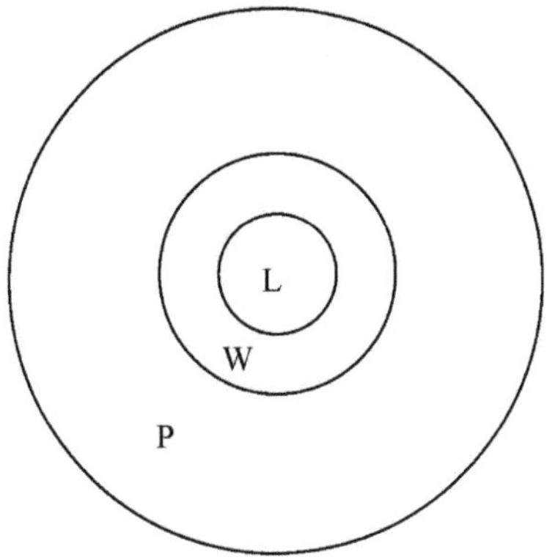

Fig. 10: Players: leadership (L), winning coalition (W), population (P)

4.2 Tools: Repression, economic transfers, political power

A breakthrough in autocracy research was Wintrobe's combination of the political question of autocratic regime stability with the language of economics (*supply*, *demand*, *price*). Wintrobe sees political life as a marketplace "in which political exchanges take place."[506] The population gives the leader political power in exchange for other goods. The difference to the economic market is that such a political contract is not enforceable because there is no higher authority. The problem of (mutual) cheating is solved by investment in loyalty. The autocrat's second tool is repression. The careful balancing of repression and loyalty rewards and its constant re-adjusting is the secret of leader survival in autocracies.[507]

Wintrobe also argues that decline in economic performance has different effects in different types of autocracies. If the autocrat only tends to minimize the costs of remaining in power to collect the fruits of office, he needs to increase repression. If the autocrat likes to maximize power (totalitarian regime), he will reduce repression in case of economic decline. In authoritarian regimes, a strong economic performance could lead in the long run even to democratization. If the authoritarian leader does not respond with repression to economic decline, he will be deposed. Wintrobe sees the fall of the Iranian shah in 1979 as an example of a wrong relaxation of repression, following the deterioration in economic

506 Wintrobe 1990, p. 851.
507 "Autocrats learn and adjust." Kagan 2008, p. 57.

conditions after 1976.[508] Many scholars since Wintrobe identify repression and loyalty rewards[509] or co-optation as the leader's main tools.[510]

4.2.1 Repression

Peksen et al. find that economic sanctions increase the regime's "coercive capacity and create incentives for the regime's leadership to commit political repression."[511] Repression is often described as the main characteristic of autocracies. It is defined as the actual or threatened use of (physical) violence against individuals or social groups, "for the purpose of imposing a cost on the target as well as deterring specific activities."[512] Almost all studies find that democratic political institutions decrease state repression, what Davenport calls domestic democratic peace,[513] analogous to the democratic peace hypothesis in International Relations theory.[514] Dahl theorizes that democratization occurs when the costs of repression become greater than the costs of toleration.[515] The price of repression includes the costs of paying police and military, maintaining the judicial system and prisons.

Bove et al. distinguish between vertical repression (elite) and horizontal repression (citizens).[516] They find that the ruler's reliance on vertical and horizontal repression is antithetically affected by the country's wealth. Other studies distinguish between high and low-intensity repression,[517] and between soft and hard repression: Soft repression is non-violent and includes harassment, surveillance, restriction of civil liberties. It aims at increasing the collective action problem of the opposition.[518] Soft repression could "prevent economic misfortune from turning into a critical juncture."[519] Escribà-Folch shows that civil liberties restrictions increase autocratic survival.[520]

---

508 Wintrobe 1990, pp. 859–860.
509 E.g., Gandhi 2008; Gershenson & Grossman 2001.
510 Tanneberg, Stefes, & Merkel 2013.
511 Peksen & Drury 2009, p. 393.
512 Davenport 2007, p. 2.
513 Davenport 2007, p. 10.
514 Russett 1993.
515 Dahl 1971, pp. 15–16.
516 Bove, Platteau, & Sekeris 2016.
517 Levitsky & Way 2010.
518 Tucker 2007.
519 Tanneberg, Stefes, & Merkel 2013, p. 119.
520 Escribà-Folch 2013.

Hard repression relies on the use of violence and includes torture, disappearances, and extra judicial imprisonment and killing of opposition members. Often, it is considered as counterproductive. It can increase the vertical threat and help the opposition to overcome the collective action problem. This so-called repression-protest paradox means that regime violence can quell popular unrest or provoke even larger mass mobilization (Syria 2011).[521] Also, it can increase the horizontal threat (defection of elite members), and exogenous threats (sanctions, war).[522] Hard repression may be ineffective in competitive authoritarian regimes because opposition groups have legal status, whereas it can be more effective in other autocratic regime types.[523]

The actual level of repression, however, must not be confused with repressive capacity. Empirical evidence suggests that repressive capacity is more important than applied repression. It is costly to change the level of repressive capacity. For outsiders, it is difficult to observe and measure it.[524] The information asymmetry is in most cases an advantage for the incumbent leader, but sometimes it can also put him at a disadvantage: The more repression he applies, the friendlier his enemies might talk to him, and the worse think of him.[525] It is a problem of trust and the credibility of commitments. Kuran describes this as a disjunction between the "private beliefs" and "publicly expressed opinions," which makes revolutions unpredictable.[526] The autocrat's dilemma is, the more power he has, the more insecure he feels. Only the right balance between repression and redistribution solves the dictator's dilemma.[527] Wintrobe explains with this dilemma the alleged paranoia of many autocrats, from the Roman emperor Tiberius to the Philippine president Marcos.[528]

Definition: Repression is the actual or threatened use of violence against individuals or groups. It can target both the population (horizontal repression) and the elite (vertical repression). Hard repression relies on physical violence (torture, murder), whereas soft repression relies on non-physical measures (harassment, surveillance).

---

521 Cf. Osa & Corduneanu-Huci 2003, p. 607.
522 Cf. Tanneberg, Stefes, & Merkel 2013, p. 119.
523 Lueders & Croissant 2014, p. 332.
524 Desai, Olofsgård, & Yousef 2009, p. 118.
525 Wintrobe 1998, p. 25.
526 Kuran 1995.
527 Wintrobe 1998, p. 337.
528 Wintrobe 1998, pp. 335–336.

4.2.2 Economic transfers

States are not necessarily repressive. The leadership can provide loyalty rewards to avoid counterproductive repression. To decrease the horizontal threat of protests and the vertical threat of elite splits and coups, a leader can reward loyalty via redistributing goods. A main finding of autocratic survival research is that the leader must choose the right balance between private and public goods.[529] Meltzer et al. develop a distributive conflict model of regime change and argue that greater inequality in a consolidated democracy increases redistribution.[530] Building on this model, both Acemoglu et al.[531] and Boix[532] think that the main division within society is the one between the poor (population) and the rich (elite), the latter also being the political elite to protect their profits. The leadership's primary tool is redistribution which can be used in case of a revolutionary threat.

Private goods benefit the leader's supporter and are necessary to keep the winning coalition together. An overreliance on the distribution of goods and co-optation results in patron-client networks, systematic corruption, clientelism, and kleptocracy. The support base in such patron-client networks is often organized along linguistic, religious or ideological lines.[533]

The leader can also provide public goods to the population in general. Citizens relinquish political influence in exchange for public spending. An autocratic leader's survival is more likely if he adopts such welfare policies.[534] Public goods benefit everyone: rule of law, security, transparency and accountability, education, antipollution legislation, communication and transportation infrastructure, welfare.[535] The provision of public goods is also connected to state capacity and governance. By providing more and more public goods, the population becomes more productive and the leader's output will increase. This is a win-win-situation and creates benefits for the leader and the population: "[A]n 'invisible hand' gives a roving bandit an incentive to make himself a

529 Desai, Olofsgård, & Yousef 2009, p. 95; cf. Bueno de Mesquita & Smith 2010; Gandhi & Przeworski 2006.

530 Meltzer & Richard 1981.

531 Acemoglu & Robinson 2001.

532 Boix 2003.

533 Acemoglu, Robinson, & Verdier 2004; Bueno de Mesquita, Smith, Siverson, & Morrow 2003; Mehlum, Moene, & Torvik 2002; Milante 2007.

534 Overland, Simons, & Spagat 2005.

535 Bueno de Mesquita, Smith, Siverson, & Morrow 2003, p. 29–31.

public-good-providing king."[536] An autocrat, therefore, is thus "not like the wolf that preys on the elk, but more like the rancher who makes sure that his cattle are protected and given water."[537] This applies, of course, only to leaders with a long-time horizon. An autocrat with a short time-horizon is more concerned about the immediate extraction of the maximum of goods, and thus behaves like a roving bandit.[538] Liberal-democratic regimes with their system of checks and balances have the advantage of "preventing significant extraction of social surplus by their leaders."[539]

What the leader does not use as public or private goods, he can keep for himself (personal goods) and future uncertainties. "The greater the discretionary resources, the greater are the incumbent's survival prospects;" the smaller the winning coalition is, the more resources the leader has.[540] The leader's revenues have legal sources (taxation; depends on the provision of public goods), illegal sources (bribes, smuggling), or free sources that are independent of the provision of public goods (natural resources, foreign aid). Pond finds that when facing a revolutionary threat, autocrats liberalize financial markets to stimulate the economy so that they can distribute more goods and undermine political opposition.[541] The distinction between private and public goods is not as easy as it seems: In real life, all policies contain somewhat aspects of private and public goods.[542] Whereas the definition in the selectorate model also includes repression, this book defines goods as economic transfers. Repression and political rights are located in separate spheres.

Definition: Economic transfers are loyalty rewards for the winning coalition or the whole population.

4.2.3 Political power

In addition to repression and economic loyalty rewards, this book adds political power as good that can be redistributed or centralized.[543] The political sphere is different from repression which mainly concerns the individual liberty

536 McGuire & Olson 1996, p. 73.
537 Olson 1993, p. 569.
538 McGuire & Olson 1996, p. 80.
539 Olson 1993, p. 574.
540 Bueno de Mesquita & Smith 2009, p. 173.
541 Pond 2017.
542 Bueno de Mesquita, Smith, Siverson, & Morrow 2003, p. 31; cf. Desai, Olofsgård, & Yousef 2009, p. 95.
543 Similar to Desai, Olofsgård, & Yousef 2009, p. 94.

of the people. The offer to participate in the political process is perhaps the cheapest – and sometimes the last – tool of the leader.

The question of whether repression and co-optation (a term usually used to describe the distribution of political rights) are substitutive or complementary strategies for autocratic survival has not been determined yet.[544] Wintrobe and Bueno de Mesquita et al. see both variables as substitutive, which means that the average autocrat who uses more co-optation tends to use less repression.[545] Wintrobe thinks that the autocrat's capacity for repression "also entails a greater tendency to redistribute income or wealth, in contrast to democracies."[546] According to Bove et al., repression increases the risk of coups, whereas co-optation decreases it.[547] Desai et al., however, find that the provision of public goods (welfare spending) and political liberalization are negatively related in authoritarian states and see both variables as a trade-off.[548] Political decentralization can decrease the vertical and the horizontal threat.

4.2.3.1 Vertical: Co-optation

Policy concessions can prolong the rule of autocrats because they can be used as a tool for co-opting potential competitors, especially if the autocrat is too greedy or not able to share his rents. "[D]ictatorships maintain institutions for systematic reasons: to mobilize cooperation and, if the opposition is threatening, also to thwart the danger of rebellion."[549] Narrow institutions (such as juntas or political bureaus) serve as a first "institutional trench against threats from rivals within the ruling elite."[550] Threats from competing elite groups or the population can be neutralized if they are incorporated into somewhat democratic institutions such as a legislature. Also, formal institutions help to co-opt actors who have strategically important resources.[551]

Institutions promote the survival of autocrats by facilitating power-sharing: "once such institutions are in place, the [regime] can maintain a more stable ruling coalition under less favorable circumstances than would be possible

544 Bove & Rivera 2015, p. 458.
545 Bueno de Mesquita & Smith 2010; Wintrobe 1990.
546 Wintrobe 1998, p. 339.
547 Bove & Rivera 2015, p. 454.
548 Desai, Olofsgård, & Yousef 2009, p. 118.
549 Gandhi & Przeworski 2006, p. 21.
550 Gandhi 2008.
551 Gerschewski, Merkel, Schmotz, Stefes, & Tanneberg 2012, p. 4.

without those institutions."[552] They are a tool to facilitate power sharing among the elite.[553] The main reason why autocrats install legislatures is to co-opt opposition groups in order to broaden their basis of support.[554] Having opposition groups within formal institutions also allows the autocrat to "negotiate over various policy realms without having to reconstitute his bargaining partner each time."[555] Also, the establishment of such institutions or the co-optation of some elite members into them builds trust, shares information, and makes credible commitments.[556]

4.2.3.2 Horizontal: Enfranchisement

Further groups of the population can be enfranchised to decrease the horizontal threat. Slow democratization pushed by the autocratic leadership, in connection with stable development, can guarantee the leader's and the elite's survival.[557] For an autocrat with a strong opposition, it is crucial to keep latter within the system. Institutions serve to divide and co-opt the opposition.[558] They can help the leader to tackle threats to the leadership.[559] Partial concessions are sometimes seen as a sign of weakness and can develop their own dynamics, see Louis XVI in 1789, the Kerensky government in Russia in 1917, or the Shah in 1978.[560] Political decentralization of centralization often occurs in times of economic crises, because "the costs of political turmoil, both to the rich and to the poor, are lower during such episodes."[561] Transition to democracy is a way to avoid a costly revolution,[562] and therefore preferred by the rich elite that wants to keep as many resources as possible, and decides to share political power with the population.[563]

---

552 Boix & Svolik 2013, p. 301.
553 Svolik 2009, p. 493.
554 Boix & Svolik 2013; Gandhi 2008; Gandhi & Przeworski 2006, 2007; Wright 2008.
555 Gandhi 2008, p. 78.
556 Gandhi 2008; Gandhi & Przeworski 2007; Wright 2008.
557 Milante 2007.
558 Gandhi & Przeworski 2006, 2007.
559 Acemoglu & Robinson 2006; Brownlee 2007; Bueno de Mesquita, Morrow, Siverson, & Smith 1999; Bueno de Mesquita, Smith, Siverson, & Morrow 2003; Gandhi 2008; Magaloni 2006, 2008; Svolik 2009.
560 Examples mentioned by Acemoglu & Robinson 2000a, p. 684.
561 Acemoglu & Robinson 2001, p. 939; cf. Acemoglu & Robinson 2006.
562 Acemoglu & Robinson 2000b.
563 Acemoglu & Robinson 2000a.

Exogenous shocks increase pressure from below:[564] “As the least well off overcome their collective action problems […], the repression cost incurred by the wealthy rise[s],” which forces the elite to make institutional compromises.[565] Democratization is nothing else than showing credible commitment. Whereas economic redistribution in case of revolutionary threat is mostly perceived as a short-term satisfaction of the masses and therefore not credible, an institutionalization of power is a credible commitment to a more equal distribution of wealth also in the long run.

An institutionalization of power may not necessarily benefit the masses. Elections and legislatures “can become instruments of authoritarian domination.”[566] Some scholars see institutions as support of autocratic rule,[567] for others, this gradual liberalization is an almost irreversible process and leads long-term to the fall of the autocratic regime.[568] In times of crises, a leader may also turn to centralization of political power.

Definition: Political power is the possession of the means of influencing the will of others.[569] *Political rights are a good that enables the receiver to participate in the political process. Such rights are redistributed by the leadership to his winning coalition or the population and can include enfranchisement, the installation of a legislature or a general institutionalization of power.*

4.3 Integrating the variables

There are three players in our market of political survival: the leader, his winning coalition, and the population. An economic crisis disrupts the domestic peace and introduces incentives for the players to act: Elite members attempt a coup d'état (vertical threat); the population protests and attempts a revolution (horizontal threat). The leader tries to re-stabilize the system by acting in three spheres: First, he can increase (or decrease) the level of repression (aimed at the population or the elite). Second, he can transfer economic benefits to everyone (public goods) or his loyal supporters (private goods). Third, he can decentralize political power by enfranchising larger parts of the population, introducing new

564 Boix 2003, pp. 28–30.

565 Boix 2003, p. 13.

566 Haggard & Kaufman 2016, p. 127.

567 Brownlee 2007; Gandhi 2008; Gandhi & Przeworski 2007; Magaloni 2008.

568 Huntington 1991, p. 137; Przeworski 1991, p. 58.

569 Based on G. C. Lewis' definition of power (1832), qtd. in Baldwin 2016, p. 1.

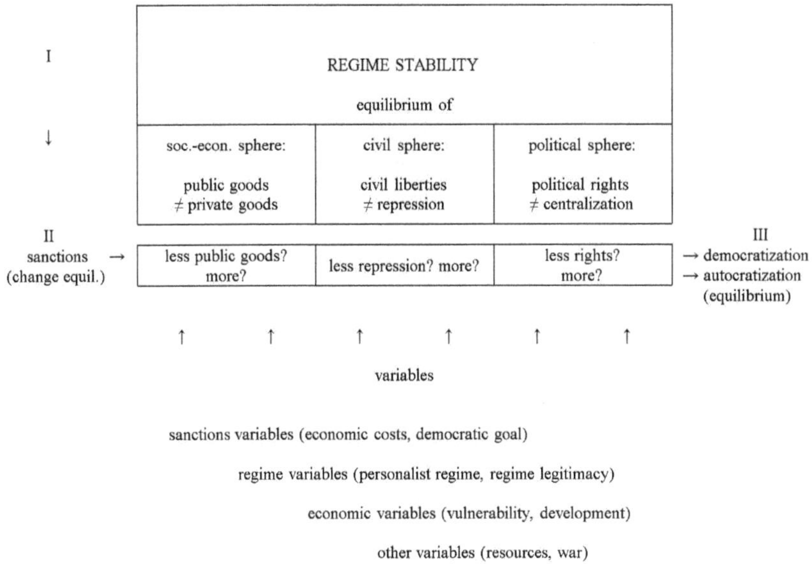

Fig. 11: Sanctions and regime stability

institutions or co-opting competing elite members or opposition groups into formal institutions – of course, the leader can also further centralize power. In analogy to Bueno de Mesquita et al.'s selectorate model,[570] this model applies not only to autocracies but to all states. Regime stability is based on an equilibrium of the socio-economic sphere, the civil sphere, and the political sphere. The three goods a leader has – economic transfers, repression, political power – mirror the tripartite definition of democracy and autocracy in the previous chapter (state capacity, civil liberties, political rights). Fig. 11 shows the impact of various factors on regime stability.

The factors that explain which strategy the players choose when the country is attacked by economic sanctions are the independent variables of this book. The following pages describe how the variables may influence regime stability and integrate them into one theoretical model.

570 Bueno de Mesquita, Smith, Siverson, & Morrow 2003.

4.3.1 Economic costs of sanctions

The hypothesis established in the previous chapter is that the higher the economic costs of sanctions, the higher the political effect. Sanctions with high costs lead to less trade, economic decline, and a budget shortfall.[571] "Revenue shocks, such as economic recession or sanctions, diminish the resources available for rewards."[572] The leader has fewer resources to redistribute, and he faces the choice between giving less to the population (public goods), to his winning coalition (private goods), or to himself (personal goods). Since it is a short-term crisis, he will probably abstain from accumulating more financial resources himself; and depending on the political system he will give more goods either to his winning coalition (vertical threat of a coup) or to the population (horizontal threat of a popular revolution). In fact, both groups may have to live without the usual amount of goods: "Fewer resources available in a period should mean a lower level of public and private goods."[573] The leader needs to be careful: When "public resources dwindle to the point where the incumbent government can no longer pay civil servants, the latter join the anti-regime protesters in the streets."[574] Sanctions make both repression and loyalty rewards more expensive.[575] If the leader has a small winning coalition, he will transfer economic goods to his winning coalition. Depending on the circumstances, the leader can even increase his budget.[576] In Yugoslavia in the 1990s, Milosevic and his coalition were able to gain the lion's share of sanctions rents, through criminal activities such as smuggling and through a centralization of the distribution of goods.[577] By investing fewer resources for the whole population, economic transfers from the population to the winning coalition contribute to an autocratization of the system. Fig. 12 shows the potential increase of the leader's budget following sanctions.

If the leader has fewer resources to redistribute, he relies on his second tool, repression. Wintrobe recommends a dictator to increase state terror when the price of loyalty increases because the price of loyalty is fixed whereas the level of repression can be increased easily.[578] Kaempfer et al. agree that more

571 Cf. Bueno de Mesquita & Smith 2017, p. 715.
572 Bueno de Mesquita & Smith 2017, p. 715.
573 Bueno de Mesquita, Smith, Siverson, & Morrow 2003, p. 283.
574 Bratton & Walle 1994, p. 460.
575 Escribà-Folch & Wright 2015, p. 123.
576 Kaempfer, Lowenberg, & Mertens 2004; Lektzian & Souva 2007.
577 Cf. Andreas 2005.
578 Wintrobe 1998, p. 47.

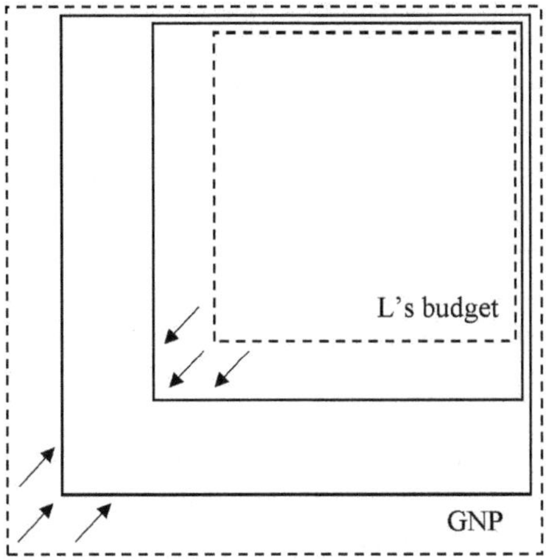

Fig. 12: Increase of the leader's budget following economic sanctions

repression is the best strategy when sanctions encourage anti-government protest.[579] Alternatively, the leadership can decrease repression to buy the loyalty of the population. In Iran, the leadership redistributed an enormous amount of wealth to its winning coalition, and slightly reduced repression. Saudi-Arabia prepares for worse economic times (after oil) by slowly increasing civil liberties. In most cases, the leadership will rely on increasing repression which contributes to an autocratization of the system.

Besides redistributing economic goods or decreasing or increasing repression, the leader can centralize political power to react better to the crisis and use the opportunity of an external threat to accumulate more power. Giving more power to the population is usually the very last strategy the leader will choose because it constrains his power and may cost his head. Indian sanctions against Nepal in the late 1980s led to protests and the legalization of political parties.[580]

4.3.2 Democratic goal of sanctions

Sanctions aimed at improving the level of democracy and human rights are most time designed differently, especially since the late 1990s. Sanctions with a goal

579 Kaempfer, Lowenberg, & Mertens 2004; cf. Escribà-Folch & Wright 2015, p. 132.
580 Escribà-Folch & Wright 2015, p. 126

that concerns the political system of the target state often threaten the support group of the leader, his winning coalition, directly. Thus, sanctions may increase the vertical threat (coup). They help unhappy members of the winning coalition to overcome the collective action problem. For them, it may be cheaper to defect to the competitor of the leader: "sanctions must be applied in such a way as to increase the political resources of those groups in the target country whose point of view is favored by the sanctioners while diminishing the resources of the groups whose position is to be thwarted."[581] Whereas sanctions with high economic costs tend to increase the horizontal threat (revolutions), sanctions targeting specific elements within the system tend to increase the vertical threat (coups).

The leader can try to shift sanctions costs from the elite to the population, thus giving his coalition more incentives to keep loyal (economic transfers). Also, he can apply repression: The coalition of the leader is in constant danger in times of economic crises. To decrease the vertical threat of a coup, strong leaders like to purge potential opposition forces or successors within their coalition. Hitler, Stalin, Saddam are typical examples of leaders who "resort to purges of their own inner circle as a means of retaining their hold on power during periods of economic decline."[582] Alternatively, he can give his coalition members more political rights: he can agree on a succession plan or an institutionalization of power which could benefit the elite. In times of economic decline, the elite may fear violent revolution or regime transition as well and thus be very interested in institutionalizing their power before a period of major transition. Latter (as well as a coup) may contribute to a positive impact on the level of democracy.

4.3.3 Personalist regime

Economic crises threaten all political systems: Some scholars see economic crises as "a truly causal determinant of democratization,"[583] whereas others see them as moments of unique opportunity for power-grabs, especially in states with weak institutions: "Economic crises offer situational incentives to institutionalize defects in an unconsolidated democracy."[584] Several scholars argue that the primary variable for sanction effectiveness (and success) is the political constitution of the target state.[585] This book distinguishes regimes with personalized power

581 Kaempfer, Lowenberg, & Mertens 2004, p. 30; cf. Escribà-Folch & Wright 2015, p. 130.
582 Bueno de Mesquita, Smith, Siverson, & Morrow 2003, p. 384.
583 Teorell 2010, p. 75.
584 Merkel 2004, p. 53.
585 Lektzian & Souva 2007, p. 847; Escribà-Folch & Wright 2015, p. 123.

from regimes with institutionalized power. All personalist leaders are autocrats, but not all autocrats are personalist leaders.

Leaders with under-institutionalized polities "rely on external revenue streams such as foreign aid or taxes on trade, especially the export of natural resources."[586] A personalist leader is very sensitive to fiscal pressure because he relies on so-called private goods (goods that benefit only his supporters and not the whole population).[587] "With ever fewer resources to distribute, political elites [face] a growing problem of how to maintain control of clientelist networks."[588] Escribà-Folch & Wright argue that sanctions may be "most harmful to citizens in personalist regimes precisely because these leaders respond to foreign economic coercion with spending cuts and increased repression."[589] Lacking money, the leader turn to repression to keep the system stable. In times of crises, the leader will spend all available resources on keeping his clientelist network alive. This further autocratizes the system. Sharing of political power through institutions is not credible because of the nature of the regime.[590] Whereas institutionalist systems provide a more peaceful regime change, credible power-sharing and perhaps even economic transfers, a personalist leader provides neither money to his supporters nor political power to oppositional forces. Thus, he increasingly relies on repression.

4.3.4 Regime legitimacy

The perceived legitimacy of the leader is an essential factor in the political marketplace. A high legitimacy of the leadership enables increasing nationalist propaganda. The common external threat can bring the population to rally around the flag,[591] which increases the loyalty to the regime. In Cuba, Castro painted U.S. sanctions as external threat to the "economic goals of the socialist project."[592] In such cases, the leader does not need to provide more resources to the people or even enfranchise them. Instead, the economic crisis provides an excellent opportunity to centralize power further and autocratize the system.

---

586 Escribà-Folch & Wright 2015, p. 128; cf. Snyder 1998; Gandhi & Przeworski 2006; Wright 2008.

587 Escribà-Folch & Wright 2015, p. 136.

588 Bratton & Walle 1997, p. 100.

589 Escribà-Folch & Wright 2015, p. 152.

590 Escribà-Folch 2012, p. 683; Escribà-Folch & Wright 2015, p. 141; Escribà-Folch & Wright 2010; Escribà-Folch & Wright 2016, p. 12.

591 Galtung 1967; Grauvogel & Soest 2014.

592 Escribà-Folch & Wright 2015, p. 126–127.

A low degree of legitimacy, however, can make the stability costs more expensive. External sanctions can work as a signal to domestic groups and increase the collective action capacity of oppositional forces. In the case of Zaire (DR Congo Kinshasa), economic sanctions against the Mobutu regime helped rebels around Kabila in 1997.[593] Depending on the leader's legitimacy, not only the economic effect of sanctions can strengthen oppositional forces but also the psychological effect.

Many hybrid regimes link their legitimacy with economic performance ("a Faustian deal"[594]). This makes them particularly vulnerable in times of economic crises. Both the winning coalition and the population may form a cross-class alliance against the incumbent leadership. When business communities lose confidence in the autocrat's ability to tackle the crisis, they ally with oppositions groups and re-calculate the costs of democratization.[595]

4.3.5 Economic vulnerability

Leader that are not vulnerable to external pressure do not change the balance of goods and repression. The more economically vulnerable a country is, the more its leader fears economic sanctions. Independently from the real economic costs, he will adapt his political system to the new situation and pursue protectionist policies to be more independent from outside influence. He will ally himself with important business communities and establish a clientelist system. He increases the size of his winning coalition and needs to provide more goods, thus decreasing the vertical threat. However, by spending less public goods that benefit the population, he shifts the economic costs of sanctions to the population. An increasing revolutionary threat forces him to apply repression and to centralize power.

4.3.6 Development

Modernization theory, as formulated by Lipset, claims that a combination of industrialization, urbanization, wealth, and education correlate with democratization or democratic consolidation.[596] A high level of development, therefore, makes repression and political centralization more expensive for the leader. Thus, the leader will pursue a path that guarantees a slow transition and his

593 Escribà-Folch & Wright 2015, p. 125.
594 Tang, Huhe, & Zhou 2017.
595 Haggard & Kaufman 1997, p. 267.
596 Lipset 1959, p. 80.

survival. Enfranchising larger parts of the population and strengthening the constitutionalist sphere of the political system may be the cheapest solution. A low level of development, however, makes it more likely that the leader will choose repression, the provision of goods to his coalition and political centralization as the best answer to the external threat of sanctions.

4.3.7 Natural resources

The resource curse hypothesis states that the availability of natural resources increases corruption, clientelism, and kleptocracy, scholars observe a positive correlation between oil and autocratic stability. Especially personalist regimes with clientelist structures depend heavily on the constant flow of cash.[597] Has a leader more wealth for disposition, he can stabilize the system much easier: He provides more public goods *and* more private goods, without the urgent need to fall back on repression or political enfranchisement.

4.3.8 Civil war

Violent conflicts in a state do not only cost large amounts of resources but do also influence the dynamics within the system. All players have fewer resources. The leader cannot provide the same level of public or private goods. Usually, political decision-making will be centralized to be more effective. Both formal constitutions in liberal democracies and informal habits in autocracies show a centralization of political power. Also, the level of repression might increase significantly to get rid of oppositional elements.

4.4 Overview process

After describing how the variables relate to regime stability, they can be integrated into one theoretical mechanism. It will be described according to different phases. The following model is not a game-theoretical analysis but a description of different steps of the process described in the previous sub-chapters, it can be the basis for further analyses.

There are three players: the leader (L), his winning coalition (W) and the population (P). In different stages of the process, there are different players in the focus. The leader can follow three strategies and mix those according to the circumstances and influencing variables. He can, first, redistribute goods (γ) to the other players (which are called public goods when benefitting P, private goods when benefitting W, and

597 Escribà-Folch & Wright 2015, p. 141.

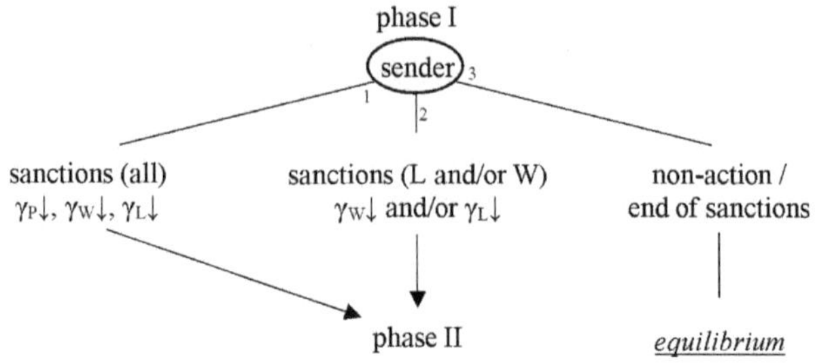

Fig. 13: Phase I

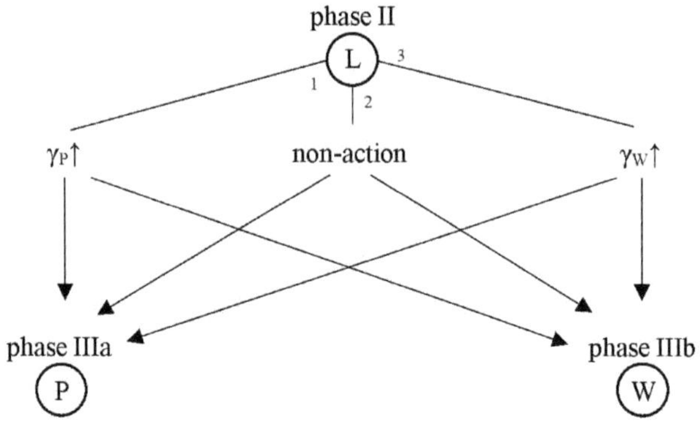

Fig. 14: Phase II

personal goods when benefitting L himself). Second, he can increase or decrease repression (ρ), and, thirdly, he can redistribute political power (π) by enfranchising parts of the population or sharing power with his coalition. In this model, the other players P (population) and W (winning coalition) have two strategies: accept L's actions (non-action), or not accept L's action. Latter is in the case of P a revolutionary attempt (horizontal threat), in the case of W a coup attempt (vertical threat).

Phase I (Fig. 13): The sender states (external player) apply sanctions. They choose between sanctions that economically (γ) hurt everyone (P, W, L) or sanctions that target specific groups within the target state (L, W). The third option is not to apply sanctions or end sanctions (equilibrium).

Phase II (Fig. 14): The leader has to react. Before applying repression or redistributing political power (step IV), he considers the redistribution of goods. He can increase goods γ to P (public goods) or W (private goods) or keep them for

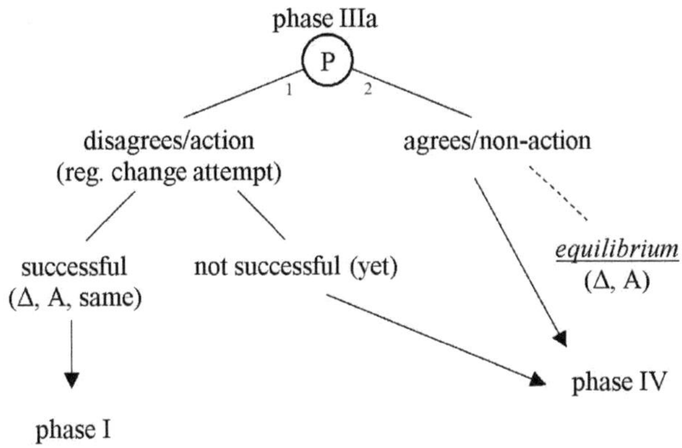

Fig. 15: Phase IIIa

himself (personal goods). In a personalist regime (variable 3), he probably has to increase goods to his coalition because the coalition supports him in exchange for monetary advantages. If the economic vulnerability of the country is low (variable 5), the leader might not need to change the mix of redistribution because the economy (and his budget) is not very much affected. If the target state is a resource-rich state (and the export of these resources is not directly affected by the sanctions), the leader can increase both the goods for the population and the goods for his coalition. He restrains from keeping too much for himself, because short-term stability is more important than the accumulation of his personal wealth. The higher the economic costs of sanctions are (variable 1), the more difficult is the remix of goods. Very high economic costs can decrease the leader's budget substantially, and he might not have any goods, neither for the population nor his coalition. Civil war (variable 8) has a similar effect: The leader needs to spend monetary resources for security purposes and not for other means.

Phase IIIa (Fig. 15): The main player of phase IIIa is the population (P). It has two choices: Accepting the leader's offer or refusing it and protesting. The revolutionary threat from the population increases when the economic costs of sanctions are very high (variable 1). A high level of development (variable 6) helps the population to decrease the information asymmetry (which is typical for many autocratic regimes) and to overcome the collective action problem. If the revolutionary attempt is successful, the regime will change which can be democratizing (Δ) or autocratizing (A) or none of both. If the revolutionary attempt is not successful, it is up to the leader to choose the next step (phase IV).

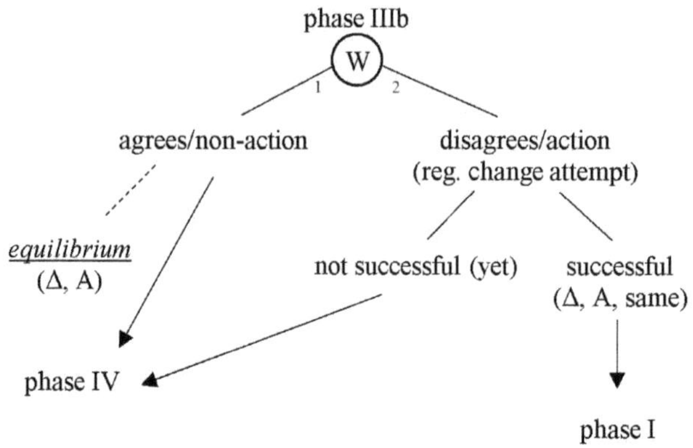

Fig. 16: Phase IIIb

Does the population, however, agree on the leader's offer (more public goods during phase II), this can lead to stability and an equilibrium. This happens especially when the level of legitimacy of the leader is very high (variable 4), and when the leader succeeds in stimulating nationalist feelings. In such cases, sanctions result in a rally around the flag. As a result, the sender states of sanctions may re-think the use of sanctions and adapt them (return to phase I).

Phase IIIb (Fig. 16): The main player of this phase is the leader's winning coalition (W). As the population, the coalition has two choices: Accept or refuse the leader's offer. If the coalition accepts, system stability (and equilibrium) may follow. Then, the sender states may reconsider the use of sanctions (phase I). If the winning coalition, however, does not accept the leader's offer, it attempts regime change (vertical threat) and stages a coup d'état. A coup is more likely if the sanctions target specific groups within the system as most democratic sanctions do (variable 2). If this regime change attempt is successful, the system may experience democratization (Δ) or autocratization or none of both. If the regime change is not successful, it is up to the leader how to react.

Phase IV (Fig. 17): After using up most of his monetary resources in phase II, the leader still has two tools: repression (ρ) and political power (π). He can decide whether to apply repression to P or W (purge) or, if repression is too expensive, he can give away his own power. Usually, this is the ultima ratio, the last resort. It can be the beginning of his end, but at least he can make sure to survive and maybe even keep some resources for himself. Giving political power to P or W can be democratizing (Δ), giving power to W can also be autocratizing (A). Also, the leader can decide to decrease repression (which is cheap but also might increase the collective action capacity of the population) or decrease the

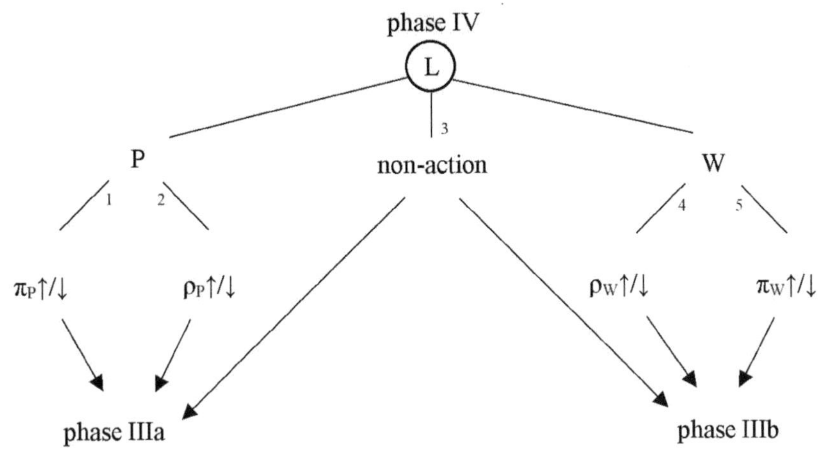

Fig. 17: Phase IV

political power of P and W and further centralize the political decision-making. In case of war (variable 8), the leader reacts with a centralization of power and sometimes increased repression ("state of emergency"). Both population and winning coalition can decide now whether to accept the leader's decision or resist (return to phases IIIa and IIIb).

All phases together can be visualized as Fig. 18 shows. The outcome of the subgames is determined by the variables. This theoretical model, based on Wintrobe, Bueno de Mesquita et al., and Tang et al.,[598] can be taken further for game-theoretical analysis and used in generating scenarios of multiple games. At the moment it offers a concise analytical model to understand the political impact of economic sanctions. The next chapter provides the methodology for the theoretical concept and operationalizes all the variables mentioned in this current chapter.

SEST	sender states	γ [gamma]	goods	Δ [delta]	democratization
L	leadership	ρ [rho]	repression	A [alpha]	autocratization
W	winning coalition	π [pi]	political power		
P	population				

598 Wintrobe 1990, 1998; Bueno de Mesquita, Smith, Siverson, & Morrow 2003; Bueno de Mesquita & Smith 2009, 2010; Tang, Huhe, & Zhou 2017.

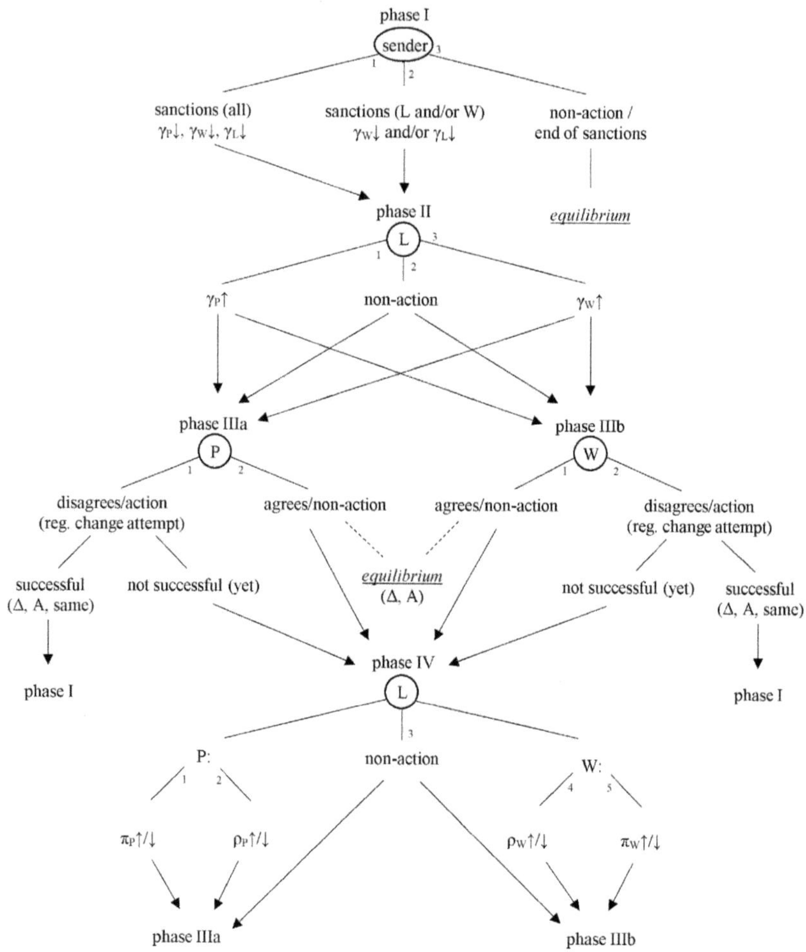

Fig. 18: Phases I–IV

5 Methodology

This chapter gives detailed information on the operationalization of the variables and the design of the model. It explains measurement and sources and prepares the data for the econometric model. It starts with the unit of analysis (including cases, excluded cases, coding, and time), then it shows the operationalization of the dependent variable, the independent and the control variables, and a final sub-chapter will reflect on some of the limitations quantitative research on sanctions has to face.

5.1 Unit of analysis

The unit of analysis is not a sanction episode or a sanction case (e.g., Algeria 1992 to 1994), but the country-year of all countries that were subjected to sanctions (Algeria 1990, Algeria 1991, Algeria 1992, etc.). Not countries are being compared to each other but country-years. All sanctions imposed between 1990 and 2015 with the United Nations, the European Union or the United States as sender are included in the analysis. All sanctions cases are listed in Appendix A.

5.1.1 Time

In many cases, the time frame has an important impact on the outcome of the analysis. Peksen & Drury come in the year 2010 to the conclusion that sanctions have a very negative impact on the level of democracy, they use cases from 1972 to 2000.[599] Around 2000, however, the design of sanctions changed a lot, and results would look differently. Therefore, this analysis will include both cases before and after 2000. Since the dynamics in international relations changed substantially at the end of the Cold War, 1990 is chosen as the starting year, and 2015 is chosen as the last year. All cases in these 25 years will be used for the analysis. All sanctions that were imposed before 1990 or after 2015 are not considered in this analysis. Since no database is that comprehensive (HSEO is using data until 2006 only, GIGA until 2010), primary research needs to be done to get a comprehensive dataset of all sanctions in the time frame. Only sanctions that were imposed for at minimum one year (within the given time frame) are included. Thus, all cases of sanctions that lasted for less than a year are excluded. This

599 Peksen & Drury 2010, p. 248.

decision needs to be taken because the unit of analysis is the country-year and not the country-month.

5.1.2 Excluded cases

Due to data issues, only sanctions with the United Nations, the European Union or the United States as sender of sanctions are used for the analysis. All sanctions targeting non-sovereign entities or areas not under state-administration are excluded, such as Transnistria, Crimea, Khmer Rouge territories in early 1990s, rebel groups/leaders and terrorist organizations (Taliban, Al Qaeda, Islamic State/Daesh), trans-national criminal organizations or former state leaders. All sovereign states with a non-sea area less than 1000 km^2 or with a population less than 500,000 are excluded. Some variables lack part of the data (see next sub-chapters for detailed information). For some countries, however, there is no data for some variables at all. This problem concerns Somalia and North Korea. Since estimates for whole variables are not appropriate, both countries are excluded completely. Furthermore, all sanctions threats are excluded from the analysis, though some quantitative analyses include them in their definition and in their analysis using the TIES dataset. The TIES dataset ends in 2005, unfortunately, and an extension of the dataset with post-2005 data proved to be too difficult, especially in regard to sources and coding. Therefore, only imposed sanction cases are used. Not excluded are targeted countries because of their political system: Peksen & Drury exclude liberal democracies (states with a Polity2 score higher than 6).[600] Similarly, Soest & Wahman exclude all democracies from their analysis. They exclude all countries with a democracy score lower than 7.5 on their 10-point scale which is a combination of Polity IV and Freedom House.[601] In contrast to those other articles, this analysis does not exclude democratic targets. The process of autocratization/democratization hypothetically concerns all countries, also countries above a specific score; therefore, it is important not to restrict the case universe.

5.1.3 Case coding

The coding of the cases proves to be difficult. Sanctions consist of a sometimes not small amount of legal regulations. Some databases homogenize such different

600 Peksen & Drury 2010, p. 248.
601 Soest & Wahman 2015, p. 963.

stages of a sanctions case into different "episodes," though the sanctions target the same country. Still, such homogenization is a simplification of the real world.

Several elements of sanctions overlap in many cases, such as the sender of sanctions. If the UN and one or both of the two other sender elements in our database (EU and US) are listed as senders, only the UN is listed as sender (because such sanctions include EU and US sanctions already). If both the EU and the US (but not the UN) apply sanctions, both are listed. If EU or US sanctions precede UN sanctions, only the UN sanctions are included.

In case of diverging data, the database uses primary data, in case of diverging databases, it uses the newer one: If the HSEO sanctions dataset and the GIGA sanctions dataset differ on a sanctions case, the data from the newer GIGA will be used. Problematic are state disintegrations, such as in the case of Yugoslavia or the Soviet Union. Concerning the variables, new countries inherit data from the predecessor country. Seldom, states also do inherit sanctions: In the case of Yugoslavia, the Belgrade government inherited the sanctions (Federal Republic of Yugoslavia, Serbia & Montenegro).

5.1.4 Sources

For collecting this data, following sources are used: academic sanctions datasets, primary data from governmental sources, and for few cases also media reports and websites. Most sanctions cases are already listed in the academic datasets. Newer datasets are used first. The Targeted Sanctions Consortium (TSC) at the Graduate Institute Geneva published a dataset (and an app) that contains all sanctions with the Security Council of the United Nations as sender since 1991.[602] It distinguishes sanctions cases into sanctions regimes (25 regimes) and sanctions episodes (70 episodes). The app provides a qualitative description and evaluation of each episode and proves to be more than necessary in the jungle of legal texts at UN level. A second dataset is the GIGA sanctions dataset, published by the German Institute for Global and Area Studies.[603] It is the basis for the dataset used for this book. This GIGA dataset includes all sanctions cases between 1990 and 2010, add give information on the official goal and the type of sanctions. The dataset is based on the older datasets TIES and HSEO. The Threat and Imposition of Economic Sanctions (TIES) is innovative because it includes the threat stage of sanctions (which helped in proving the sanctions may be

602 Biersteker, Eckert, Tourinho, & Hudáková 2018.

603 Portela & Soest 2012.

successful at the threat level).[604] It includes data from 1945 to 2005. The oldest and most influential sanctions dataset is the one by Hufbauer et al. (HSEO) that includes episodes from 1914 to 2006.[605]

Except TSC, none of these datasets include data until 2015. Therefore, primary sources are consulted and also used for controlling older cases. The United Nations publishes all resolutions by the Security Council online but treats them as merely legal texts without any overview that could be helpful for concerned businesses or interested academics.[606] The resolutions are collected on a central list but can only be found via resolution number, not via country. The European Union, however, lists all sanctions in a single document – "Restrictive measures (sanctions) in force" – with the target countries listed in alphabetical order.[607] In 2017, the Estonian presidency of the Council established a website dedicated to EU sanctions. A world map and a table with the types of measures give an excellent overview of all sanctions in place.[608] Both websites, however, do not list historical cases. In the United States, the Office for Foreign Assets Control lists all current sanctions and publishes a business-friendly overview.[609]

In some cases, additional sources need to be consulted because data is missing in both academic datasets and official notes. In such rare cases, media reports and websites are used as sources. Several legal firms and open source blogs offer overviews and further information and links.

5.2 Operationalizing the dependent variable

Definition: A liberal-democratic state is a state with an overall high level of political rights, civil liberties, and state capacity.

The dependent variable is the change of the level of democracy/autocracy. A positive change can also be defined as democratization, a negative one as autocratization or autocratic backsliding.[610] The unit of analysis of the dependent variable is the target state. To measure such a variable, a continuous scale is necessary. The previous chapters clearly pointed out that a democracy is not merely an electoral regime but consists of three main indicators: political rights, civil

604 Morgan, Bapat, & Kobayashi 2013.
605 Hufbauer, Schott, Elliott, & Oegg 2007.
606 United Nations Security Council 2018.
607 Commission of the EU 2017.
608 Commission of the EU 2018.
609 U.S. Department of Treasury 2018.
610 Cf. Shirah 2012, p. 10, for a binary operationalization of authoritarian backsliding.

liberties and a third indicator that can be described as state capacity, governance, or the provision of public goods. These three indicators need to be included in the operationalization of the dependent variable. For the last indicator, however, there is no data available for all countries over several decades. As mentioned in the previous chapters, the measurement of this variable is just in the beginning; "there is no consensus metric to operationalize 'state capacity' across countries and time, let alone a metric that is exogenous."[611]

Several democracy scores are available: the Polity IV Index (data since 1800), Freedom in the World Index (data since 1973), the Vanhanen Index (data since 1810), the Combined Index of Democracy (data since 1996, biennially only), and others. Each score uses another categorization and has its flaws and strengths.[612]

One of the more popular scores, Polity IV, is a combination of two different scores, the democracy score and the autocracy score.[613] The democracy scale is derived from the sub-indicators competitiveness of political participation, openness and competitiveness of executive recruitment, and constraints on the chief executive. The autocracy scale is derived from the same sub-indicators, adding a fourth one, regulation of participation. Based on the combined scale, countries can be categorized as democracies, anocracies, or autocracies. This index is related to the electoral sphere of democracy and focuses less on the other elements of our definition.

The Freedom in the World Index is using two indicators, political rights and civil liberties.[614] The political rights indicator is derived from the following sub-indicators: electoral process, political pluralism and participation, functioning of government. The civil liberties indicator is derived from the following sub-indicators: freedom of expression and belief, associational and organizational rights, rule of law, personal autonomy and individual rights. FH's civil liberties score can also be used as measurement of repression.[615] Whereas Polity IV is strongly related to the political sphere, Freedom in the World does focus on freedom and what is defined as "First-Amendment-type rights."[616] Other civil liberties such as economic rights are not included. Through including a sub-indicator "functioning of the government," state capacity is somewhat included.

611 Haber & Menaldo 2011, p. 2.
612 Cf. Gunitsky 2015 for a detailed analysis.
613 Marshall, Gurr, & Jaggers 2017.
614 Freedom House 2018.
615 Wintrobe 1990, p. 851.
616 Cf. Møller & Skaaning 2013, p. 84.

Depending on their overall rating, Freedom in the World categorizes states as free, partly free, or not free.

Hadenius & Teorell find that a combined score of Freedom in the World (FH) and Polity IV (PIV) outperforms all other democracy indices;[617] it compensates for the flaws of both scores. The Polity IV scale, originally from -10 (autocracy) to +10 (democracy), is rescaled to the scale from 1 to 21. The Freedom in the World index, originally from 2 (free) to 14 (not free), is first rearranged to the scale from 2 (not free) to 14 (free), and then rescaled to the Polity IV scale using the formula: (40-5xFH)/3. The combined scale ranges then from 2 (least democratic) to 42 (most democratic). For single observations (country-years) with missing PIV data, only FH data is used. If the observation lacks data completely (because the country did not exist yet), the next observation is used (for Azerbaijan 1990 the data from Azerbaijan 1991 was used). This concerns almost no sanctions case. In the end, the country-year when sanctions were not applied is replaced with zero to include only the sanctions-years.

5.3 Operationalizing the independent variables

5.3.1 Economic costs of sanctions

Definition: Economic costs of sanctions is the amount of wealth of the target state that gets lost due to sanctions.

The variable economic costs of sanctions is not only the most important variable but also the most difficult one to operationalize. "It seems that each sanctions incident is unique and, therefore, any generalization is impossible," writes Tsebelis, and he adds that all classifications and models are "abstractions and simplifications of real situations, and each one of them will present unrealistic or undesirable features."[618] Sanctions consist of a variety of legal texts of which most have no economic impact at all. Therefore, this variable analyzes the economic impact of sanctions. Despite the importance of the economic mechanism, other articles entirely ignore the economic mechanism and use a dummy variable for sanctions instead. Peksen & Drury distinguish only between extensive sanctions and limited sanctions, whereby extensive sanctions refer to sanctions that completely disrupt all trade and financial economic exchange, and limited sanctions to all other sanctions such as asset freeze or travel ban.[619] Soest

617 Hadenius & Teorell 2005; Hadenius & Teorell 2007; cf. Soest & Wahman 2015, p. 962.

618 Tsebelis 1990, p. 6.

619 Peksen & Drury 2010, pp. 249–250.

& Wahman only use a dummy variable for sanctions, in an additional model they distinguish roughly between comprehensive and targeted sanctions.[620] However, both articles have no variable accounting for the real economic impact of sanctions. Their variables are sanctions-related, not impact-related.

As mentioned in Chapter 3, the North Korea case shows how misleading such a measurement is: According to the GIGA sanctions dataset, North Korea is subjected to "comprehensive" U.S. sanctions since 1950.[621] Therefore, North Korea is coded since 1950 as subjected to comprehensive trade sanctions. However, this is more than just misleading: Pre-sanctions trade level between the U.S. and North Korea was probably close to 0; the sanctions have, therefore, an economic impact on North Korea's GNP close to 0. Another example is the U.S. sanctions regime against PR China, imposed in 1989 (and still in place), considered as unsuccessful. In both articles (Peksen & Drury, Soest & Wahman), such cases are coded in the same way as UN sanctions against Iraq in the 1990s that accounted for a loss of more than 50 percent of its GNP.[622] Obviously, such coding is not only not helping but even suggesting wrong results.

The question, then, is: How can the economic impact of sanctions be measured in a better way? The first idea is to look at the change of the GNP or other economic indicators such as inflation, unemployment, export. The problem is that there are too many other variables influencing such absolute numbers. The case of post-2014 sanctions against Russia shows this dilemma par excellence: Capital flight doubled in 2014 to USD 130 billion by December 2014. In 2014, the ruble lost 58 percent of its value.[623] Now, is that the effect of sanctions? Or is it an effect of the dramatic decline in oil prices in 2014,[624] of the alarming economic slowdown close to stagnation, and/or of the failed diversification of the economy?[625] For sure, all of these factors contributed to the economic problems in 2014 and later. The impact of economic sanctions, however, is very difficult to measure.

A second idea is to use the trade linkage. For a calculation, Wallensteen suggests using target's trade dependence on sender/target's total trade; and actual reduction of total trade the first year of sanctions/percent of year preceding year of sanctions.[626] Wolf differentiates between absolute trade linkage

---

620 Soest & Wahman 2015, p. 970.
621 Portela & Soest 2012.
622 Hufbauer, Schott, Elliott, & Oegg 2007, p. 118.
623 Rutland 2014, p. 4.
624 Connolly 2015, p. 30.
625 Vatansever 2015, pp. 1–2.
626 Wallensteen 1968, pp. 255–256.

and proportional trade linkage. Absolute trade linkage is: (export target to sender + import target from sender)/(total export target + total import target). Proportional trade linkage uses the target's national income instead: (export target to sender + import target from sender)/(national income of target).[627]

Even better than measuring the trade linkage between sender and target is to relate the trade linkage to the affected area. In the case of coffee sanctions against Uganda, not the trade linkage between the U.S. and Uganda is relevant but only the coffee exports to the U.S.[628] Unfortunately, such exact data is in most cases not available.

The fourth possibility is the most used one: Scholars and policymakers simply estimate the economic costs of sanctions. The calculation that sanctions cost Russia more than 1 percent of the GDP between summer of 2014 and summer of 2015 is an official estimate.[629] Hufbauer et al. apply in their database a complicated econometric method to determine the economic costs of sanctions (as percent of GNP), at the core of their method, however, is an estimate.[630] The second available dataset, TIES, applies a much simpler coding and categorizes sanction costs as minor, major or severe – again as vague estimates by evaluators.[631] Both groups of researchers do not use a simple change of GNP because they cannot control for other economic factors or simply changes in economic growth. In both sanctions datasets that include costs of sanctions, the costs of sanctions are estimated. Hufbauer et al. provide a four pages long methodology for estimation. First, they estimate the initial deprivation of markets or supplies, then they use their "own judgment to estimate the 'sanctions multiplier' that should be applied in the particular episode."[632] The TIES dataset asks the analysts to "examine the narratives for evidence as to the costs of the sanctions ex-post," and to "fit their response into one of the following categories": minor (economic health of the target not affected), major (significant macroeconomic difficulties on the target's economic health, e.g., increase over 5 percent in the inflation or unemployment rate), severe (economy does not function anymore: loss of ability to obtain critical supplies such as food, water, electricity, oil; increase of mortality rate).[633]

---

627 Wolf 1983, qtd. in Bergeijk 2009, p. 127.

628 For coffee sanctions against Uganda, cf. Escribà-Folch & Wright 2015, pp. 144–149.

629 Galbert 2015, p. V.

630 Hufbauer, Schott, Elliott, & Oegg 2007, pp. 211–214, cf. pp. 101–102.

631 Morgan, Bapat, & Kobayashi 2014 (TIES Users' Manual, p. 8).

632 Hufbauer, Schott, Elliott, & Oegg 2007, p. 214.

633 Morgan, Bapat, & Kobayashi 2013, p. 11.

Bergeijk offers a fifth way for the measurement of economic costs of sanctions. He distinguishes between the ex-post damage and the ex-ante threat (potential damage): Is latter successful, no ex-post damage can be measured. Ex-ante damage is the anticipated cost which is, so Bergeijk, more effective than the ex-post damage and more reliable for empirical analysis.[634]

This book follows Bergeijk's argument that a combination of both may be the best way to compute the economic costs of sanctions. The variable economic costs of sanctions, thus, consists of two indicators, the ex-ante damage and the ex-post damage. The ex-ante damage is calculated using the GIGA sanctions dataset which categorizes sanctions according to their design.[635] Along with many types that have no remarkable impact or no impact on the macro-economy at all (such as visa ban, diplomatic sanctions, etc.), some types of sanctions do influence the targeted macro-economy: A comprehensive trade embargo (CT) is always coded as 3; financial sanctions (FS), commodity embargo (CE), aid sanctions (AS) are coded as either 2 or 3, AS alone as 2. If the sanctions do not fall in any of the mentioned categories, they are coded as 1. The data for ex-post damage is taken from TIES dataset (for operationalization, see previous paragraph). 1 (minor) is coded as 0; 2 (major) as 0.25; 3 (severe) as 0.5. If there is no TIES data available, HSEO data is adapted with TIES methodology. If there is neither TIES nor HSEO data available, and estimates based on media reports are not possible, then ex-ante data will be used twice. Is a country targeted by several sanctions and senders at the same time, the higher number will be used in case of doubt.

5.3.2 Democratic goal

Definition: The democratic goal of sanctions is the explicitly stated aim of sanctions senders to increase the level of democracy by using these sanctions.

For the variable democratic goal of sanctions, the GIGA sanctions dataset can be used. GIGA scholars distinguish sanctions according to their officially stated purpose (de jure goal): democratization, support human rights, fight against narcotics, stop biological and chemical weapons of mass destruction, end nuclear proliferation, termination of bellicosities and/or establishment of peace agreement, fight terrorism (including releasing of hostages), enforcement of sanctions, other goals.[636] In this book, each sanction episode that explicitly focuses on democratization/democracy is coded as 1; all other episodes are

634 Bergeijk 2009, pp. 126–127.
635 Portela & Soest 2012, pp. 5–6.
636 Portela & Soest 2012, p. 6.

coded as 0. In case of doubt, it will be coded as 1. If the sanctions are not included in the GIGA dataset, other datasets and primary sources (legal texts) are used.

5.3.3 Personalist regime

Definition: A personalist regime is a regime in which power is institutionalized on a low level. Effective rule and leadership succession depend on one person or his personal network.

For the variable personalist regime, the Autocratic Regimes dataset by Geddes et al. (GWF) is used.[637] It distinguishes autocratic regimes into party-based, military, monarchist and personalist regimes. In personalist regimes, the leader is ruling through personal networks – a strongman is ruling the country. Following Escribà-Folch & Wright and as described in the previous chapters, party-based, military and monarchist regimes will be categorized as institutionalist regimes, as opposed to personalist regime.[638] Referring to the DAPI regime matric (Democratic Autocratic Personalist Institutionalist), presented in Chapter 3, liberal democracies are categorized as institutionalist too (Freedom in the World score of maximum 4). Electoral democracies, however, are not necessarily coded as institutionalist. Based on the coding by Geddes et al., electoral democracies can be coded as personalist. Therefore, the whole universe of political regimes can be somewhat categorized. In the original concept by Geddes et al., only autocratic regimes fit their categorization. Since this variable is a dummy variable, only regimes that can be clearly defined as personalist will be coded with 1. All other regimes, including all cases in doubt, will be coded as 0. Countries that experience phases of transition, war, civil war, are usually coded as 0.

5.3.4 Regime legitimacy

Definition: Regime legitimacy is the acceptance of political authority by the population.

Some scholars use expert interviews for the operationalization of legitimacy.[639] This book uses the State Fragility Index and Matrix 2016 (SFIM).[640] The legitimacy score consists of the indicators security legitimacy, political legitimacy, economic legitimacy, and social legitimacy. Each sub-indicator is rated on a four-point scale: no fragility (0), low fragility (1), medium fragility (2), and high

---

637 Geddes, Wright, & Frantz 2014.

638 Escribà-Folch & Wright 2015, pp. 30–38.

639 E.g., Grauvogel & Soest 2014.

640 Marshall & Elzinga-Marshall 2016.

fragility (3). The sub-indicator security legitimacy is based on the Political Terror Scale (PTS);[641] the sub-indicator political legitimacy is based on Gurr et al., Gurr & Harff and on other datasets;[642] the sub-indicator economic legitimacy is based on UN and World Bank data (trade with manufactured goods); the sub-indicator social legitimacy is based on social issues such as infant mortality rate.[643]

This variable uses the indicator political legitimacy that consists of the sub-indicators factionalism, ethnic group political discrimination, political salience of elite ethnicity, polity fragmentation, exclusionary ideology of ruling elite. Unfortunately, the State Fragility Index and Matrix starts in 1995 only. In the few cases of sanctions episodes between 1990 and 1994, data from 1995 was used. The final scale ranges from 1 (low level of legitimacy) to 3 (high level of legitimacy). There is no collinearity with the dependent variable democracy (confirmed by tests); legitimacy is based on perception by the people. It seems logical that liberal democracies have a higher level of legitimacy than autocracies: In real life, however, institutions of liberal democracies are sometimes perceived as not very legitimate because citizens think that only directly elected institutions are legitimated by the citizens, whereas in authoritarian countries, theocratic leaders, strongmen or monarch-like rulers enjoy highest levels of legitimacy. Military dictators and countries with institutionalized power such as dominant-party-regimes may struggle more with their claim to legitimacy if they cannot establish a good narrative, refer to a founding myth or create nationalist feelings.

5.3.5 Economic vulnerability

Definition: Vulnerability is the ability to be influenced or hurt. The economic vulnerability of a country is an indicator for the degree how much a country may be affected by external economic shocks. It can be measured by the economy's dependence on export and import with the world.

The variable economic vulnerability of the target state can also be described as autarky or export dependence. It can be measured by its degree of exposure to the global economy, such as using the ratio of international trade to GDP.[644] The classic article by Galtung about Rhodesia measures vulnerability with the percentage of the GNP comprising foreign trade (exports plus imports).[645] Peksen

641 Gibney, Cornett, Wood, Haschke, Arnon, & Pisanò 2017; Wood & Gibney 2010.

642 Marshall, Gurr, & Jaggers 2017; Gurr, Marshall, & Asal 2016; Gurr & Harff 2016.

643 For details, cf. Marshall & Elzinga-Marshall 2016.

644 United Nations Development Programme 2011; Briguglio, Cordina, Farrugia, & Vella 2009.

645 Galtung 1967, pp. 385–387.

et al. measure it with the amount of total foreign direct investment (FDI) flows as a percentage of GDP in a given year.[646] This book uses the comprehensive data provided by World Bank on the exports of goods and services in percent of the GDP.[647]

5.3.6 Development

Definition: Development is a process of change and advance. The development level of a country is an indicator that measures how advanced a country is in important areas such as wealth, education and healthcare.

For the variable development, data from the Human Development Index (HDI) can be used. The HDI consists of the sub-indicators life expectancy at birth, expected years of schooling, mean years of schooling, and GNI per capita.[648] The scale ranges from 0 (minimum) to 1 (maximum).

5.4 Operationalizing the control variables

5.4.1 Natural resources

Definition: Resources are valuable possessions of a country; natural resources are valuable possessions provided by nature.

Ideally, the variable resources should include all natural resources. Historical data for natural resources, however, is not sufficiently available. Therefore, only fuel exports as percent of merchandise exports are used for this variable. If the fuel exports exceed one third (33 percent) of the merchandise exports, the observation will be coded as 1, otherwise 0. Most data comes from the World Bank; additional data is taken from Simoes & Hidalgo, Ross, and media reports.[649] The provision of a dataset that includes all natural resources in the last few decades is urgently needed because there is no reason to assume that the resource curse hypothesis applies to countries with oil resources only.

---

646 Peksen & Drury 2010, p. 252.

647 World Bank 2018a.

648 United Nations Development Programme 2018.

649 World Bank 2018b; Simoes & Hidalgo 2011; Ross 2011.

5.4.2 Civil war

Definition: Civil war is an armed conflict within a country.

The civil war variable measures whether a country experienced a civil war in a certain year. For this variable, the dataset Major Episodes of Political Violence (MEPV) can be used that provides data from 1946 to 2016.[650] Indicators are: civil violence, civil war, ethnic violence, and ethnic war. The total summed magnitudes of all these indicators results in a 11-point scale from 0 to 10: sporadic or expressive political violence (1), limited political violence (2), serious political violence (3), serious warfare (4), substantial and prolonged warfare (5), extensive warfare (6), pervasive warfare (7), technological warfare (8), total warfare (9), extermination and annihilation (10). For the present book, 0 is coded as 0 and all data between 1 and 10 as 1. The coding by MEPV is better than the absolute number of battle-related deaths per year such as the Armed Conflict Dataset of the International Peace Research Institute[651] – that is used by Peksen & Drury 2010 – because those dead would need to be seen relative to the total population of the country.

5.5 Limitations

The main problem of social science is that experiments (with all variables known) are not possible. In place of an ex-ante explanation scholars need to be happy with ex-post explanations, based on observations. However, confirmed explanatory variables still cannot guarantee causality because too many variables are unknown.[652] Depending on the number of observations, only a very limited number of explanatory variables can be used. The selection of variables is, therefore, fundamental. This book selects the variable based on the state of the art in sanctions literature and democratization literature: sanctions variables, regime variables, and economic variables. Many other factors, however, are excluded, such as regional variables, cultural variables, other economic variables, other variables for the political system of the target state, variables of international relations (allies), etc.

Another challenge is the measurement of variables. Among the present variables, the variable economic costs was most difficult to measure. It is based on estimates by scholars. Several other variables are, eventually, based on estimates, such as the dependent variable, the regime variables, etc. Most difficult proved to be the definition and measurement of sanctions. What is a sanction? When

---

650 Marshall 2018.
651 Gleditsch, Wallensteen, Eriksson, Sollenberg, & Strand 2002.
652 Sandschneider 1995, pp. 23–24.

do sanctions begin, when do they end? To define a sanctions episode with all these legal texts as sources is a difficult undertaking. A large amount of sometimes irrelevant legal updates makes it tough for scholars to define different episodes of sanctions. Sanctions are difficult to operationalize. Previous approaches used a dummy variable or related the costs to the sender. This book tries to define a target-related costs variable by using ex-ante costs and ex-post costs as indicators. In order to further distinguish sanctions, one variable measures the aim of sanctions and a subsequent model looks at different types of sanctions. Despite these efforts, it is still challenging to use sanctions in quantitative analyses.

The main critique of previous articles on similar questions is the endogeneity issue. Sanctions do not only influence the political system; sanctions are caused by a political decision-making process. This book logs the dependent variable (two years) to mitigate this problem. Still, autocratization does not always happen within two years. In the case of Russia, a long-term autocratization can be observed; and the event that led to the imposition of sanctions (the annexation of Crimea in 2014) is perhaps a result of the same autocratizing process. In other cases, such as classical coup d'états in several African cases of sanctions, the lagged variable helps. Despite lags and robustness checks, the endogeneity issue is the main reason why the main findings of articles such as Peksen et al. need to be read with caution.[653]

Similarly, some sanctions scholars mention selection bias: First, some regimes are targeted exactly because of variables that may make sanctions effective. A state that is quite small and economically weak is more likely to get sanctioned than an economic superpower. Second, "selection bias may be caused by regimes' self-selection into sanction episodes," and variables for this may not be observable because we simply do not know the reasons for it.[654] Several political decisions seem to be irrational to outsiders, such as the increasingly aggressive behavior North Korea's towards its protector China that led to an increasingly active participation China's in the sanctions regime. There may be (or may not be) reasons for it; it is just not possible to see them from the outside.

The current research question only asks under which conditions sanctions have a negative impact on the level of democracy. This does not answer the question, *do* sanctions have a positive or negative impact on the level of democracy? Marinov points out: "If the question is 'Does coercion work?,' we need to compare cases in which pressure was applied, to those in which it was not."[655] What

653 Peksen & Drury 2010.
654 Escribà-Folch & Wright 2015, pp. 142–143; cf. Nooruddin 2002; Marinov 2005.
655 Marinov 2005, p. 565.

he writes about the question of sanctions success applies to the question of political impact too. The current research question and the model do not answer to that question. A small-N comparison might be more helpful to answer that question. The design and imposition of sanctions is just too diverse to find enough similar cases for a large-N analysis.

5.6 Econometric model

The econometric model for the variables is:

$$democracy = \alpha_1 economic\_costs + \alpha_2 democratic\_goal + \alpha_3 personalist\_regime + \alpha_4 regime\_legitimacy + \alpha_5 vulnerability + \alpha_6 development + \beta_1 resources + \beta_2 civil\_war + \mu_{it}$$

In this model, democracy is the dependent variable. Economic costs, democratic goal, personalist regime, regime legitimacy, vulnerability, and development are the independent variables. Resources and civil war are the control variables. α_1–α_7 are the coefficients of the variables which need to be estimated by the regression. α refers to the independent variables; β refers to the control variables; μ is the interaction term (random variable).

For the panel data, a linear dynamic regression model will be used – the two-step system GMM; specifically, SYSGMM (SYS=system). The generalized method of moments (GMM) estimator was derived by Arellano & Bond, Arellano & Bover, and finally Blundell and Bond who added moment conditions.[656] Thus, the model is also called Arellano–Bover/Blundell–Bond linear dynamic panel-data model. The dynamic GMM model is suitable for such data with change over the years; it is thus better than a static model. Furthermore, the GMM model is the best choice to deal with the endogeneity problem, which is relevant for the present research question.

The total number of observations of the main model is 1440. This number includes all countries, which were subjected to sanctions within the time frame 1990–2015. However, most sanctions last only for a few years. A comparison of the whole time period would be strongly distorting. Therefore, the dependent variable is coded as 0 in the year when sanctions were not applied to the country, in other years the dependent variable is coded with normal data. The dependent variable is lagged two years to control for endogeneity. The regression analysis is done with the statistical software Stata 14.

656 Arellano & Bond 1991; Arellano & Bover 1995; Blundell & Bond 1998.

The next part of the book which is also the last one evaluates the results. Chapter 6 presents the models and the results and interpret the results regarding the theory. Chapter 7 shows which implications these findings have, on a macro- and metatheoretical level and also for the heated success debate. Policy and research recommendations and a list of research contributions conclude the book.

Part III Evaluating

"The Security Council [r]eaffirms its decisions that the DPRK [North Korea] shall not conduct any further launches that use ballistic missile technology, nuclear tests, or any other provocation [and d]ecides that the DPRK shall not supply, sell or transfer [...] coal, iron, and iron ore, [...] gold, titanium ore, vanadium ore, and rare earth minerals, [...] aviation fuel, including aviation gasoline, naptha-type jet fuel, kerosene-type jet fuel, and kerosene-type rocket fuel."

—UNSC Resolution 2270, 2016-03-02

"Since 30 years we're imposing sanctions on North Korea. [...] Sanctions do not work!"

—Wolfgang Nowak, former Head of Planning at the German Federal Chancellery, dealing with the North Korea issue, 2017-09-04[657]

"[W]e will discontinue nuclear test and inter-continental ballistic rocket test-fire from April 21, Juche 107 (2018). The northern nuclear test ground of the DPRK will be dismantled to transparently guarantee the discontinuance of the nuclear test."

—Resolution of the Central Committee of the Worker's Party of Korea, 2018-04-20[658]

---

657 Interviewed by ZDF, 2017-09-04.

658 Resolution "On Proclaiming Great Victory of the Line of Simultaneous Development of Economic Construction and Building of Nuclear Force," 3rd Plenary Meeting of the 7th Central Committee of the Workers' Party of Korea, held in presence of Chairman Kim Jong Un. Rodong Sinmun, 2018-04-21.

6 Findings

This chapter is the empirical core of the book. A large-N analysis uses all sanction cases as observations (country-year as the unit of analysis) and shows correlations between the dependent variable and the independent variables. The chapter starts with the main model, continues with extensive robustness checks to see whether the results are valid, and ends with an interpretation of the results referring back to the original hypotheses.

6.1 Main model

The main model tests the independent variables (IV); they focus on the design of sanctions and the political and economic constitution of the target state.[659] The dependent variable (DV) is the level of democracy, for which a combination of Polity IV and Freedom in the World (Freedom House) is used. It is lagged two years.

	(1) *main model*		
	Coef.		***P>|z|***
economic costs	18.593	***	0.003
democratic goal	9.397	***	0.003
regime legitimacy	0.149		0.897
personalist regime	-0.146		0.949
vulnerability	-0.062	*	0.065
development	18.412	*	0.066
natural resources	-0.908		0.756
civil war	0.935		0.650
AR(1)	0.000		
AR(2)	0.483		
Sargan	1.000		

*** p<0.01, ** p<0.05, * p<0.1

659 AR = Arellano-Bond test, Sargan = Sargan test. Full models including standard errors are in appendix C.

Surprisingly, none of the sanctions variables has a negative impact on the DV, the level of democracy. Both IV economic costs (α = 18.593, p = .003) and IV democratic goal (α = 9.397, p = .003) are significant and have a high coefficient.[660] The coefficients of the regime variables (IV personalist regime, IV regime legitimacy) are not significant at all, and their impact is very low. IV economic vulnerability is the only significant variable with a negative impact on the level of democracy: A high level of economic interdependence of the target state correlates with a lower level of democracy (α = -0.062, p = .065). This correlation, however, is close to zero.[661] The coefficient of IV development is significant and very high (α = 18.412, p = .066).[662] Model 1 confirms some of the hypotheses established in Chapter 3 and disconfirm others. Based on the previous chapters, another factor to consider are the effects of the types and senders of sanctions. A second and third model replace the original sanctions variables with types (2) and senders (3) of sanctions.

<table>
<tr><th></th><th colspan="3">(2)
types of sanctions</th><th colspan="2">(3)
sender of sanctions</th></tr>
<tr><th></th><th>Coef.</th><th></th><th>P>|z|</th><th>Coef.</th><th>P>|z|</th></tr>
<tr><td>arms embargo</td><td>6.544</td><td>**</td><td>0.045</td><td>–</td><td></td></tr>
<tr><td>asset freeze</td><td>-0.968</td><td></td><td>0.874</td><td>–</td><td></td></tr>
<tr><td>aid sanctions</td><td>12.068</td><td>***</td><td>0.000</td><td>–</td><td></td></tr>
<tr><td>commodities embargo</td><td>10.391</td><td>*</td><td>0.056</td><td>–</td><td></td></tr>
<tr><td>comprehensive trade embargo</td><td>0.277</td><td></td><td>0.984</td><td>–</td><td></td></tr>
<tr><td>diplomatic sanctions</td><td>4.395</td><td></td><td>0.528</td><td>–</td><td></td></tr>
<tr><td>flight ban</td><td>-11.544</td><td></td><td>0.380</td><td>–</td><td></td></tr>
</table>

660 The variable democratic goal is a dummy variable. The additional model (14) inverts the data of IV democratic goal. The coefficient of IV democratic goal changes to α = -9.397, p = .003. The other variables do not change. Cf. appendix C.

661 In an additional model (12) without time lag, vulnerability (α = -.044, p = .201) got insignificant. The other variables got very similar results: economic costs (α = 15.188, p = .071), democratic goal (α = 8.457, p = .014), development (α = 21.074, p = .023). Cf. appendix C.

662 The original wording of the hypothesis is that a low level of development correlates with a lower level of democracy. Model 1 tests a high level of development, therefore, an additional model (13) inverts the data. The coefficient of IV development now changed to α = -0.020, p = .047. The other variables do not change substantially. Cf. appendix C.

	(2) types of sanctions			(3) sender of sanctions		
financial sanctions	8.146	*	0.054	–		
interrupted military cooperation	1.375		0.759	–		
visa ban	1.782		0.637	–		
EU	–			8.116	***	0.000
US	–			13.660	***	0.000
UN	–			8.572	**	0.040
regime legitimacy	0.217		0.662	-1.066		0.146
personalist regime	2.457		0.211	0.589		0.674
vulnerability	0.003		0.903	-0.006		0.718
development	19.284	**	0.047	-2.899		0.687
resources	-1.340		0.398	-0.105		0.935
civil war	1.531		0.413	0.644		0.573
AR(1)	0.002			0.001		
AR(2)	0.093			0.476		
Sargan	1.000			1.000		

*** $p<0.01$, ** $p<0.05$, * $p<0.1$

Model 2 shows four correlations: The coefficients of the variables arms embargo, aid sanctions, commodity embargo, and financial sanctions are all significant and positive. These correlations are interesting and need to be interpreted and discussed further. The other variables do not change substantially, except IV vulnerability.

Model 3 looks at the effects of dominant senders of sanctions. All sender coefficients are significant, and the impact is positive. What is particularly striking is the impact of the variable U.S. ($\alpha = 13.660$, $p = .000$): It is much higher than that the variables EU ($\alpha = 8.116$, $p = .000$) and UN ($\alpha = 8.572$, $p = .040$).

6.2 Robustness checks

Before comparing the results with the hypotheses, several robustness checks are necessary to check the validity of model 1. Several important topics ask for a closer look. The following models look at multicollinearity, the control variables, time, autocracies, global trend; they compare with the main model how the coefficients change.

6.2.1 Multicollinearity

Though legitimacy is based on perception, it could be possible that it is connected to the dependent variable. In the main model, IV regime legitimacy is based on political indicators (factionalism, ethnic group political discrimination, political salience of elite ethnicity, polity fragmentation, exclusionary ideology of ruling elite). To be sure that none of the sub-indicators is indirectly part of the DV, model 5 uses only non-political indicators of regime legitimacy (security, economic, social), and model 6 uses a comprehensive measurement of all relevant spheres of legitimacy (political, security, economic, social).

	(1) *main model*			*(4)* *other legitimacy*			*(5)* *combined legitimacy*		
	Coef.		*P>|z|*	*Coef.*		*P>|z|*	*Coef.*		*P>|z|*
economic costs	18.593	***	0.003	20.172	***	0.000	19.770	***	0.000
democratic goal	9.397	***	0.003	8.582	***	0.001	8.435	***	0.001
personalist regime	0.149		0.897	0.110		0.955	0.140		0.946
regime legitimacy	-0.146		0.949		–			–	
vulnerability	-0.062	*	0.065	-0.061	*	0.082	-0.059	*	0.068
development	18.412	*	0.066	18.694		0.171	17.349		0.121
natural resources	-0.908		0.756	-1.141		0.647	-0.820		0.761
civil war	0.935		0.650	0.740		0.785	0.709		0.788
other legitimacy		–		-0.015		0.981		–	
combined legitimacy		–			–		0.051		0.924
AR(1)	0.002			0.000			0.000		
AR(2)	0.093			0.529			0.511		
Sargan	1.000			1.000			1.000		

*** $p<0.01$, ** $p<0.05$, * $p<0.1$

Comparing all three models, the results do not change substantially. Following our definition of significance, IV development is narrowly non-significant in model 5 ($\alpha = 18.694$, $p = .171$) and 6 ($\alpha = 17.349$, $p = .121$). Not to prove significance does not necessarily mean there is no significance at all; the significance just cannot be proven with the current model. Absence of evidence is not evidence of absence.

6.2.2 Resource-rich states and civil war states

Natural resources and civil war are standard control variables in most large-N analyses on similar issues. States that benefit from natural resources and suffer from civil war are included in the main model because a high number of observations is crucial. The more observations there are, the more precise are the estimates. The following models exclude observations based on the control variables to see if the results of the main variables change. Model 9 excludes resource-rich states (385 of 1440 observations); model 10 excludes states that are affected by civil war (504 of 1440 observations).

	(1)			*(6)*			*(7)*		
	main model			*exclude resource-rich states*			*exclude civil war states*		
	Coef.		*P>|z|*	*Coef.*		*P>|z|*	*Coef.*		*P>|z|*
economic costs	18.593	***	0.003	18.988	***	0.002	22.336	***	0.000
democratic goal	9.397	***	0.003	9.087	**	0.020	11.778		0.666
personalist regime	0.149		0.897	0.497		0.795	-2.114		0.952
regime legitimacy	-0.146		0.949	0.028		0.974	0.034		0.978
vulnerability	-0.062	*	0.065	-0.056		0.143	-0.041		0.653
development	18.412	*	0.066	15.682		0.150	36.765		0.486
natural resources	-0.908		0.756		–		0.443		0.993
civil war	0.935		0.650	0.871		0.547		–	
AR(1)	0.002			0.001			0.536		
AR(2)	0.093			0.123			0.965		
Sargan	1.000			1.000			1.000		

*** $p<0.01$, ** $p<0.05$, * $p<0.1$

The results do not change much. When excluding resource-rich states, the economic variables (IV vulnerability and development) are narrowly non-significant but the number does not change much or even changes the sign. When excluding civil war states, the coefficient of IV democratic goal got non-significant too ($\alpha = 11.778$, $p = .666$).

6.2.3 Time

In the years around 2000, the United Nations re-evaluated the use of sanctions and re-designed them. Instead of targeting the macro-economy of the target state and hurting innocents, sanctions increasingly target the leadership and the supporting elite. The design of sanctions changed substantially, that's why a look at different time periods may provide more insights:

	(1) *time 1990–2015*			*(8)* *time 1990–2000*			*(9)* *time 2001–2015*		
	Coef.		**P>|z|**	***Coef.***		**P>|z|**	***Coef.***		**P>|z|**
economic costs	18.593	***	0.003	31.595	***	0.000	16.769	**	0.023
democratic goal	9.397	***	0.003	3.054		0.267	12.496	***	0.000
personalist regime	0.149		0.897	-1.538		0.316	0.385		0.848
regime legitimacy	-0.146		0.949	1.686		0.248	-0.008		0.992
vulnerability	-0.062	*	0.065	-0.045		0.282	-0.021		0.653
development	18.412	*	0.066	24.782		0.151	20.539		0.110
natural resources	-0.908		0.756	0.679		0.805	0.085		0.960
civil war	0.935		0.650	0.087		0.944	0.848		0.787
AR(1)	0.002			0.016			0.019		
AR(2)	0.093			0.509			0.548		
Sargan	1.000			0.488			0.965		

*** p<0.01, ** p<0.05, * p<0.1

The change of IV democratic goal is noteworthy: Sanctions with a democratic goal have a much higher (and significant) coefficient after 2001 ($\alpha = 12.496$, $p = .000$) than in the 1990s ($\alpha = 3.054$, $p = .267$).

6.2.4 Autocracies and global trend

Similar research contributions analyze only autocratic states and exclude all democratic states from their large-N analysis. Based on the combined index of Polity IV and Freedom in the World, model 11 excludes all democracies. The combined score ranges from 2 (most autocratic) to 42 (most democratic). All states above 30 – roughly one fourth on the scale – are excluded. This concerns 390 of 1440 observations.

	(1)			*(10)*			*(11)*		
	main model			*exclude democracies*			*global trend*		
	Coef.		*P>|z|*	*Coef.*		*P>|z|*	*Coef.*		*P>|z|*
economic costs	18.593	***	0.003	14.349	***	0.000	16.112	***	0.002
democratic goal	9.397	***	0.003	6.718	***	0.001	8.937	***	0.002
personalist regime	0.149		0.897	-0.262		0.850	0.508		0.811
regime legitimacy	-0.146		0.949	0.762		0.316	0.359		0.728
vulnerability	-0.062	*	0.065	-0.001		0.983	-0.043		0.181
development	18.412	*	0.066	22.820	***	0.008	17.456	**	0.030
natural resources	-0.908		0.756	-1.534		0.392	-1.270		0.681
civil war	0.935		0.650	0.198		0.900	2.540		0.228
global trend		–			–		1.569		0.351
AR(1)	0.002			0.000			0.000		
AR(2)	0.093			0.706			0.560		
Sargan	1.000			1.000			1.000		

*** p<0.01, ** p<0.05, * p<0.1

When just looking at autocracies (model 11), the coefficient of IV development is only considerably higher and more significant (α = 22.820, p = .008). The coefficient of IV vulnerability is not significant anymore (α = -0.001, p = .983).

An important topic that needs to be addressed is a global or regional trend. It is often a trigger for democratization or autocratization; simultaneous sanctions may simply be irrelevant. During periods of liberal and authoritarian hegemonies, the hegemon is more likely to promote like-minded regimes.[663] The 20th century was shaped by waves (and counter-waves) of democratization.[664] The end of the Cold War resulted in a wave of democratization, as can be seen in Fig. 19.

Model 12 adds a variable accounting for the global trend to the main model. The results do not change much: The sanctions variables are still significant; IV vulnerability got not significant (α = -0.043, p = .181).

---

663 Boix 2011; confirmed by Gunitsky 2014, p. 592; cf. Levitsky & Way 2010.

664 Huntington 1991.

6.3 Interpretation

After several robustness checks to test the validity of the variables and the model, the results can be compared to the hypotheses established in Chapter 3:

Variable	*Hypothesis*	*Result*
IV 1: Economic costs	The higher the economic costs of the sanctions to the target state are, the more likely is a negative impact on the level of democracy in the target state.	Not confirmed, opposite correlation: The higher the economic costs of the sanctions to the target state are, the higher is the level of democracy.
IV 2: Democratic goal	The less sanctions focus on democracy, the more likely is a negative impact on the level of democracy.	Confirmed. Furthermore, sanctions with a democratic goal correlate with a higher level of democracy.
IV 3: Personalist regime	The more personalized rule in the target country is, the more likely is a negative impact on the level of democracy.	Not confirmed, no correlation.
IV 4: Regime legitimacy	The higher the level of legitimacy of the targeted regime is, the more likely is a negative impact on the level of democracy.	Not confirmed, no correlation.
IV 5: Economic vulnerability	The higher the level of economic vulnerability of the target economy is, the more likely is a negative impact on the level of democracy.	Confirmed, but weak and negligible impact.
IV 6: Development	The less developed the target country is, the more likely is a negative impact on the level of democracy.	Confirmed. Furthermore, the more developed the target country is, the more likely is a positive impact on the level of democracy.

The original research question was: *Why do some economic sanctions have a negative impact on the level of democracy in the target state but others not?* The

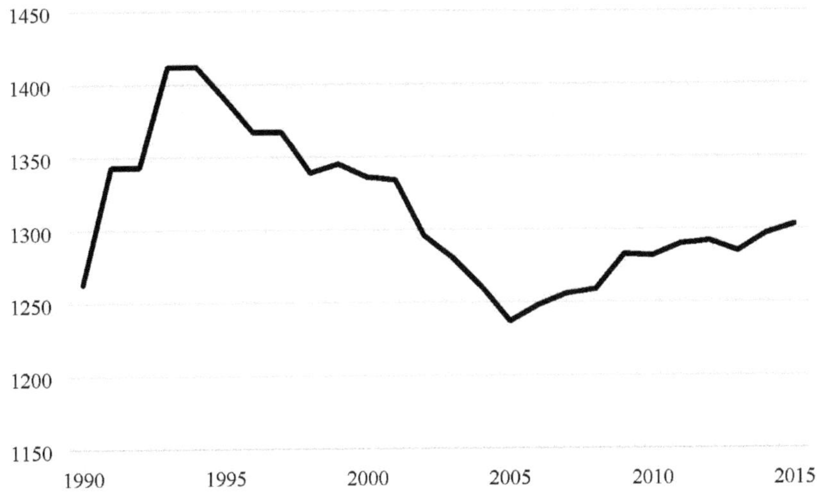

Fig. 19: Global democracy trend 1990–2015 (combined FH index, worldwide)

answer is: Sanctions that are not intended and designed at improving the level of democracy correlate with a lower level of democracy. Sanctions targeting a country that is economically vulnerable may also correlate with a lower level of democracy, but this finding is questionable. Both findings do not implicate a causal correlation. Otherwise, no variables could be found that correlate with a lower level of democracy. However, the analyses showed several interesting results that need to be interpreted in light of the literature and the theories mentioned in the previous chapters; also, the theoretical mechanism proposed in the previous chapters needs to be re-conceptualized.

6.3.1 Variable 1: Economic costs of sanctions

Previous literature argued that sanctions have a negative impact on the level of democracy, especially when they are comprehensive. Economic theory suggests an even stronger political impact with higher economic costs. The present analysis, however, did not confirm that. Instead, a correlation with a higher degree of democracy was measured. This does not necessarily mean that sanctions are a cause of democratization, but it shows that anecdotal evidence of cases of sanctions with a negative impact on the level of democracy cannot be generalized. Economic sanctions do not cause autocratization, both variables do not even correlate. Instead, sanctions with high economic costs correlate with a higher level of democracy. This is in line with the most basic sanctions mechanism that was described as naïve: Sanctions with high economic costs disrupt the targeted political system and have transitional effects, perhaps in the context of a global, regional or temporal trend. External punishment legitimizes oppositional forces and may help the citizens to overcome their collective action problem.

6.3.2 Variable 2: Democratic goal of sanctions

Chapter 3 built the hypothesis that democratic sanctions have a positive impact on the level of democracy, based on Soest & Wahman who find a "significant correlation between democratic sanctions and increased levels of democracy."[665] The model confirmed the hypothesis. The coefficient is remarkably high and significant. The hypothesis was formulated in a negative way to be in line with the other hypotheses which point to a negative impact of sanctions. Therefore, this hypothesis was also tested in their original (negative) wording. As a dummy variable, the results mirror exactly the result of the positive formulation: Non-democratic sanctions correlate with a lower level of democracy. Sanctions that specifically aim at democracy may be smart enough to target the right groups within the political system of the targeted state (public choice approach). Sanctioning the right groups deprives the leader of crucial support and strengthens oppositional forces.

6.3.3 Variable 3: Personalist regime

According to the DAPI regime matrix (Democratic Autocratic Personalist Institutionalist) introduced in Chapter 3, regimes can be classified on two scales: Once scale measures how democratic the regime is, another one how much power is institutionalized. Based on empirical findings, a personalist leader is more sensitive to external pressure because his survival in office depends on his ability to provide goods to his supports. He depends on resources much more than leaders with a more institutionalized system of power do. Sanctions harm those revenues and, in most cases, decrease the leader's budget substantially.

The analysis does not confirm the mechanism proposed by theory. In none of the models is the variable personalist regime significant. One reason can be that the distinction in personalist and institutionalist regimes is not precise enough, and many regimes are somewhat hybrids. Svolik questions the validity of Geddes' regime classification.[666] Furthermore, the operationalization provided by Geddes et al. may not be accurate enough. It is difficult to look into closed

665 Soest & Wahman 2015, p. 957.
666 Svolik 2012, p. 29.

systems and evaluate if power belongs more to persons or institutions. Another reason is the fact that most regimes in the 1990s were simply non-consolidated and in a phase of transition – not necessarily to democracy, but for example from a secluded Soviet republic to a globally connected autocracy.[667] This leads to a fourth reason, which is the constant change of autocracies. Due to missing accountability and legitimacy, autocratic systems are less "consolidated" than liberal democracies. Autocracies, especially with non-institutionalized rule, tend to instability or at least remarkable change. Autocracies pretend to be strong and stable and sometimes repressive (information asymmetry is crucial for real stability). The missing institutionalization of power, however, may lead to constant instability and *aggiornamento* (adaption). The last century shows how often major autocracies adapted their system: Almost all of the remaining communist states embraced in some form market economy, thus abandoning the central element of communist economic theory, central planning.

6.3.4 Variable 4: Regime legitimacy

Theory and qualitative research suggest that a high degree of legitimacy strengthens autocratic rule in case of sanctions.[668] The quantitative analysis, however, did not find any correlation between legitimacy and democracy. One explanation is that legitimacy is perceived very differently. Scholars may evaluate a leader's legitimacy in another way than his citizens may do it. Another study on the impact of economic crises on the political system similarly questioned measurements and use of legitimacy.[669] A sound operationalization of legitimacy is a challenging task for the future generation of political scholars.

6.3.5 Variable 5: Economic vulnerability

In the main model, a high level of vulnerability (economic interdependency or interconnectedness) correlates with a lower level of democracy, but the coefficient is negligible and varies substantially in different robustness checks. The evidence for this variable is weak.

6.3.6 Variable 6: Development

As theory and empirical evidence suggests, a high level of development correlates with a high level of democracy. In Chapter 3, the hypothesis was formulated in

667 Cf. Cooley & Heathershaw 2017.
668 Grauvogel & Soest 2014, p. 635.
669 Tanneberg, Stefes, & Merkel 2013, p. 124.

a negative way, similar to all other hypotheses. Therefore, this hypothesis was also tested in their original (negative) wording. The coefficient was negative but not significant. In total, the result confirms modernization theory that assumes a relation between economic and political development. A high level of development – education, income, health – decreases the information asymmetry of autocracies and helps the population to overcome the collective action problem. A high level of development makes repression and centralization of power more expensive. It is cheaper for the leader – and perhaps the only way to survive in times of crises – to enfranchise larger parts of the population, to strengthen civil liberties, and to increase public goods benefitting everyone.

6.3.7 Sanction design

One of the most interesting findings is the correlation between some types of sanctions and a higher level of democracy. The variables arms embargoes, aid sanctions, commodity embargoes, and financial sanctions are all significant on a high level, and the impact on the dependent variable democracy is positive. The sanctions types commodity embargo and financial sanctions are related to the first variable economic costs of sanctions, they stand for comprehensive and real sanctions, as opposed to symbolic sanctions.

Arms embargoes hurt government forces most; they can hurt their repressive capacity. Arms are crucial for repression and internal deterrence. Restricting access to arms in a substantial way means that the target's leader has less leverage regarding his main tool repression. Hultman et al. find that arms embargoes are likely to reduce conflict violence.[670] In order to keep on power, this may force him to rely on other tools such as decentralizing political power and giving more civil rights.

Aid sanctions – the cut of financial aid – also correlate with a higher level of democracy. Foreign aid is often aimed at state building and promoting rule of law, democracy, and social welfare; however, "leader with the political incentive to do just the opposite."[671] An external revenue source helps him providing private goods to his supports, thus financing kleptocratic structures. This applies especially to personalist regimes.[672] Aid sanctions are very harmful, and their impact is immediate. Once these revenue streams disappear, the leader needs other means to keep the system stable such as providing more political rights.

---

670 Hultman & Peksen 2017.

671 Bueno de Mesquita & Smith 2009, p. 196.

672 Wright 2010, p. 735.

Improving the level of democracy is also the best way to make sure that foreign aid will re-appear in the future. So, the leader may not be forced to provide more political rights but simply be interested in gaining as much money as possible and voluntarily refrain from too much political power. Wintrobe describes such leaders as tin-pot dictators – leaders who are more interested in collecting the fruits of office than in maximizing power (totalitarian leaders).[673] Aid sanctions hurt a paternalistic autocrat much more than a democratic system with institutionalized power.

This finding is interesting in light of Bueno de Mesquita et al. who find that leaders who have access to "free" revenue sources such as natural resource rents or foreign aid reply to revolutionary pressure by reducing public goods and increasing autocratic features. A leader who doesn't have such sources responds to a revolutionary threat by "by increasing the provision of public goods and democratizing."[674] Foreign aid might retard democratization. The authors suggest increasing the size of the winning coalition. This offers the "best long-term prospects for improving their economic and social welfare because the nature of political competition in such systems encourages leaders who want to survive in office to produce policies with these goals in mind."[675]

Another interesting finding regarding sanction design concerns the sender of sanctions. The analysis includes only sanction cases with the EU, the U.S. or the UN as senders. Using the senders as independent variables, the results show that all variables correlate with a higher level of democracy. The variable U.S. is double as high as the other variables. One interpretation is that American sanctions have less autocratizing collateral damage because they are designed in a better way. This is noteworthy regarding different implementation mechanisms and institutions among U.S., EU, and UN. Another interpretation is that the U.S. sanctions countries more often than the EU and the UN in regard to democracy issues (selection bias), challenging the view of the EU as a normative power in opposition to the U.S.

Looking at the time period when sanctions were imposed, it is surprising that the coefficient of sanctions with a democratic goal increased dramatically after 2000. Assuming a causal correlation between this variable and the level of democracy, one could argue that democratic sanctions became much more successful after the re-design of sanctions around 2000.

673 Wintrobe 1990, p. 849.
674 Bueno de Mesquita & Smith 2009, p. 167.
675 Bueno de Mesquita & Smith 2009, p. 195.

6.3.8 Re-conceptualizing

Theoretical and empirical literature suggest a negative impact of sanctions on the level of democracy. The analysis found no quantitative evidence for such sanctions – autocratization mechanism. Instead, the results show correlations between some variables and a higher level of democracy. Fig. 20 shows the variables in Coleman's bathtub model that relates micro and macro level.[676]

The state leader is the one who has the most power and can do most in changing the system. Depending on the many variables – sanction design, economic variables, regime variables, but also many other variables that were not included in this model – will the leader choose the best strategy to stay on power. He can increase or decrease repression (civil liberties), centralize or decentralize political power, and provide more or fewer goods to the population or his clients. The analysis showed that when economic costs of sanctions are high, sanctions are aimed at democracy, and the level of development is high, sanctions correlate indeed with a higher level of democracy.

676 The macro-to-macro link is controversial in social theory. In one article, Coleman himself does not include a macro-to-macro line at all. For him, "the macro level is an abstraction." Coleman 1990, p. 12; cf. Coleman 1986, p. 1322.

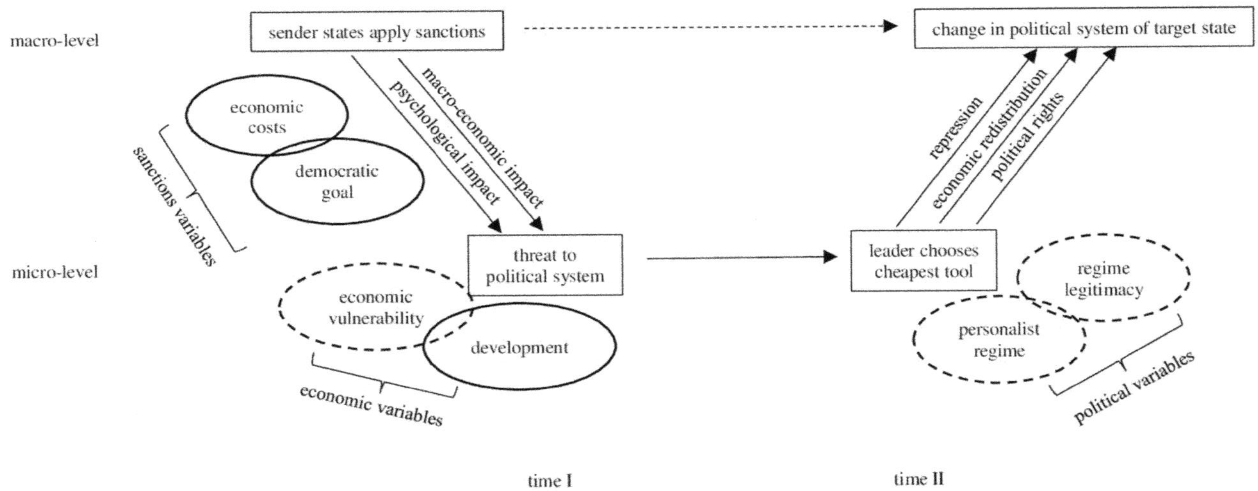

Fig. 20: Adaption of Coleman's bathtub model

Circles with continuous line: independent variables that correlate with dependent variable

Circles with dashed line: independent variables that do not correlate with dependent variable

7 So what? Implications and recommendations

> "[T]ools can only perform well when they are employed with a proper strategy; one can't blame the saw if it fails to perform the work of a screwdriver."[677]

In 2015, sanctions scholars described Zimbabwe as an example of how sanctions enhance the cohesion of the ruling elite.[678] Two years later, the military ousted long-time dictator Mugabe. In 2017, North Korea was described as insensitive to economic sanctions because the regime adapts so well to sanctions.[679] Half a year later, North Korea announced to discontinue the nuclear tests. Both examples should not make us assume that sanctions are successful. Nobody knows which political impact the sanctions had in both cases. However, they show that even the most spectacular "failures" of sanctions can quickly prove those wrong who enjoy quoting them as evidence against the use of sanctions.

Based on literature, this book established hypotheses and tested them with new and reliable data. Though not many of the hypotheses proved to be right, the results of the quantitative analysis provide us with valuable information on the impact of sanctions. These findings need to be seen in light of current debates within and outside academia to make sense of them. The final chapter discusses metatheoretical implications for the academic sanctions debate (ontological, methodological, epistemological), provides research recommendations (related to sanctions research and regime research) and policy recommendations, reflects the use of economic statecraft in international relations today, and concludes with a list of research contributions. A comprehensive summary can be found at the very beginning of the book (*executive summary*).

7.1 Metatheoretical implications

7.1.1 Ontology of success

The present results show that sanctions with the aim of democratic improvement correlate indeed with a better democratic performance (confirmed hypothesis 2).

677 Nephew 2018, pp. 4–5.
678 Grauvogel & Soest 2015.
679 E.g., Haggard & Noland 2017; interview with W. Nowak, ZDF, 2017-09-04.

Though the success of sanctions is not part of the puzzle in this book, the results suggest that democratic sanctions are rather successful than non-successful. But what is success? Many articles in the sanctions debate skip this abstract ontological question. The disagreement over apparently "neutral" quantitative results has its roots, partly, in different definitions and ontological assumptions – such as the definition of sanctions success.

As mentioned in the introductory chapter, the definition of success was in the center of an emotional debate between Pape, Elliott, and Baldwin in the late 1990s.[680] Most scholars define success as compliance with the publicly stated goal. Baldwin is puzzled by the hitherto "persistence of the zero-sum conception of military conflict,"[681] and by the fact that scholars of economic sanctions use this "oversimplifying"[682] dichotomy of victory and defeat/failure too. Though the overwhelming majority of scholars heavily argued against applying economic sanctions, policymakers continued using them with even increasing frequency.[683] Some scholars explain this basic paradox of the sanction debate by describing policymakers as fools,[684] others reply that the "answer lies less in the ignorance of government officials than in the naiveté of the research on […] sanctions."[685]

One explanation for the sanctions paradox is that "policymakers and scholars are addressing different questions."[686] Baldwin suggests separating the questions 'do sanctions work' and 'should sanctions be used'.[687] Policymakers are, in opposition to academics, not concerned with the usefulness of sanctions per se but choose the best possible answer in a specific situation under specific circumstances.[688] Sometimes an apparently non-successful tool may still be better than the alternative. Sanctions do not exist in a vacuum. In the toolkit of foreign policy, economic coercion is only one tool and always co-exists with information, military and political-diplomatic tools.[689] The success of all of these tools is

680 Pape's first article was "Why Economic Sanctions Do Not Work" (1997) as a reply to Hufbauer et al. 1990. After a reply by one of Hufbauer's co-authors (Elliott 1998), he published the follow-up article "Why Economic Sanctions Still Do Not Work" (1998). Baldwin 1999 replied that effectiveness needs to be analyzed together with costs.
681 Baldwin 1999, p. 94.
682 Portela 2010, p. 14.
683 Baldwin 1999, p. 80.
684 Cf. the article "Fools Suffer Gladly" by Morgan & Schwebach 1997.
685 Lindsay 1986, p. 153.
686 Baldwin 1999, p. 81.
687 Baldwin 1999, p. 81.
688 O'Sullivan 2003.
689 Baldwin 1985, pp. 13–14.

usually difficult to evaluate.[690] Sanctions do not simply "succeed" or "fail," rather, they are "either helpful to achieving the desired end result of a sanctioning state or not."[691]

The spectacular announcement of North Korea in April 2018 to discontinue the nuclear tests follows the comprehensive economic sanctions implemented just two years before; China too as biggest North Korean trading partner participated in the sanction round. Independently from the question whether North Korea will pursue the announced path: What caused the announcement? Economic sticks (UN including China), political carrots (South Korea's Moon's appeasement policies), military threat (US), or the combination of all of them? Sanctions are only part of a larger strategy. Economic policies are one tool in the foreign policy toolbox, along with military, diplomacy, and propaganda.[692] Sanctions need to be understood "as a tool embedded in a larger strategic setting."[693] In the case of North Korea, the combination of these tools in 2017 and 2018 changed substantially from the previous years with less military threat, less economic pressure, and a remote South Korean administration.

An important issue in this book was the distinction between comprehensiveness of sanctions and economic costs of sanctions. If the sender and the target state have a low level of trade linkage, and if the sender state employs neither military threats nor propaganda or diplomatic negotiations, how can such sanctions be "successful"? How should they change a policy in the target state? Instead, such sanctions send a signal; they are a symbol in the international arena. Only when we include the variable economic costs (and do not see sanctions as a dummy variable), we can have a look behind the curtain, and start distinguishing (and evaluating) sanctions according to their real goal.

The research results of the book made it clear that sanctions are not a binary variable. Two sanctions variables and an additional model that tested types of sanctions showed that the design of sanctions is one of the most important variables when researching the impact of sanctions. Further quantitative research should incorporate non-quantitative research such as Giumelli's tripartite taxonomy of sanction goals or Baldwin's fourfold foreign policy toolbox. In traditional sanctions literature, the answer to the question how to measure success is simply compliance of the target.[694] As mentioned in the introductory

690 Baldwin 2011, p. 708.
691 Nephew 2018, pp. 4–5.
692 Baldwin 1985, pp. 13–14.
693 Eriksson & Wallensteen 2015.
694 Jones & Portela 2014, p. 1.

chapter, sanctions are not always intended to succeed in their ostensible goal, and there may be multiple targets and goals.[695] This book adds the distinction between the *de jure goal* and the *de facto goal*. Whereas the de jure goal refers to the stated goal in the legal texts – denuclearization, democratization, the return of territory – the de facto goal refers to the mechanism-oriented purpose that Giumelli describes as coercing, constraining or signaling.[696] In 2018, a first sanctions dataset applied Giumelli's de facto goal to UN sanctions (TSC), using it for the measurement of effectiveness.[697]

7.1.2 Epistemological issues

This book does not claim that economic sanctions lead to an increase of the level of democracy, even though the results may indirectly suggest that. There are too many variables that cannot be included, there are too many variables that cannot be measured. The claim, however, that sanctions have an autocratizing effect, cannot be backed with the present findings. Peksen & Drury claim that comprehensive sanctions (defined as sanctions with high economic impact) have a strong negative impact on the level of democracy.[698] The large-N findings with better variables and newer data falsify that claim. Sanctions with economic costs cannot cause autocratization because they don't even correlate with it. Falsification of a theory is even more important than its verification.[699]

All studies in the 70s and 80s were single case studies analyzing prominent cases – which became prominent due to their failure.[700] In 1985 only, the HSEO dataset provided data for quantitative analyses.[701] Whereas the heated debate concerned the success of sanctions, some scholars pointed at the humanitarian damage done by comprehensive sanctions and, eventually, at the political impact. The fact that quantitative results apparently confirmed anecdotal evidence made the case crystal clear: Comprehensive economic sanctions cause a deterioration of the political system and the liberal-democratic system.

695 Baldwin 1985, p. 371; Dashti-Gibson, Davis, & Radcliff 1997, p. 616.

696 Giumelli 2010, 2011.

697 Biersteker, Eckert, Tourinho, & Hudáková 2018.

698 Peksen & Drury 2010, p. 254.

699 Popper 1963 (Conjectures and Refutations), p. 215; cf. Popper 2002 [1959] (The Logic of Scientific Discovery).

700 Morgan, Bapat, & Kobayashi 2014.

701 Hufbauer & Schott 1985 (second edition in 1990 and third edition in 2007).

Another epistemological and methodological problem is the incommensurability of sanctions. Independently from their strategical setting, it proved to be difficult to measure the sanction itself. The basic problem of all quantitative sanction research is the quantification of sanctions. Many scholars use a dummy variable for sanctions, they see sanctions as a binary being – it's either on or off. A more refined measurement could make use of the a-priori design of sanctions, focusing on design, scope, depth, type, targets, senders, etc. An a-posteriori approach could measure the real impact of sanctions: compliance, economic costs, unintended side-effects, etc. Each sanctions episode consists of a complex process of legal texts and implementation. We cannot observe and measure sanctions per se, we can just observe and measure specific features such as the ones mentioned above. But even those features proved to be a challenge. They are different in every case.

The question, then, is how can we compare sanctions if we cannot even describe them? Just looking at one feature (such as economic costs) is unsatisfying for a general evaluation of sanctions, using a dummy is simply misleading. The incommensurability[702] of sanctions has an important implication: Large-N analyses have only limited validity. This does not mean that positivist scientific realism cannot make use of them. It means that some quantitative large-N analyses may have less explanatory power than some case studies. Area studies are crucial not only for the analysis of sanctions cases but especially for the application of sanctions.

7.1.3 Methodological bias and manipulation

Using newest data and employing the best possible statistical tools, the present book indicates surprisingly the opposite of what previous large-N studies claim. This is a real puzzle. Can the design of quantitative studies be manipulated? Scholars who argue that sanctions lead to autocratization are not necessarily cheating, the results, however, can be biased or adjusted in many ways. The better statistical expertise is, the easier it is to get the results one wishes for. Including additional variables can have a significant impact on the whole model. The results presented in the previous chapter show how some variables change. How can one prevent himself from unintentionally manipulating the models? First of all, the methodology and the results should be fully transparent. The results need to be discussed comprehensively, problems need to be mentioned, changes to the model need to be made seen. Second, and even more important, the hypotheses

702 The term is not used in a Kuhnian or Feyerabendian sense but in its literal meaning.

need to be based on the literature review and be integrated into a proper theoretical model. Only then, a quantitative analysis can look for correlations.

Regarding the articles on the current puzzle – the impact of economic sanctions on the political system – it is clear that the selection of cases was a perhaps unintentional mean of manipulation. Peksen & Drury analyze in both articles on the same puzzle only cases between 1970/1972 and 2000,[703] despite their case source, the Hufbauer dataset, provides data until 2007.[704] The design of sanctions changed that much around 2000 that the selection of the time frame very much influences the results of a quantitative analysis. Selection bias is an important argument in the sanctions debate.

When reviewing the whole sanctions debates, it is striking that many debate contributions come from few authors. It is very surprising that even quantitative analyses by some scholars confirm their own previous findings. One example for a devote sanctions opponent is Doxey,[705] one example for sanctions proponents are Cortright & Lopez.[706] Relevant for our puzzle – the negative consequences of sanctions independent from the success questions – is the academic work of Peksen & Drury. In an impressive number of papers, they cover many governance-related topics: the impact of sanctions on women's rights, on ethnic discrimination, on private property and wealth, on public health, on press freedom, on human rights, on political rights, on democracy.[707] All of their articles come to a negative evaluation of sanctions. Their often-quoted articles contributed to the negative image of sanctions. Lakatos described how scholars stick to degenerating research programs: Scholars strengthen their own position, build auxiliary hypotheses around their core hypotheses.[708] Abandoning a self-built research program comes with high costs. This does not necessarily mean that the mentioned scholars manipulated data and models to strengthen their

703 Peksen & Drury 2009, 2010.

704 Hufbauer, Schott, Elliott, & Oegg 2007.

705 Doxey 1971, 1972, 1980, 1996.

706 Cortright 2007; Cortright, Gerber, & Lopez 2005; Cortright & Lopez 1995; Cortright & Lopez 2000a; Cortright & Lopez 2000b; Cortright & Lopez 2000c; Cortright & Lopez 2001; Cortright & Lopez 2007; Cortright, Lopez, & Gerber-Stellingwerf 2008; Lopez 2011; Lopez 2012; Lopez 2013; Lopez & Cortright 1997; Lopez & Cortright 2010; Lopez & Cortright 2011.

707 Drury & Peksen 2014; Drury & Li 2006; Peksen 2009; Peksen 2010; Peksen 2011; Peksen 2014; Peksen 2017; Peksen & Drury 2009; Peksen & Drury 2010; Peksen, Peterson, & Drury 2014.

708 Lakatos 1978, p. 6.

academic reputation. It may, however, be an indicator for an unintentional bias of scholars in favor of themselves.

A serious issue is the manipulation of raw data. Part I of this book started with the quote: "[E]conomic sanctions [...] may have contributed to more deaths during the post-Cold War era than all weapons of mass destruction throughout history."[709] The claim refers to the catastrophic humanitarian "collateral damage" to the Iraqi population during the comprehensive economic sanctions in the 1990s. According to data by UN agencies, these sanctions killed around 500,000 Iraqis.[710] A major demographic survey by UNICEF – the Iraq Child and Maternal Mortality Survey (ICMMS) – found that the child mortality rate had increased dramatically after the imposition of comprehensive sanctions.[711] After the world learned of the devastating humanitarian impact of sanctions in Iraq, sanctions scholars shifted their attention from sanctions success to unintended side-effects of sanctions. Many studies since quote the case of Iraq as paradigmatic example of sanctions.[712]

In 2017, a meta-study exposed that the 1999 UNICEF study was very likely a hoax. It was conducted together with the Iraqi government. Three other retrospective surveys found no significant increase of the child mortality rate. The small gap between Iraq and the neighbor countries existed already in the 1980s and did not significantly increase in the 1990s. For the authors of the meta-study it is clear that Saddam Hussein manipulated the data "to shake international opinion so that the UN economic sanctions would be lifted."[713] Despite the fact that other surveys exist since the early 2000s and quickly proved to be more reliable, sanction scholars continue citing the UNICEF/Saddam survey from 1999. No sanctions study could be found that doubts the fantastic data. "[T]he more mundane truth that has emerged has received much less attention than the original spectacular lie."[714] Latter definitely matches better the narrative of ineffective and inhumane sanctions.

709 Mueller & Mueller 1999, p. 43.
710 Mueller & Mueller 1999, p. 49.
711 Dyson & Cetorelli 2017, p. 1.
712 E.g., Afesorgbor & Mahadevan 2016; Batniji, Khatib, Cammett, et al. 2014; Devakumar, Birch, Osrin, et al. 2014; Gorji 2014; Neuenkirch & Neumeier 2015; Neuenkirch & Neumeier 2016; Peksen 2011; Escribà-Folch & Wright 2015, p. 151.
713 Mueller & Mueller 1999, p. 49.
714 Dyson & Cetorelli 2017, p. 1.

7.2 Research recommendations

7.2.1 Sanctions-related research recommendations

The analysis clearly showed the limits of quantitative sanctions research. "[E]ach sanctions incident is unique and, therefore, any generalization is impossible," writes Tsebelis.[715] Generalizations are not impossible but very difficult. The structure of a sanctions policy in combination with other foreign policy tools (military, diplomacy, propaganda) makes it difficult to describe and measure sanctions. This book tried to use the economic impact of sanctions as the main characteristic. Such quantitative research is only fruitful if the sanctions are comparable. If sanctions target only individual groups and not the macro-economy, alternative methodological approaches are necessary. Area studies may complement sanctions research also on topics of worldwide relevance.

Such an approach might help to answer another question: How does a targeted leadership actively behave after the threat or imposition of sanctions? Drezner complains about a "sender bias of the literature."[716] Few studies look at targeted leadership as active agents – they are not only subjected to sanctions, they react to the imposition of sanctions and have a wide opportunity of actions. Most papers are written from a neutral or the sender's perspective. At least equally interesting is what the targeted leader does: Does he increase taxes? Does he try to bring financial assets abroad home? How does he increase propaganda? How does he subvert sanctions? The theoretical explanation of this book, based on Wintrobe, is abstract and generalizing. Case studies should look in detail into the actions of the targeted leader following the imposition of sanctions.

A third sanctions-related research recommendation concerns the implementation on a regional level. Most studies look at sanctions imposed by the United Nations, the European Union or the United States, probably due to data availability. A trend that is not well described by academia is the regionalization of sanctions impositions. More and more, regional organizations impose sanctions, especially in the Southern hemisphere (the Organization of American States, the African Union, OPEC, ECOWAS). The increasing importance of regional economic blocks in the last decades led to an increase of sanctions imposition by regional organizations. Such sanctions are easier applicable than UNSC sanctions. A comparative study could give more insight into the power of regional sanctions.

---

715 Tsebelis 1990, p. 6.

716 Drezner 2011, p. 96.

7.2.2 Regime-related research recommendations

It proved to be difficult to define the opposite of a liberal-democratic state. "Autocracy" is not a well-defined concept but a residual category for everything that does not match the definition of a liberal-democratic state. Democracy is described as an "essentially contested concept,"[717] but autocracy is not even a concept. The many regime types summarized by the term autocracy have not much in common, except their opposition to liberal-democratic values. Political theory is needed to establish a proper categorization of regimes that can be used by quantitative science too. The mechanisms in different types of regimes are fundamentally different. A military dictator has other tools than a monarch in a resource-rich state, and the winning coalition he needs to satisfy looks very differently. Future research might be advised to focus on single types of regimes.

A further question is, which path do failed regimes follow: Why do some regimes transition to military dictatorships, others to one-party-regimes? Regimes do not necessarily transform from autocracy to democracy.[718] The traditional continuous scale with a utopian democracy at one end and a dystopian autocracy at the other is helpful for a first overview. When analyzing the impact of some factors on the regime, other features may be more illuminating: the quality of government, regime performance or state capacity,[719] the degree of institutionalization of power,[720] technocratic/meritocratic versus non-meritocratic (elected or personalized) elements, the centralization of different policy areas (local, regional, national), and so on. Such features may add more epistemological value to a general democracy-autocracy score. Another important regime characteristic is the perceived legitimacy of the regime by the population. So far, the measurement of regime legitimacy is unsatisfying.[721]

717 Gallie 1956, p. 168.
718 Escribà-Folch & Wright 2015, pp. 38–48.
719 Schmitter 2015, p. 37; Haber 2011, p. 2; Fukuyama 2013, p. 347.
720 Geddes 1999, pp. 121–122; Escribà-Folch & Wright 2015, p. 137.
721 Tanneberg, Stefes, & Merkel 2013, p. 124. Grauvogel et al. use expert interviews for establishing a legitimacy score. Grauvogel & Soest 2014, pp. 641–642.

7.3 Policy recommendations

1. Policymakers need to be careful with countries with a low level of development, with a high level of vulnerability, or a high level of legitimacy of the leadership. The research results showed that in such countries a negative impact of economic sanctions may be stronger than in others.
2. Policymakers need to listen primarily to area studies and public choice approaches, not only to large-N studies. The basic problem of all quantitative research on sanctions is the quantification of sanctions. Sanctions are not a binary variable. It is not possible to observe and measure sanctions, we can just serve a specific output, e.g., economic costs. Large-N analysis have only limited validity.
3. Policymakers need to know what they want. They need to be aware of different mechanisms of sanctions. This book distinguishes between the *de jure goal* and the *de facto goal*. The de jure goal refers to the stated goal in the legal texts, the de facto goal refers to the inherent mechanism (coercing, constraining, signaling).[722] This distinction shows the importance of theory for policy making and analyzing. Often, sanctions pursue multiple goals and cannot be categorized easily. This is fine if sanctions are intended to be unclear – information is an important good in international relations, and information asymmetry can be part of a strategy. When the sanctions are intended to coerce, however, they should be designed in the respective way to achieve the desired outcome. Both policymakers and policy analysists should be aware of this important theoretical distinction.
4. Policymakers need to recognize so-called secondary sanctions as "normal sanctions" against their state. An insight from data collection and organization is that secondary sanctions – sanctions that force a state to impose sanctions on a third state – are not some sort of collateral damage of normal sanctions. Instead, they directly target a state and its economy. Through economic means, they pursue a policy change. Such sanctions are a new development but will appear more frequently in future. It is important for the target state to recognize such sanctions as sanctions, as direct (economic) attack, and not as an unintentional by-product. In 2018, U.S. president Trump announced to leave the Joint Comprehensive Plan of Action, an international agreement on nuclear proliferation in Iran, that was signed by Iran, the permanent five of the UNSC, Germany, and the EU. Following the retreat, the U.S. administration announced to impose the "strongest sanctions in history"[723] on Iran, including

722 Giumelli 2010, 2011.
723 BBC, 2018-05-21.

so-called secondary sanctions. This euphemism means that all companies investing in Iran are restricted from doing business in the U.S. States hurt most by this measure are those who have a high level of trade relations with both the U.S. and Iran. The measure does not hurt the North Korean or the Syrian Iran-trade (both exist), but mainly European business. The U.S. forces companies in the EU and the EU to comply with U.S. sanctions. The policy recommendation is to recognize such "secondary" sanctions as sanctions. Only then, counter-sanctions capabilities can be developed.

5. Policymakers need to develop sanctions and counter-sanctions capabilities. Sanctions need to be implemented properly. The imposition and implementation of sanctions is a highly complicated process that needs legal expertise, trade expertise, and financial and regional intelligence. The findings show that U.S. sanctions have a much stronger effect on the level of democracy than sanctions by other senders. Though such results need to be read with care, they could indicate a higher effectiveness regarding democratic sanctions. This may be related to different implementation mechanisms and institutions of the senders analyzed in this book.

The United Nations does impose sanctions via its Security Council. The member states are responsible for implementing them.[724] For major sanctions regimes, the UNSC establishes sanctions committees, comprising all members of the UNSC, that oversee the measures. A Panel of Experts analyzes the implementation by the UN member states and gives recommendations. An example is the Security Council Committee Established Pursuant to Resolution 1718, established in 2006 with the aim of overseeing UN sanctions on North Korea. In the U.S., the Office of Economic Sanctions Policy and Implementation within the Department of State is responsible for developing sanctions. The Office of Foreign Assets Control (OFAC), a financial intelligence agency of the Treasury Department, then targets (and hunts) individuals and entities, not only in the financial but also in the economic sector. The EU has a sanctions unit within the European External Action Service; the member states are responsible for the implementation. As an example, in the EU member state Germany the responsible authorities are a unit within *Deutsche Bundesbank* (the German central bank) for financial sanctions and a unit within *Bundesamt für Wirtschaft und Ausfuhrkontrolle* (an agency of the Federal Ministry for Economic Affairs) for trade-related sanctions.

It is interesting to compare the size of the institutions: The U.S. Office of Foreign Assets Control has around 170 employees working full-time on the

724 Cf. Carisch, Rickard-Martin, & Meister 2017.

design and implementation of sanctions. A scholar estimated the number of employees working full-time on the design and implementation of sanctions in the EU at four to five in the EEAS (only one in 2011) and at one to three in most member states such as Germany.[725] An insider doubted this estimate as too low;[726] exact numbers do not exist. The respective Bundesamt could not give a number because the employees do not work full-time on sanctions. They do not hunt potential targets of sanctions or design sanctions but advise companies on legal and technical implications for their business.[727] Within the financial sanctions unit of Deutsche Bundesbank, seven employees are responsible for the "operative implementation" (not the design) of EU financial sanctions.[728]

The estimated numbers make clear that sanction design and implementation capabilities in the EU are not comparable to those in the U.S. This confirms the image of the EU as an economic superpower that does not make use of its political capacities. Anecdotal evidence supports this argument: In 2017, the official UNSC panel of experts report rebuked Germany for enabling North Korea to commercialize its diplomatic property, which is clearly prohibited by the UNSC.[729] A whole paragraph describes the German reluctance (or inability) to enforce binding UNSC sanctions regulations.[730]

Sanctions needs expertise. The design and imposition of sanctions is at least as tricky as counter-sanctions capabilities: The 2018 U.S. sanctions against Iranian trade partners such as the EU showed once again that the EU is not only a sender but also a target of sanctions. For the EU, it is necessary to develop both sanction and counter-sanction capabilities to protect the values and interests of the Union.

The last policy advice is to have a grand strategy for economic statecraft. Economic sanctions are part of economic statecraft as much as economic aid, tariffs and free trade agreements are. The problems and challenges liberal democracies face today make it urgently necessary to include economic statecraft into

725 E-mail by Richard Nephew (2013–2015 Principal Deputy for the Coordinator for Sanctions Policy, U.S. State Department) to the author, 2018-05-14 (publication forthcoming).

726 E-mail to the author, 2018-06-02.

727 E-mail by Bundesamt für Wirtschaft und Ausfuhrkontrolle to the author, 2018-05-23.

728 E-mail by Deutsche Bundesbank, Servicezentrum Finanzsanktionen, to the author, 2018-06-05.

729 UNSC Panel of Experts 2017, p. 25.

730 Ironically, the property is situated next to the German Foreign Office.

a political strategy. The following, last chapter of the book presents how a grand strategy of economic statecraft could look like.

7.4 A Kantian use of economic statecraft

> "Pugnant [...] inter se mali et mali. Item pugnant inter se mali et boni. Boni vero et boni, si perfecti sunt, inter se pugnare non possunt." ([...] there are battles of evil against evil. There are also battles of evil against good and good against evil. But the good, if they have achieved perfection, cannot fight among themselves.)
>
> —*Augustine, De civitate Dei, 15,5*

Comparing economic sanctions with a non-trade situation is more than a metaphor. The application of economic sanctions isolates the target state and lead to more autarky indeed, whereas the non-application leads to economic interdependence.[731] Looking at economic sanctions in a larger context, they can be defined more precisely as negative economic sanctions. The opposite term is positive economic sanctions that refers to measures increasing economic interdependence: decreasing of tariffs, establishing a common market. Such positive economic measures are not less powerful. In 19th century's central Europe, Prussia created the *Deutscher Zollverein* (German Customs Union). This economic community excluded the old hegemon Austria and was a crucial step towards the creation of the so-called *Deutsches Reich* under Prussian dominance. Historical evidence and large-N evidence show that the economy is a powerful weapon. The question is how to use it. Even not doing anything contributes to a broader strategy.[732] The non-application of economic sanctions might have even a greater political impact than the application of sanctions. Two arguments help to get an answer of how to use economic statecraft in international relations.

The first argument is that economic interdependence among (liberal-democratic) republics leads to overall peace and prosperity. The Kantian triad sees peace as result of a liberal-democratic (republican) constitution within the states, international institutions above the states, and economic interdependence between the states (Fig. 21).[733] Such states do not wage war against

731 Bergeijk 2009, pp. 119–120; Pond 2017; Dizaji & Bergeijk 2013, p. 725.

732 无为而无不为 [Non-action is not non-action], says Laozi (Daodejing, ch. 37).

733 Russett & Oneal 2001 ("Triangulating Peace: Democracy, Interdependence, and International Organizations"); cf. Doyle 1986; Hegre, Oneal, & Russett 2010; Oneal & Russett 1997, 1999a, 1999b; Oneal, Russett, & Davis 1998; Oneal 2003.

Fig. 21: Kantian triangle, based on Russett & Oneal[734]

each other. This liberal peace theory is based on Immanuel Kant's writing *Perpetual Peace* from 1795/1796, in which he describes requirements of a perpetual peace: "The civil constitution in every state shall be republican;" the "right of nations shall be founded on a federation of free states;" and "commercial spirit […] cannot exist along with war."[735] Whereas some approaches focus on his last argument (commercial peace hypothesis), Kant emphasizes that perpetual peace applies to republics only, states with a separation of power. (He distinguishes republics from "despotic" democracies – a Greek-style tyranny of majority without laws protecting the individuals – and other despotic states.[736])

The second argument is that economic interdependence with corrupt regimes leads not to peace and prosperity for everyone. Nili argues that trading with corrupt regimes strengthens them even more.[737] In the late 20th century, some European powers believed in changing their Eastern neighbors through

734 Russett & Oneal 2001, p. 35.

735 Kant 2010 [1796], pp. 13, 17, 32.

736 Russett equals Kant's concept of republics to modern liberal representative democracies. Russett 1993, p. 4; in contrast to Zakaria 1997, pp. 36–37. Kant does not directly mention which other types government do not count as republics. It must be added that at the time Kant wrote his pamphlet, numerous (city) republics with institutionalized power and collective decision-making bodies existed.

737 Nili 2011, p. 355.

economic exchange (*Wandel durch Handel*). Politicians and academics argued that economic engagement would lead to political reforms.[738] However, the "modernization" effect can easily be manipulated by corrupt leaders. Economic interdependence with a corrupt regime makes the leader richer and provides resources for strengthening his power position and increasing his military budget. In most autocracies, the political and the economic elite are the same or interwoven. Economic interdependence increases the GDP per capita, but it benefits the regime's winning coalition more than it does the population. Thanks to the export of natural resources, Equatorial Guinea had the fourth-highest average income in the world in 2008. At the same time, three-quarters of the country's people were malnourished.[739]

Putting both arguments together, it follows that liberal democracies should increase economic dependence on friendly states and decrease economic dependence on corrupt regimes. In analogy to Rousseau's social contract, liberal democracies should replace dependence on corrupt regimes with interdependence between equals.[740] This has three advantages. First, economic disengagement helps not to enrich kleptocrats. (Based on this argument, economic sanctions against corrupt regimes at least prevent companies in the sender state from enriching the elite of the target state, even if they seem to fail on every account.) Second, economic engagement with partners strengthens the political alliance. Decreasing tariffs is one way to manage trade flows. Following from these two advantages, states are less vulnerable to economic sanctions from enemies. Though decreasing economic engagement with corrupt regimes hurts the sanction capabilities, not being vulnerable to economic sanctions by corrupt regimes is an important long-term counter-sanction capability.

A darkening political-economic landscape asks for adequate strategies. The economy is a powerful tool in the foreign policy toolbox. Decreasing the dependence on corrupt regimes and increasing interdependence with states that share the same values serves the long-term interests of the free world. It is, perhaps, the best way to strengthen Kantian resilience in a Hobbesian world.

738 E.g., Haggard & Noland 2017, pp. 10–11; for the commercial peace hypothesis, cf. McDonald 2004, 2007, 2010.

739 Wenar 2008, pp. 6–7.

740 Nili 2011, p. 358.

7.5 Lessons learned

This book does not end with the sentence "We are still confused, but on a higher level." The book contributes to academic knowledge with quantitative findings and on a theoretical level. Before looking at the lessons learned, it needs to be clarified what this book does not do: This book does not claim that sanctions cause democracy. That issue is not part of the research question. This book does not claim that democratic sanctions are "successful." Democratic sanctions correlate with a higher level of democracy indeed, but such findings need to be read with caution. This book does not claim that its quantitative findings are the last truth. The measurement of sanctions is as "maddeningly difficult"[741] as the search for causes of democratization is. Future research may provide more insights. This book does not claim that all previous literature is wrong. Many contributions to the academic debate provide excellent data and analytical tools for the evaluation of sanctions. Instead, this book contributes with four central innovations to the academic debate.

1. Sanctions with high economic costs do not cause autocratization. The findings of this book debunk the argument that such sanctions are responsible for an autocratization of the targeted state as a myth. Peksen & Drury write that comprehensive economic sanctions "significantly reduce the level of democratic freedoms in the target."[742] With their large-N analysis they confirm what previous case studies already found. They argue that high economic costs cause the autocratizing effect. Using newer data, this finding cannot be reproduced. Instead, the analysis conducted in this book finds a significant correlation between sanctions with high economic costs and the level of democracy. Cases that suggest otherwise are not prototypical sanctions cases but infamous anomalies, particularly known for their "failure". In other cases, sanctions follow (not cause) autocratization, such as post-2014 sanctions against Russia. This book does not claim that sanctions with high economic costs cause democratization, but it claims that they do not cause autocratization – there is no correlation, so the claimed causality cannot be true. Policymakers should always be careful with the imposition of sanctions, but these results suggest that sanctions with high economic costs do not automatically have a negative impact on the level of democracy.
2. Aid sanctions and arms embargoes correlate with a higher level of democracy. The type of sanction is crucial for its side-effects. Previous large-N studies

741 Coppedge 1997.
742 Peksen & Drury 2010, p. 240.

on the political impact of sanctions did not look at different types. Arms embargoes hurt the repressive capacity in the targeted state. Aid sanctions are particularly harmful to an autocratic leader because they directly hurt his revenue streams. Once they disappear, he needs to rely on other tools to keep the system stable – such as granting political rights. This will also guarantee the lifting of sanctions. This finding should be an incentive for further research.

3. Sanctions are not a binary variable and should, therefore, not be used as such in quantitative analyses. This seems to be self-evident, but the reference articles for the present research puzzle use sanctions more or less as a dummy variable: Dury et al. distinguish between extensive and limited sanctions;[743] Soest et al. between comprehensive and targeted sanctions;[744] Drury et al. just use a dummy variable;[745] Wood refers to the comprehensiveness of the design.[746] One problem following from a binary modeling of sanctions is that scholars equal comprehensive sanctions with high economic costs. This is wrong. High economic costs result from the potentially affected trade linkage (ex-ante damage) and the de facto implementation of sanctions (ex-post damage). The North Korea case shows how misleading this confusion is: In the 1990s, the U.S. applied (and lifted) unilateral sanctions that are described as comprehensive. The pre-sanctions trade level between these two countries, however, was already at zero before the imposition of sanctions. The sanctions regime did not concern the North Korean economy at all, it merely functioned as signal. In most databases and analyses, these sanctions are coded in the same way as the most comprehensive UN sanctions against Iraq in the 1990s. Sanctions consist of a complex net of legal regulation and laws, from different bodies, and their goal, design, and scope need to be included in a quantitative analysis of sanctions. Using sanctions as a binary variable is misleading and may lead to wrong findings.
4. Sanctions have a de jure goal and a de facto goal; an evaluation of sanctions that is only based on the de jure goal is misleading. Whereas the de jure goal refers to a publicly stated purpose of sanctions, the de facto goal refers to the inherent mechanism (coercing, constraining, signaling). When a state annexes territory, sanctions against that state may ask for its return. In praxis, it is very difficult to coerce a state on "high politics" issues. The sanctions may be

743 Peksen & Drury 2010.
744 Soest & Wahman 2015.
745 Peksen & Drury 2009.
746 Wood 2008, p. 500.

nothing else than a signal in the international arena and show other countries that such behavior will be punished. In this case, the de jure goal differs substantially from the de facto goal, but traditional sanctions researchers would evaluate these sanctions as non-successful as long as the targeted country does not return the territory. In fact, these sanctions may have punished the target state and perhaps even prevented it from annexing other territories. An evaluation of sanctions needs to include the de facto goal, though it may be very difficult to establish in most cases.

To sum up: Economic sanctions are not as bad as many academic and non-academic contributions suggest. The economy is a powerful tool in the international arena and should not be forgotten by political decision-makers. If they want to employ economic sanctions properly, they should not forget that economic policy is only one tool in the foreign policy toolbox. A sound strategy needs to consider all spheres of foreign policy to achieve a goal. The rise of new alliances and the danger of a resulting new Cold War between liberal democracies and autocracies asks for adequate ideas and strategies.

E tenebris autem quae sunt in luce tuemur.

—*Lucretius, De Rerum Natura*

Appendix

A. Cases of economic sanctions

Target	Main sender	Start	End	Type	Main source
Afghanistan	UN	1999	2001	FB, AE, FS, VB	GIGA
Algeria	EU	1992	1994	AS	GIGA
Angola	UN	1993	2002	AF, DS, AE, CE	TSC
Azerbaijan	US	1992	2002	AS	GIGA
Belarus	EU	1998	1999	VB	GIGA
Belarus	EU	2000	ongoing	VB, AF, DS, AE	GIGA
Belarus	US	2004	ongoing	VB, AF, AS	GIGA
Bosnia and Herzegovina	EU	1992	2006	AE	GIGA
Bosnia and Herzegovina	UN	1992	1996	AE	GIGA
Burundi	US	1996	2005	AS	GIGA
Cameroon	US	1992	1998	AS, AE	GIGA
Central African Republic	EU	2003	2005	AS	GIGA
Central African Republic	US	2003	2005	IM	GIGA
Central African Republic	UN	2013	ongoing	AF, AE	TSC
Colombia	US	1996	1998	FS, AS, AE, IM	GIGA
Comoros	EU	1999	2000	AS	GIGA
Côte d'Ivoire	EU	2000	2002	AS	GIGA
Côte d'Ivoire	UN	2004	2016	AE, VB, AF, CE	TSC
Côte d'Ivoire	US	1999	2002	AE, AS	GIGA
Croatia	EU	1992	2000	AE	GIGA
Croatia	UN	1992	1996	AE	GIGA
Cuba	EU	2003	2005	DS	GIGA
Cuba	US	1990	ongoing	CT, FS	HSEO
Congo, DR (Kinshasa)	EU	1992	1997	AE, AS, VB	GIGA

Target	Main sender	Start	End	Type	Main source
Congo, DR (Kinshasa)	EU	1997	2008	AE	GIGA
Congo, DR (Kinshasa)	UN	2003	ongoing	AF, AE, VB	TSC
Congo, DR (Kinshasa)	US	1990	1997	IM, AS, VB, AE	GIGA
Ecuador	US	1995	1998	CE, FS	HSEO
El Salvador	US	1990	1993	FS	HSEO
Equatorial Guinea	EU	1992	2010	AS	GIGA
Eritrea	UN	2000	2001	AE	GIGA
Eritrea	UN	2009	ongoing	AE	GIGA
Eritrea	US	2006	ongoing	AE	GIGA
Ethiopia	UN	2000	2001	AE	GIGA
Fiji	EU	2001	2003	AS	GIGA
Fiji	EU	2006	2014	AS	GIGA
Fiji	US	2006	2014	AS	GIGA
Gambia	EU	1994	2002	IM, AS	GIGA
Gambia	US	1994	1998	IM, AS	GIGA
Guinea	EU	2002	2006	AS	GIGA
Guinea	EU	2009	ongoing	VB, AE, AF	GIGA
Guinea	US	2009	2010	AF, VB	GIGA
Guinea-Bissau	US	2003	2004	AS	GIGA
Guinea-Bissau	UN	2012	ongoing	VB	TSC
Haiti	EU	2001	2005	AS	GIGA
Haiti	UN	1993	1994	CE, AE, FS, CT	GIGA
Haiti	US	1991	2006	AE	GIGA
Honduras	EU	2009	2010	AS, DS	GIGA
Honduras	US	2009	2010	AS	GIGA
India	US	1998	2001	FS, CE	HSEO
Indonesia	EU	1998	1999	AE	GIGA
Indonesia	US	1992	2005	IM, AS, FS	GIGA
Iran	UN	2006	ongoing	FS, AE, VB, CE	GIGA
Iraq	UN	1990	2003	CT	GIGA
Jordan	US	1990	1997	AS	GIGA
Kenya	US	1990	1993	IM, AS	GIGA
Lebanon	UN	2005	ongoing	AF, VB	TSC

Target	Main sender	Start	End	Type	Main source
Lebanon	EU	2006	ongoing	AE	EU
Lebanon	US	2007	ongoing	AF	US
Liberia	UN	1992	2016	AF, VB, DS, AE, CE	TSC
Libya	UN	1992	2003	FB, CE, AE	GIGA
Libya	UN	2011	ongoing	AE, AF, VB	TSC
Macedonia	EU	1991	2000	AE	GIGA
Macedonia	UN	1991	1996	AE	GIGA
Madagascar	EU	2009	2011	AS	GIGA
Madagascar	US	2010	ongoing	AS	GIGA
Malawi	EU	1992	1994	AS	GIGA
Malawi	US	1992	1994	AS	GIGA
Mauritania	EU	2008	2009	AS	GIGA
Mauritania	US	2008	2009	VB, AS	GIGA
Myanmar	EU	1996	ongoing	AE, VB, FS, AS, AF	GIGA
Nicaragua	US	1992	1995	AS	GIGA
Niger	EU	1996	1999	AS	GIGA
Niger	US	1996	2000	AS, IM, FS	GIGA
Niger	US	2009	2011	VB, AS	GIGA
Nigeria	EU	1993	1999	AS, AE, DS, VB	GIGA
Nigeria	US	1993	1998	IM, AS, DS, FB, VB	GIGA
Pakistan	US	1999	2001	AS	GIGA
Peru	EU	2000	2001	AS	GIGA
Peru	US	1991	1998	AS, ab 1995 IM	GIGA
Romania	US	1990	1993	FS, CE	HSEO
Russian Federation	EU	2014	ongoing	AE, FS	EU
Russian Federation	US	2014	ongoing	AF, FS	US
Rwanda	EU	1994	1995	AS	GIGA
Rwanda	UN	1994	2008	AE	TSC
Serbia (Yugoslavia)	EU	1991	1997	AE, AS	GIGA
Serbia (Yugoslavia)	EU	1998	2001	AE, AF, CE, FB, FS, VB	GIGA
Serbia (Yugoslavia)	UN	1991	1996	AE, AS, DS, FB, FS	TSC

Target	Main sender	Start	End	Type	Main source
Serbia (Yugoslavia)	UN	1998	2001	AE	GIGA
Serbia (Yugoslavia)	US	1991	2003	AE, AS, FS, DS, FB; after 1995 FS, DS, FB; after 1999 AS, FS, AE	GIGA
Sierra Leone	UN	1997	2010	AE, CE, DS, VB	TSC
Sri Lanka	US	2008	2016	AE	GIGA
Sudan	EU	1994	ongoing	AE, AS	GIGA
Sudan	UN	1996	2001	AE, DS, VB	TSC
Sudan	UN	2004	ongoing	AE	TSC
Sudan	US	1993	2017	AS, CE, DS, FS	GIGA
Sudan	EU	2014	ongoing	AE, AF, VB	EU
Syria	US	2004	ongoing	AE, AF	GIGA
Syria	EU	2011	ongoing	AF	EU
Syria	US	2011	ongoing	CE, CT, FS	US
Thailand	US	1991	1992	IM, AS	GIGA
Togo	EU	1992	1995	AS	GIGA
Togo	EU	1998	2004	AS	GIGA
Uzbekistan	EU	2005	2009	VB, AE, DS	GIGA
Uzbekistan	US	2005	ongoing	IM	GIGA
Venezuela	US	2006	ongoing	AE	GIGA
Yemen	US	1990	1997	AS, AE	GIGA
Yemen	UN	2014	ongoing	AF, VB, AE	TSC
Zambia	US	1996	1998	FS	HSEO
Zambia	EU	1996	1999	AS	GIGA
Zimbabwe	EU	2002	ongoing	AE, AF, AS, VB	GIGA
Zimbabwe	US	2002	ongoing	FS, VB	GIGA

B. Types and goals of sanctions

Types of sanctions[747]

AE	arms embargo	encompasses export restrictions of weapons or weapons-related technology
AF	asset freeze	freezing of financial assets held by individuals on a personal capacity
AS	aid sanctions	entails the partial or full suspension of aid, including redirection of aid
CE	commodity embargo	encompasses import and export sanctions on selected commodities, such as timber, cocoa, oil or diamonds (subtype arms embargo is treated in a separate category)
CT	comprehensive trade embargo	entails the complete ban of trade and financial relations (commercial transactions) with the targeted country
DS	diplomatic sanctions	encompasses limitation of contacts, recall of ambassadors or reduction of diplomatic personnel, expulsion from or suspension of membership in international organizations or vetoing accession
FB	flight ban	entails the prohibition of operating flights to and from the sender(s) or using the airspace of the sender countries
FS	financial sanctions	includes investment bans, bans on financial transactions, decisions to vote against the granting of loans by the international financial institutions and bilateral donors (EU, US), freezing of assets, ban on export credits
IM	interruption of military cooperation	concerns also military training and advisory services
VS	visa ban	entails restrictions on entry or prohibition on the issuing of visa

747 Taken from the GIGA sanctions dataset (Portela & Soest 2012, pp. 5–6). It also includes enforcement of sanctions as separate type ("sanctions imposed against a target to enforce sanctioning of other sanctioned units"). This book sees enforcement of sanctions neither as type nor as goal because so-called secondary sanctions directly attack a state and pursue a policy goal.

De jure goal (officially stated goal) of sanctions[748]

DM	democratization
HR	support human rights
NR	fight against narcotics
MD	stop biological and chemical weapons of mass destruction
NW	end nuclear proliferation
PC	termination of bellicosities, establishment of peace agreement
TR	fight terrorism, including releasing of hostages

De facto goal (mechanism)[749]

	Impact	***Feasibility***
coercing	high	high
constraining	high	low
signaling	low	low or high

C. Results

The statistical software Stata 14 was used for all quantitative analyses. The comprehensive log file containing the codes and the replication data is available via tobias.lechner@fu-berlin.de. All models are controlled with Arellano-Bond test and Sargan test. All models are controlled for standard error in the regression (using command *vce robust*).

748 Taken from Portela & Soest 2012, p. 5.
749 Giumelli 2010, p. 137.

```
------------------------------------------------------------------------------------


Model 1: main model

System dynamic panel-data estimation              Number of obs      =      1,440
Group variable: count                             Number of groups   =         60
Time variable: year
                                                  Obs per group:
                                                                min =         24
                                                                avg =         24
                                                                max =         24

Number of instruments =    142                    Wald chi2(10)      =     367.96
                                                  Prob > chi2        =     0.0000
Two-step results
------------------------------------------------------------------------------------
                  |              WC-Robust
        democracy |      Coef.   Std. Err.      z    P>|z|     [95% Conf. Interval]
------------------+-----------------------------------------------------------------
        democracy |
              L1. |   .4150492   .0704125     5.89   0.000     .2770432    .5530552
              L2. |  -.0097794   .0584187    -0.17   0.867     -.124278    .1047193
                  |
    economiccosts |   18.59276   6.180702     3.01   0.003     6.478807    30.70671
   democraticgoal |   9.396561   3.147674     2.99   0.003     3.227234    15.56589
personalistregime |  -.1455421   2.263205    -0.06   0.949    -4.581342    4.290257
 regimelegitimacy |   .1486448   1.150067     0.13   0.897    -2.105445    2.402735
    vulnerability |  -.0617011   .0334315    -1.85   0.065    -.1272256    .0038235
      development |   18.41247   9.999834     1.84   0.066    -1.186839    38.01179
 naturalresources |   -.907722   2.924605    -0.31   0.756    -6.639843    4.824399
         civilwar |   .9348371   2.061581     0.45   0.650    -3.105787    4.975462
            _cons |  -9.896592   6.020726    -1.64   0.100      -21.697    1.903814
------------------------------------------------------------------------------------

Arellano-Bond test for zero autocorrelation in first-differenced errors
  +-----------------------+
  |Order |  z     Prob > z|
  |------+----------------|
  |   1  |-3.6602  0.0003 |
  |   2  |-.70151  0.4830 |
  +-----------------------+
   H0: no autocorrelation

Sargan test of overidentifying restrictions
        H0: overidentifying restrictions are valid

        chi2(131)     =  52.03364
        Prob > chi2   =    1.0000


------------------------------------------------------------------------------------
```

Model 2: types

```
System dynamic panel-data estimation         Number of obs      =      1,440
Group variable: count                        Number of groups   =         60
Time variable: year
                                             Obs per group:
                                                          min =         24
                                                          avg =         24
                                                          max =         24

Number of instruments =    150               Wald chi2(17)      =    1710.70
                                             Prob > chi2        =     0.0000
Two-step results
```

democracy	Coef.	WC-Robust Std. Err.	z	P>|z|	[95% Conf.	Interval]
democracy						
L1.	.2535702	.0608147	4.17	0.000	.1343756	.3727649
L2.	-.0022442	.0287884	-0.08	0.938	-.0586684	.05418
armsembargo	6.543824	3.262168	2.01	0.045	.1500913	12.93756
assetfreeze	-.968316	6.098075	-0.16	0.874	-12.92032	10.98369
aidsanctions	12.06794	2.87723	4.19	0.000	6.428669	17.7072
commoditiesembargo	10.3915	5.426643	1.91	0.056	-.2445271	21.02752
comprtradeembargo	.2774912	13.96445	0.02	0.984	-27.09232	27.6473
diplomatsanctions	4.395092	6.968727	0.63	0.528	-9.263363	18.05355
flightban	-11.54378	13.15012	-0.88	0.380	-37.31754	14.22998
financialsanctions	8.145824	4.219241	1.93	0.054	-.1237366	16.41538
interruptmilitcoop	1.375349	4.491084	0.31	0.759	-7.427013	10.17771
visaban	1.782277	3.7761	0.47	0.637	-5.618744	9.183298
personalistregime	2.456693	1.964045	1.25	0.211	-1.392765	6.30615
regimelegitimacy	.216634	.495252	0.44	0.662	-.7540421	1.18731
vulnerability	.0030503	.0250437	0.12	0.903	-.0460344	.0521349
development	19.28406	9.686988	1.99	0.047	.2979074	38.2702
naturalresources	-1.339987	1.585818	-0.84	0.398	-4.448132	1.768158
civilwar	1.531072	1.872194	0.82	0.413	-2.13836	5.200505
_cons	-13.66181	6.116761	-2.23	0.026	-25.65044	-1.673184

Arellano-Bond test for zero autocorrelation in first-differenced errors

Order	z	Prob > z
1	-3.1559	0.0016
2	-1.6816	0.0926

H0: no autocorrelation

Sargan test of overidentifying restrictions
H0: overidentifying restrictions are valid

```
chi2(131)     =   41.7822
Prob > chi2   =    1.0000
```

```
--------------------------------------------------------------------------------

Model 3: sender of sanctions

System dynamic panel-data estimation            Number of obs      =      1,440
Group variable: count                           Number of groups   =         60
Time variable: year
                                                Obs per group:
                                                              min =         24
                                                              avg =         24
                                                              max =         24

Number of instruments =    143                  Wald chi2(11)      =    1459.88
                                                Prob > chi2        =     0.0000
Two-step results
------------------------------------------------------------------------------------
                  |              WC-Robust
        democracy |      Coef.   Std. Err.       z    P>|z|     [95% Conf. Interval]
------------------+-----------------------------------------------------------------
        democracy |
              L1. |   .2336342   .0548222     4.26   0.000      .1261846    .3410837
              L2. |  -.0325835   .0378792    -0.86   0.390     -.1068253    .0416583
                  |
               eu |   8.115667   1.789783     4.53   0.000      4.607756    11.62358
               us |   13.66023   1.349082    10.13   0.000      11.01607    16.30438
               un |    8.57248   1.728501     4.96   0.000       5.18468    11.96028
personalistregime |   .5892242     1.4016     0.42   0.674     -2.157861     3.33631
 regimelegitimacy |  -1.065765   .7334184    -1.45   0.146     -2.503239    .3717088
    vulnerability |  -.0063482   .0175833    -0.36   0.718     -.0408109    .0281146
      development |  -2.898576   7.202301    -0.40   0.687     -17.01483    11.21767
 naturalresources |  -.1051924   1.293549    -0.08   0.935     -2.640503    2.430118
         civilwar |   .6443659   1.143988     0.56   0.573      -1.59781    2.886542
            _cons |   1.650313   4.407611     0.37   0.708     -6.988445    10.28907
------------------------------------------------------------------------------------

Arellano-Bond test for zero autocorrelation in first-differenced errors
  +-----------------------+
  |Order |  z     Prob > z|
  |------+----------------|
  |   1  |-3.4893  0.0005 |
  |   2  |-.71315  0.4758 |
  +-----------------------+
   H0: no autocorrelation

Sargan test of overidentifying restrictions
        H0: overidentifying restrictions are valid

        chi2(131)     =  39.25347
        Prob > chi2   =    1.0000

--------------------------------------------------------------------------------
```

```
------------------------------------------------------------------------------

Model 4: other legitimacy

System dynamic panel-data estimation          Number of obs      =      1,440
Group variable: count                         Number of groups   =         60
Time variable: year
                                              Obs per group:
                                                             min =         24
                                                             avg =         24
                                                             max =         24

Number of instruments =    142                Wald chi2(10)      =     375.49
                                              Prob > chi2        =     0.0000
Two-step results
------------------------------------------------------------------------------
                  |              WC-Robust
        democracy |      Coef.   Std. Err.      z    P>|z|     [95% Conf. Interval]
------------------+-----------------------------------------------------------
        democracy |
              L1. |   .4104318   .0637486     6.44   0.000     .2854868    .5353768
              L2. |  -.0138712   .0565866    -0.25   0.806    -.1247789    .0970365
                  |
    economiccosts |   20.17174   5.466436     3.69   0.000      9.45772    30.88576
   democraticgoal |   8.582425   2.619662     3.28   0.001     3.447983    13.71687
personalistregime |   .1096879   1.958005     0.06   0.955    -3.727931    3.947306
    othlegitimacy |  -.0147054   .6297719    -0.02   0.981    -1.249036    1.219625
    vulnerability |  -.0609917   .0350716    -1.74   0.082    -.1297308    .0077473
      development |   18.69437   13.64064     1.37   0.171    -8.040782    45.42953
 naturalresources |  -1.141371   2.495606    -0.46   0.647    -6.032668    3.749926
         civilwar |   .7404063   2.715685     0.27   0.785    -4.582239    6.063052
            _cons |  -9.925104   5.767616    -1.72   0.085    -21.22942    1.379216
------------------------------------------------------------------------------

Arellano-Bond test for zero autocorrelation in first-differenced errors
  +-----------------------+
  |Order |  z     Prob > z|
  |------+----------------|
  |   1  |-3.5688  0.0004 |
  |   2  |-.62917  0.5292 |
  +-----------------------+
   H0: no autocorrelation

Sargan test of overidentifying restrictions
        H0: overidentifying restrictions are valid

        chi2(131)     =  52.26921
        Prob > chi2   =    1.0000

------------------------------------------------------------------------------
```

```
Model 5: combined legitimacy

System dynamic panel-data estimation           Number of obs      =      1,440
Group variable: count                          Number of groups   =         60
Time variable: year
                                               Obs per group:
                                                             min =         24
                                                             avg =         24
                                                             max =         24

Number of instruments =    142                 Wald chi2(10)      =     334.54
                                               Prob > chi2        =     0.0000
Two-step results
------------------------------------------------------------------------------
                 |              WC-Robust
       democracy |      Coef.   Std. Err.      z    P>|z|     [95% Conf. Interval]
-----------------+------------------------------------------------------------
       democracy |
             L1. |   .4221851   .0624804     6.76   0.000      .2997257    .5446445
             L2. |  -.0128376   .0560048    -0.23   0.819     -.1226051    .0969298
                 |
   economiccosts |    19.7699   5.564413     3.55   0.000      8.863854    30.67595
  democraticgoal |   8.434663   2.639023     3.20   0.001      3.262273    13.60705
personalistregime|   .1401222   2.078383     0.07   0.946     -3.933434    4.213678
  comblegitimacy |   .0510599   .5384642     0.09   0.924     -1.004311     1.10643
   vulnerability |  -.0594341   .0326141    -1.82   0.068     -.1233565    .0044883
     development |   17.34933   11.18223     1.55   0.121     -4.567437     39.2661
naturalresources |  -.8198488   2.697238    -0.30   0.761     -6.106339    4.466641
        civilwar |   .7094911   2.638923     0.27   0.788     -4.462704    5.881686
           _cons |  -9.716407   5.481221    -1.77   0.076      -20.4594    1.026588
------------------------------------------------------------------------------

Arellano-Bond test for zero autocorrelation in first-differenced errors
  +-----------------------+
  |Order |  z     Prob > z|
  |------+----------------|
  |   1  |-3.6212  0.0003 |
  |   2  |-.65763  0.5108 |
  +-----------------------+
   H0: no autocorrelation

Sargan test of overidentifying restrictions
        H0: overidentifying restrictions are valid

        chi2(131)     =  52.33271
        Prob > chi2   =    1.0000
```

```
-----------------------------------------------------------------------------------


Model 6: exclude resource-rich states

System dynamic panel-data estimation           Number of obs      =      1,061
Group variable: count                          Number of groups   =         49
Time variable: year
                                               Obs per group:
                                                             min =          1
                                                             avg =   21.65306
                                                             max =         24

Number of instruments =    141                 Wald chi2(9)       =     226.26
                                               Prob > chi2        =     0.0000
Two-step results
-----------------------------------------------------------------------------------
                 |              WC-Robust
       democracy |      Coef.   Std. Err.      z    P>|z|     [95% Conf. Interval]
-----------------+-----------------------------------------------------------------
       democracy |
             L1. |   .3944255    .0765057     5.16   0.000      .2444771    .5443739
             L2. |   .0045608    .0334948     0.14   0.892     -.0610878    .0702094
                 |
   economiccosts |   18.98757     6.04678     3.14   0.002      7.136097    30.83904
  democraticgoal |   9.087081    3.906574     2.33   0.020      1.430337    16.74383
personalistregime |   .4971953    1.912427     0.26   0.795     -3.251093    4.245483
regimelegitimacy |   .0276038    .8595673     0.03   0.974     -1.657117    1.712325
   vulnerability |  -.0561655    .0383523    -1.46   0.143     -.1313346    .0190036
     development |   15.68172    10.90107     1.44   0.150     -5.683986    37.04742
        civilwar |   .8714085    1.447341     0.60   0.547     -1.965328    3.708145
           _cons |  -8.994569    6.208793    -1.45   0.147     -21.16358    3.174442
-----------------------------------------------------------------------------------

Arellano-Bond test for zero autocorrelation in first-differenced errors
  +-----------------------+
  |Order |  z     Prob > z|
  |------+----------------|
  |   1  | -3.194  0.0014 |
  |   2  |-1.5432  0.1228 |
  +-----------------------+
   H0: no autocorrelation

Sargan test of overidentifying restrictions
        H0: overidentifying restrictions are valid

        chi2(131)     =   35.9636
        Prob > chi2   =    1.0000


-----------------------------------------------------------------------------------
```

```
------------------------------------------------------------------------------

Model 7: exclude civil war states

System dynamic panel-data estimation            Number of obs      =       906
Group variable: count                           Number of groups   =        52
Time variable: year
                                                Obs per group:
                                                              min =          1
                                                              avg =   17.42308
                                                              max =         24

Number of instruments =    141                  Wald chi2(9)       =    690.36
                                                Prob > chi2        =    0.0000
Two-step results
------------------------------------------------------------------------------
                  |              WC-Robust
        democracy |      Coef.   Std. Err.      z    P>|z|     [95% Conf. Interval]
------------------+-----------------------------------------------------------
        democracy |
              L1. |   .4066354   .7386483     0.55   0.582    -1.041089    1.854359
              L2. |  -.0005407   .0993634    -0.01   0.996    -.1952894     .194208
                  |
    economiccosts |   22.33578   4.390791     5.09   0.000     13.72999    30.94158
   democraticgoal |   11.77786   27.31623     0.43   0.666    -41.76096    65.31668
personalistregime |  -2.114014   35.07044    -0.06   0.952    -70.85081    66.62279
 regimelegitimacy |   .0337955   1.204659     0.03   0.978    -2.327294    2.394885
    vulnerability |   -.041461   .0921889    -0.45   0.653    -.2221478    .1392259
      development |   36.76508   52.75008     0.70   0.486    -66.62318    140.1533
 naturalresources |   .4429555   49.59688     0.01   0.993    -96.76514    97.65105
            _cons |  -21.04418   37.90451    -0.56   0.579    -95.33566    53.24729
------------------------------------------------------------------------------

Arellano-Bond test for zero autocorrelation in first-differenced errors
  +-----------------------+
  |Order |  z     Prob > z|
  |------+----------------|
  |   1  |-.61828  0.5364 |
  |   2  |-.04444  0.9646 |
  +-----------------------+
   H0: no autocorrelation

Sargan test of overidentifying restrictions
        H0: overidentifying restrictions are valid

        chi2(131)     =  39.54138
        Prob > chi2   =    1.0000

------------------------------------------------------------------------------
```

```
-------------------------------------------------------------------------------

Model 8: time 1990-2000

System dynamic panel-data estimation           Number of obs      =       540
Group variable: count                          Number of groups   =        60
Time variable: year
                                               Obs per group:
                                                             min =          9
                                                             avg =          9
                                                             max =          9

Number of instruments =      52                Wald chi2(10)      =    160.63
                                               Prob > chi2        =    0.0000
Two-step results
------------------------------------------------------------------------------
                 |              WC-Robust
       democracy |      Coef.   Std. Err.      z    P>|z|     [95% Conf. Interval]
-----------------+------------------------------------------------------------
       democracy |
             L1. |    .346592   .1108213     3.13   0.002     .1293863    .5637976
             L2. |  -.0553986   .0744166    -0.74   0.457    -.2012523    .0904552
                 |
  economiccosts |   31.59476   4.866034     6.49   0.000     22.05751    41.13201
  democraticgoal |   3.053625   2.752416     1.11   0.267    -2.341011    8.448261
personalistregime |  -1.538478   1.534472    -1.00   0.316    -4.545987    1.469031
 regimelegitimacy |   1.685959   1.458656     1.16   0.248    -1.172954    4.544872
    vulnerability |  -.045478   .0422454    -1.08   0.282    -.1282776    .0373215
      development |   24.78212   17.23713     1.44   0.151    -9.002038    58.56628
 naturalresources |   .6794205   2.746065     0.25   0.805    -4.702769     6.06161
         civilwar |   .0870239   1.249636     0.07   0.944    -2.362218    2.536266
           _cons |  -14.64494   10.37642    -1.41   0.158    -34.98235    5.692464
------------------------------------------------------------------------------

Arellano-Bond test for zero autocorrelation in first-differenced errors
  +-----------------------+
  |Order |  z     Prob > z|
  |------+----------------|
  |   1  |-2.4188  0.0156 |
  |   2  | .6612   0.5085 |
  +-----------------------+
   H0: no autocorrelation

Sargan test of overidentifying restrictions
        H0: overidentifying restrictions are valid

        chi2(41)      =  40.60455
        Prob > chi2   =    0.4881

-------------------------------------------------------------------------------
```

```
------------------------------------------------------------------------------

Model 9: time 2001-2015

System dynamic panel-data estimation           Number of obs      =       780
Group variable: count                          Number of groups   =        60
Time variable: year
                                               Obs per group:
                                                            min =        13
                                                            avg =        13
                                                            max =        13

Number of instruments =     76                 Wald chi2(10)      =    407.56
                                               Prob > chi2        =    0.0000
Two-step results
------------------------------------------------------------------------------
                |              WC-Robust
      democracy |      Coef.   Std. Err.      z    P>|z|     [95% Conf. Interval]
----------------+-------------------------------------------------------------
      democracy |
            L1. |   .3034452    .094044     3.23   0.001     .1191224    .4877681
            L2. |   .0250428   .0419202     0.60   0.550    -.0571193    .1072049
                |
  economiccosts |   16.76915   7.362575     2.28   0.023     2.338764    31.19953
 democraticgoal |   12.49587   2.639637     4.73   0.000      7.32228    17.66947
personalistregime |  .3849408   2.014119     0.19   0.848     -3.56266    4.332542
regimelegitimacy | -.0078145    .779508    -0.01   0.992    -1.535622    1.519993
  vulnerability |  -.0205294   .0457296    -0.45   0.653    -.1101579     .069099
    development |   20.53912   12.84805     1.60   0.110    -4.642593    45.72083
naturalresources |   .0851131   1.705613     0.05   0.960    -3.257827    3.428053
       civilwar |   .8483342   3.136113     0.27   0.787    -5.298333    6.995002
          _cons |  -12.48475   6.919061    -1.80   0.071    -26.04586    1.076356
------------------------------------------------------------------------------

Arellano-Bond test for zero autocorrelation in first-differenced errors
  +-----------------------+
  |Order |  z     Prob > z|
  |------+----------------|
  |   1  |-2.3485  0.0188 |
  |   2  |-.60162  0.5474 |
  +-----------------------+
   H0: no autocorrelation

Sargan test of overidentifying restrictions
        H0: overidentifying restrictions are valid

        chi2(65)     =  45.8634
        Prob > chi2  =   0.9655


------------------------------------------------------------------------------
```

```
------------------------------------------------------------------------------------


Model 10: exclude democracies

System dynamic panel-data estimation            Number of obs      =      1,025
Group variable: count                           Number of groups   =         55
Time variable: year
                                                Obs per group:
                                                              min =          4
                                                              avg =   18.63636
                                                              max =         24

Number of instruments =    142                  Wald chi2(10)      =     365.32
                                                Prob > chi2        =     0.0000
Two-step results
------------------------------------------------------------------------------------
                 |              WC-Robust
       democracy |      Coef.   Std. Err.      z    P>|z|     [95% Conf. Interval]
-----------------+------------------------------------------------------------------
       democracy |
             L1. |   .4046379   .0693238     5.84   0.000     .2687658    .5405101
             L2. |  -.0732876   .0585382    -1.25   0.211    -.1880204    .0414452
                 |
   economiccosts |    14.3491    4.06694     3.53   0.000     6.378041    22.32015
  democraticgoal |   6.717508    2.03066     3.31   0.001     2.737487    10.69753
personalistregime |  -.2618211   1.382136    -0.19   0.850    -2.970758    2.447115
 regimelegitimacy |   .7621037    .759614     1.00   0.316    -.7267125     2.25092
   vulnerability |  -.0005488   .0258381    -0.02   0.983    -.0511905    .0500929
     development |   22.82042   8.534979     2.67   0.008     6.092165    39.54867
 naturalresources |  -1.534169   1.794018    -0.86   0.392    -5.050379    1.982041
        civilwar |   .1984661   1.580806     0.13   0.900    -2.899857     3.29679
           _cons |  -13.38122   5.098852    -2.62   0.009    -23.37478   -3.387649
------------------------------------------------------------------------------------

Arellano-Bond test for zero autocorrelation in first-differenced errors
  +-----------------------+
  |Order |  z     Prob > z|
  |------+----------------|
  |   1  |-3.4241  0.0006 |
  |   2  |-.37734  0.7059 |
  +-----------------------+
   H0: no autocorrelation

Sargan test of overidentifying restrictions
        H0: overidentifying restrictions are valid

        chi2(131)     =   47.0675
        Prob > chi2   =    1.0000


------------------------------------------------------------------------------------
```

```
------------------------------------------------------------------------------

Model 11: global trend

System dynamic panel-data estimation             Number of obs      =      1,440
Group variable: count                            Number of groups   =         60
Time variable: year
                                                 Obs per group:
                                                               min =         24
                                                               avg =         24
                                                               max =         24

Number of instruments =    143                   Wald chi2(11)      =     423.89
                                                 Prob > chi2        =     0.0000
Two-step results
------------------------------------------------------------------------------
                 |              WC-Robust
       democracy |      Coef.   Std. Err.      z    P>|z|     [95% Conf. Interval]
-----------------+------------------------------------------------------------
       democracy |
             L1. |   .3853007    .067702     5.69   0.000     .2526073     .517994
             L2. |  -.0214226   .0498346    -0.43   0.667    -.1190966    .0762513
                 |
   economiccosts |   16.11174   5.257391     3.06   0.002     5.807439    26.41603
  democraticgoal |   8.937135   2.847193     3.14   0.002     3.356739    14.51753
personalistregime |   .5082184   2.122925     0.24   0.811    -3.652639    4.669076
 regimelegitimacy |   .3586108   1.030763     0.35   0.728    -1.661647    2.378869
   vulnerability |  -.0427251   .0319439    -1.34   0.181    -.1053341    .0198838
     development |   17.45563   8.048525     2.17   0.030     1.680813    33.23045
 naturalresources |  -1.270188   3.088128    -0.41   0.681    -7.322808    4.782431
        civilwar |   2.540122    2.10753     1.21   0.228    -1.590561    6.670804
     globaltrend |   1.568591   1.682412     0.93   0.351    -1.728876    4.866058
           _cons |  -10.92368   4.645851    -2.35   0.019    -20.02938   -1.817981
------------------------------------------------------------------------------

Arellano-Bond test for zero autocorrelation in first-differenced errors
  +-----------------------+
  |Order |  z     Prob > z|
  |------+----------------|
  |   1  |-3.5789  0.0003 |
  |   2  |-.58256  0.5602 |
  +-----------------------+
   H0: no autocorrelation

Sargan test of overidentifying restrictions
        H0: overidentifying restrictions are valid

        chi2(131)     =  44.96787
        Prob > chi2   =    1.0000

------------------------------------------------------------------------------
```

```
------------------------------------------------------------------------------

Model 12: without lag

System dynamic panel-data estimation            Number of obs      =      1,500
Group variable: count                           Number of groups   =         60
Time variable: year
                                                Obs per group:
                                                              min =         25
                                                              avg =         25
                                                              max =         25

Number of instruments =    143                  Wald chi2(9)       =     302.24
                                                Prob > chi2        =     0.0000
Two-step results
------------------------------------------------------------------------------
                 |              WC-Robust
       democracy |      Coef.   Std. Err.      z    P>|z|     [95% Conf. Interval]
-----------------+------------------------------------------------------------
       democracy |
             L1. |   .4246887   .0578417     7.34   0.000       .311321    .5380564
                 |
   economiccosts |   15.18831   8.421356     1.80   0.071     -1.317248    31.69386
  democraticgoal |   8.457073   3.449764     2.45   0.014      1.695659    15.21849
personalistregime|   1.176612     1.6325     0.72   0.471      -2.02303    4.376254
 regimelegitimacy|   .5912228   .7475751     0.79   0.429     -.8739976    2.056443
   vulnerability |  -.0440297   .0344303    -1.28   0.201     -.1115118    .0234524
     development |   21.07406   9.243395     2.28   0.023      2.957334    39.19078
naturalresources |  -1.040647   1.802573    -0.58   0.564     -4.573625    2.492331
        civilwar |   2.245115   1.761535     1.27   0.202     -1.207431     5.69766
           _cons |  -12.80216   5.364287    -2.39   0.017     -23.31597   -2.288352
------------------------------------------------------------------------------

Arellano-Bond test for zero autocorrelation in first-differenced errors
  +-----------------------+
  |Order |  z     Prob > z|
  |------+----------------|
  |   1  |-3.8633  0.0001 |
  |   2  |-1.5024  0.1330 |
  +-----------------------+
   H0: no autocorrelation

Sargan test of overidentifying restrictions
        H0: overidentifying restrictions are valid

        chi2(133)     =  46.05565
        Prob > chi2  =    1.0000

------------------------------------------------------------------------------
```

```
--------------------------------------------------------------------------------

Model 13: inverted development

System dynamic panel-data estimation            Number of obs      =      1,440
Group variable: count                           Number of groups   =         60
Time variable: year
                                                Obs per group:
                                                              min =         24
                                                              avg =         24
                                                              max =         24

Number of instruments =    142                  Wald chi2(10)      =     341.70
                                                Prob > chi2        =     0.0000
Two-step results
------------------------------------------------------------------------------------
                    |              WC-Robust
          democracy |      Coef.   Std. Err.      z    P>|z|     [95% Conf. Interval]
--------------------+---------------------------------------------------------------
          democracy |
                L1. |   .4094557    .079749     5.13   0.000     .2531506    .5657609
                L2. |  -.0181679   .0557192    -0.33   0.744    -.1273756    .0910397
                    |
      economiccosts |   14.42859   5.852395     2.47   0.014     2.958106    25.89907
     democraticgoal |   9.855487    2.32067     4.25   0.000     5.307058    14.40392
  personalistregime |   .2410975   1.682763     0.14   0.886    -3.057057    3.539252
   regimelegitimacy |  -.3915722    1.10237    -0.36   0.722    -2.552178    1.769034
      vulnerability |  -.0362776   .0367073    -0.99   0.323    -.1082226    .0356673
developmentinverted |   -.019984   .0100572    -1.99   0.047    -.0396957   -.0002723
   naturalresources |  -1.877871   2.975695    -0.63   0.528    -7.710126    3.954384
           civilwar |    .613724   2.332207     0.26   0.792    -3.957317    5.184765
              _cons |   189.8583   94.69428     2.00   0.045     4.260911    375.4557
------------------------------------------------------------------------------------

Arellano-Bond test for zero autocorrelation in first-differenced errors
  +-----------------------+
  |Order |  z     Prob > z|
  |------+----------------|
  |   1  |-3.7366  0.0002 |
  |   2  |-.60479  0.5453 |
  +-----------------------+
   H0: no autocorrelation

Sargan test of overidentifying restrictions
        H0: overidentifying restrictions are valid

        chi2(131)    =  46.50057
        Prob > chi2  =    1.0000

--------------------------------------------------------------------------------
```

```
--------------------------------------------------------------------------------

Model 14: inverted democratic goal

System dynamic panel-data estimation            Number of obs      =      1,440
Group variable: count                           Number of groups   =         60
Time variable: year
                                                Obs per group:
                                                              min =         24
                                                              avg =         24
                                                              max =         24

Number of instruments =    142                  Wald chi2(10)      =     367.96
                                                Prob > chi2        =     0.0000
Two-step results
------------------------------------------------------------------------------------------
                       |              WC-Robust
             democracy |      Coef.   Std. Err.      z    P>|z|     [95% Conf. Interval]
-----------------------+------------------------------------------------------------------
             democracy |
                   L1. |   .4150492   .0704125     5.89   0.000      .2770432    .5530552
                   L2. |  -.0097794   .0584187    -0.17   0.867      -.124278    .1047193
                       |
         economiccosts |   18.59276   6.180702     3.01   0.003      6.478807    30.70671
democraticgoalinverted |  -9.396561   3.147674    -2.99   0.003     -15.56589   -3.227234
     personalistregime |  -.1455421   2.263205    -0.06   0.949     -4.581342    4.290257
      regimelegitimacy |   .1486448   1.150067     0.13   0.897     -2.105445    2.402735
         vulnerability |  -.0617011   .0334315    -1.85   0.065     -.1272256    .0038235
           development |   18.41247   9.999834     1.84   0.066     -1.186839    38.01179
      naturalresources |   -.907722   2.924605    -0.31   0.756     -6.639843    4.824399
              civilwar |   .9348371   2.061581     0.45   0.650     -3.105787    4.975462
                 _cons |  -.5000316   6.552287    -0.08   0.939     -13.34228    12.34221
------------------------------------------------------------------------------------------

Arellano-Bond test for zero autocorrelation in first-differenced errors
  +-----------------------+
  |Order |  z     Prob > z|
  |------+----------------|
  |   1  |-3.6602  0.0003 |
  |   2  |-.70151  0.4830 |
  +-----------------------+
   H0: no autocorrelation

Sargan test of overidentifying restrictions
        H0: overidentifying restrictions are valid

        chi2(131)     =  52.03364
        Prob > chi2   =    1.0000

--------------------------------------------------------------------------------
```

List of figures

Bibliography

Acemoglu, Daron, Johnson, Simon, Robinson, James A., & Yared, Pierre. (2008). Income and Democracy. American Economic Review, 98 (3), 808–842.

Acemoglu, Daron, Johnson, Simon, Robinson, James A., & Yared, Pierre. (2009). Reevaluating the Modernization Hypothesis. Journal of Monetary Economics, 56 (8), 1043–1058.

Acemoglu, Daron, & Robinson, James A. (2000a). Democratization or Repression? European Economic Review, 44 (4–6), 683–693.

Acemoglu, Daron, & Robinson, James A. (2000b). Why Did the West Extend the Franchise? Democracy, Inequality, and Growth in Historical Perspective. Quarterly Journal of Economics, 115 (4), 1167–1199.

Acemoglu, Daron, & Robinson, James A. (2001). A Theory of Political Transitions. The American Economic Review, 91 (4), 938–963.

Acemoglu, Daron, & Robinson, James A. (2006). Economic Origins of Dictatorship and Democracy. New York: Cambridge University Press.

Acemoglu, Daron, Robinson, James A., & Verdier, Thierry. (2004). Kleptocracy and Divide-and-Rule: A Model of Personal Rule. Journal of the European Economic Association, 2 (2–3), 162–192.

Afesorgbor, Sylvanus, & Mahadevan, Renuka. (2016). The Impact of Economic Sanctions on Income Inequality of Target States. World Development, 83 (C), 1–11.

Albertus, Michael, & Menaldo, Victor. (2014). Gaming Democracy: Elite Dominance during Transition and the Prospects for Redistribution. British Journal of Political Science, 44 (3), 575–603.

Alemán, José, & Yang, David D. (2011). A Duration Analysis of Democratic Transitions and Authoritarian Backslides. Comparative Political Studies, 44 (9), 1123–1151.

Alfoneh, Ali. (2013). Iran Unveiled. How the Revolutionary Guards is Transforming Iran from Theocracy into Military Dictatorship. Lanham: Rowman & Littlefield.

Allen, Susan H. (2005). The Determinants of Economic Sanctions Success and Failure. International Interactions, 31 (2), 117–138.

Allen, Susan H. (2008a). Political Institutions and Constrained Response to Economic Sanctions. Foreign Policy Analysis, 4 (3), 255–274.

Allen, Susan H. (2008b). The Domestic Political Costs of Economic Sanctions. Journal of Conflict Resolution, 52 (6), 916–944.

Allen, Susan H., & Lektzian, David J. (2013). Economic Sanctions: A Blunt Instrument? Journal of Peace Research, 50 (1), 121–135.

Almond, Gabriel A., & Verba, Sidney. (1963). The Civic Culture. Princeton, NJ: Princeton University Press.

Alvarez, Mike, Cheibub, José, Limongi, Fernando, & Przeworski, Adam. (1996). Classifying Political Regimes. Studies in Comparative International Development, 31 (2), 3–36.

Andreas, Peter. (2005). Criminalizing Consequences of Sanctions: Embargo Busting and Its Legacy. International Studies Quarterly, 49 (2), 335–360.

Ang, Adrian U-Jin, & Peksen, Dursun. (2007). When Do Economic Sanctions Work? Asymmetric Perceptions, Issue Salience, and Outcomes. Political Research Quarterly, 60 (1), 135–145.

Arellano, Manuel, & Bond, Stephen. (1991). Some Tests of Specification for Panel Data. Monte Carlo Evidence and an Application to Employment Equations. Review of Economic Studies, 58 (2), 277–297.

Arellano, Manuel, & Bover, Olympia. (1995). Another Look at the Instrumental Variable Estimation of Error-Components Models. Journal of Econometrics, 68 (1), 29–51.

Askari, Hossein, Forrer, John, Teegen, Hildy, & Yang, Jiawen. (2003). Economic Sanctions: Examining Their Philosophy and Efficacy. Westport, CT: Praeger.

Augustine. (1945 [5th cent. CE]). The City of God. De civitate dei. London: Dent.

Bader, Julia, Grävingholt, Jörn, & Kästner, Antje. (2010). Would Autocracies Promote Autocracy? A Political Economy Perspective on Regime-Type Export in Regional Neighbourhoods. Contemporary Politics, 16 (1), 81–100.

Baldwin, David A. (1971). The Power of Positive Sanctions. World Politics, 24 (1), 19–38.

Baldwin, David A. (1985). Economic Statecraft. Princeton, NJ: Princeton University Press.

Baldwin, David A. (1999). The Sanctions Debate and the Logic of Choice. International Security, 24 (3), 80–107.

Baldwin, David A. (2011). Economic Statecraft. In Bertrand Badie, Dirk Berg-Schlosser, & Leonardo Morlino (eds.), The International Encyclopedia of Political Science (Vol. 3, pp. 706–708). Los Angeles et al.: Sage.

Baldwin, David A. (2016). Power and International Relations. A Conceptual Approach. Princeton, NJ: Princeton University Press.

Bapat, Navin A., Heinrich, Tobias, Kobayashi, Yoshiharu, & Morgan, T. Clifton. (2013). Determinants of Sanctions Effectiveness: Sensitivity Analysis Using New Data. International Interactions, 39 (1), 79–98.

Bapat, Navin A., & Kwon, Bo R. (2015). When Are Sanctions Effective? A Bargaining and Enforcement Framework. International Organization, 69 (1), 131–162.

Bapat, Navin A., & Morgan, T. Clifton. (2009). Multilateral Versus Unilateral Sanctions Reconsidered: A Test Using New Data. International Studies Quarterly, 53 (4), 1075–1094.

Barber, James. (1979). Economic Sanctions as a Policy Instrument. International Affairs, 55 (3), 367–384.

Batniji, Rajaie, Khatib, Lina, Cammett, Melani, Sweet, Jeffrey, Basu, Sanjay, Jamal, Amaney, Wise, Paul, & Giacaman, Rita. (2014). Governance and Health in the Arab World. The Lancet, 383 (9914), 343–355.

Bazoobandi, Sara. (2015). Sanctions against Iran: winners and losers. In Iana Dreyer & José Luengo-Cabrera (eds.), On Target? EU Sanctions as Security Policy Tools (Vol. 25, pp. 57–65). Paris: EU Institute for Security Studies.

BBC. (2018-05-21). US Vows 'Strongest Sanctions in History' on Iran. Retrieved from http://www.bbc.com/news/world-us-canada-44200621 (accessed on 2019-10-01).

Becker, Gary S. (1985). Public Policies, Pressure Groups, and Dead Weight Costs. Journal of Public Economics, 28 (3), 329–347.

Beladi, Hamid, & Oladi, Reza. (2015). On Smart Sanctions. Economics Letters, 130, 24–27.

Benhabib, Jess, & Przeworski, Adam. (2006). The Political Economy of Redistribution under Democracy. Economic Theory, 29 (2), 271–290.

Bergeijk, Peter A. G. van. (1989). Success and Failure of Economic Sanctions. Kyklos, 42 (3), 385–404.

Bergeijk, Peter A. G. van. (1994). Economic Diplomacy, Trade and Commercial Policy: Positive and Negative Sanctions in a New World Order. Aldershot: Elgar.

Bergeijk, Peter A. G. van. (1995). The Impact of Economic Sanctions in the 1990s. The World Economy, 18 (3), 443–453.

Bergeijk, Peter A. G. van. (2009). Economic Diplomacy and the Geography of International Trade. Cheltenham: Edward Elgar.

Bergeijk, Peter A. G. van. (2015). Sanctions against Iran: a preliminary economic assessment. In Iana Dreyer & José Luengo-Cabrera (eds.), On Target? EU Sanctions as Security Policy Tools (pp. 49–56). Paris: EU Institute for Security Studies.

Bergeijk, Peter A. G. van, & Marrewijk, Charles van. (1995). Why Do Sanctions Need Time to Work? Adjustment, Learning and Anticipation. Economic Modelling, 12 (2), 75–86.

Biersteker, Thomas, & Bergeijk, Peter A. G. van. (2015). How and when do sanctions work? The evidence. In Iana Dreyer & José Luengo-Cabrera (eds.), On Target? EU Sanctions as Security Policy Tools (pp. 17–28). Paris: EU Institute for Security Studies.

Biersteker, Thomas, Eckert, Sue E., Romaniuk, Peter, Halegua, Aaron, & Reid, Natalie. (2001). Targeted Financial Sanctions: A Manual for Design and Implementation. Contributions from the Interlaken Process. Providence: Watson Institute, Brown University. Retrieved from http://www.watsoninstitute.org/pub/TFS.pdf (accessed on 2019-10-01).

Biersteker, Thomas, Eckert, Sue E., Tourinho, Marcos, & Hudáková, Zuzana. (2013). The Effectiveness of United Nations Targeted Sanctions. Findings from the Targeted Sanctions Consortium (TSC). Retrieved from http://graduateinstitute.ch/files/live/sites/iheid/files/sites/internationalgovernance/shared/Effectiveness%20of%20UN%20Targeted%20Sanctions%20-%206.Nov.2013%20.pdf (accessed on 2019-10-01).

Biersteker, Thomas J., Eckert, Sue E., Tourinho, Marcos, & Hudáková, Zuzana. (2018). UN Targeted Sanctions Datasets (1991–2013). Journal of Peace Research, 55 (3), 404–412.

Biersteker, Thomas, Hudáková, Zuzana, & Tourinho, Marcos. (2016). SanctionsApp. Computer Software, iOS and Android App, Version 4.0 (July 2016).

Blundell, Richard, & Bond, Stephen. (1998). Initial Conditions and Moment Restrictions in Dynamic Panel Data Models. Journal of Econometrics, 87 (1), 115–143.

Boix, Carles. (2003). Democracy and Redistribution. Cambridge: Cambridge University Press.

Boix, Carles. (2011). Democracy, Development, and the International System. American Political Science Review, 105 (4), 809–828.

Boix, Carles, & Svolik, Milan W. (2013). The Foundations of Limited Authoritarian Government: Institutions, Commitment, and Power-Sharing in Dictatorships. The Journal of Politics, 75 (2), 300–316.

Bolks, Sean M., & Al-Sowayel, Dina. (2000). How Long Do Economic Sanctions Last? Examining the Sanctioning Process through Duration. Political Research Quarterly, 53 (2), 241–265.

Bonetti, Shane. (1998). Distinguishing Characteristics of Degrees of Success and Failure in Economic Sanctions Episodes. Applied Economics 30 (6), 805–813.

Boudreaux, Christopher J., & Holcombe, Randall G. (2017). Economic Institutions and the Durability of Democracy. Atlantic Economic Journal, 45 (1), 17–28.

Bove, Vincenzo, Platteau, Jean-Philippe, & Sekeris, Petros G. (2016). Political Repression in Autocratic Regimes. Journal of Comparative Economics, 45 (2), 1–19.

Bove, Vincenzo, & Rivera, Mauricio. (2015). Elite Co-optation, Repression, and Coups in Autocracies. International Interactions, 41 (3), 543–479.

Bratton, Michael, & Walle, Nicolas van de. (1994). Neopatrimonial Regimes and Political Transitions in Africa. World Politics, 46 (4), 453–489.

Bratton, Michael, & Walle, Nicolas van de. (1997). Democratic Experiments in Africa: Regime Transitions in Comparative Perspective. Cambridge: Cambridge University Press.

Briguglio, Lino, Cordina, Gordon, Farrugia, Nadia, & Vella, Stephanie. (2009). Economic Vulnerability and Resilience: Concepts and Measurements. Oxford Development Studies, 37 (3), 229–247.

Brinks, Daniel M., & Coppedge, Michael. (2006). Diffusion Is No Illusion. Neighbor Emulation in the Third Wave of Democracy. Comparative Political Studies, 39 (4), 463–489.

Brooks, Risa A. (2002). Sanctions and Regime Type: What Works, and When? Security Studies, 11 (4), 1–50.

Brownlee, Jason. (2007). Authoritarianism in an Age of Democratization. Cambridge: Cambridge University Press.

Brownlee, Jason. (2009). Portents of Pluralism: How Hybrid Regimes Affect Democratic Transitions. American Journal of Political Science, 53 (3), 515–532.

Brumberg, Daniel. (2002). The Trap of Liberalized Autocracy. Journal of Democracy, 13 (4), 56–68.

Brzoska, Michael. (2001a). Design and Implementation of Arms Embargoes and Travel and Aviation Related Sanctions. Results of the Bonn-Berlin Process. Bonn: Bonn International Center for Conversion. Retrieved from http://www.watsoninstitute.org/tfs/CD/booklet_sanctions.pdf (accessed on 2019-10-01).

Brzoska, Michael. (2001b). Smart Sanctions: The Next Steps. The Debate on Arms Embargoes and Travel Sanctions within the 'Bonn-Berlin Process' (vol. 6). Baden-Baden: Nomos.

Brzoska, Michael. (2008). Measuring the Effectiveness of Arms Embargoes. Peace Economics, Peace Science and Public Policy, 14 (2), 1–32.

Brzoska, Michael. (2015). International Sanctions before and beyond UN Sanctions. International Affairs, 91 (6), 1339–1349.

Bueno de Mesquita, Bruce, & Downs, George W. (2005). Development and Democracy. Foreign Affairs, 84 (5), 77–86.

Bueno de Mesquita, Bruce, Downs, George W., Smith, Alastair, & Cherif, Feryal M. (2005). Thinking Inside the Box: A Closer Look at Democracy and Human Rights. International Studies Quarterly, 49 (3), 439–458.

Bueno de Mesquita, Bruce, Morrow, James D., Siverson, Randolph M., & Smith, Alastair. (1999). An Institutional Explanation of the Democratic Peace. The American Political Science Review, 93 (4), 791–807.

Bueno de Mesquita, Bruce, & Smith, Alastair. (2009). Political Survival and Endogenous Institutional Change. Comparative Political Studies, 42 (2), 167–197.

Bueno de Mesquita, Bruce, & Smith, Alastair. (2010). Leader Survival, Revolutions, and the Nature of Government Finance. American Journal of Political Science, 54 (4), 936–950.

Bueno de Mesquita, Bruce, & Smith, Alastair. (2011). The Dictator's Handbook. Why Bad Behavior Is Almost Always Good Behavior. New York: Public Affairs.

Bueno de Mesquita, Bruce, & Smith, Alastair. (2017). Political Succession: A Model of Coups, Revolution, Purges, and Everyday Politics. Journal of Conflict Resolution, 61 (4), 707–743.

Bueno de Mesquita, Bruce, Smith, Alastair, Siverson, Randolph M., & Morrow, James D. (2003). The Logic of Political Survival. Cambridge, MA: MIT Press.

Burgsdorff, Sven Kühn von. (2009). Effectiveness of Economic Sanctions: The Case of Cuba. Intercultural Human Rights Law Review, 4, 31–51.

Burke, Paul J., & Leigh, Andrew. (2010). Do Output Contractions Trigger Democratic Change? American Economic Journal, 2 (4), 124–157.

Burnell, Peter. (2010). Is there a new autocracy promotion? Working Paper 96: Fundación para las Relaciones Internacionales y el Diálogo Exterior (FRIDE).

Carisch, Enrico, Rickard-Martin, Loraine, & Meister, Shawna R. (2017). The Evolution of UN Sanctions From a Tool of Warfare to a Tool of Peace, Security and Human Rights. Cham: Springer.

Carneiro, Cristiane L. (2014). Economic Sanctions and Human Rights: An Analysis of Competing Enforcement Strategies in Latin America. Revista Brasileira de Política Internacional, 57 (1), 197–215.

Carneiro, Cristiane L., & Elden, Dominique. (2009). Economic Sanctions, Leadership Survival, and Human Rights. Journal of International Law, 30 (3), 969–998.

Carothers, Thomas. (2007). The 'Sequencing' Fallacy. Journal of Democracy, 18 (1), 12–27.

Cheibub, José. (2007). Presidentialism, Parliamentarism, and Democracy. New York: Cambridge University Press.

Choi, Seung-Whan. (2014). Causes of Domestic Terrorism: Economic Sanctions as a Violence Trigger Structure. The Korean Journal of International Studies, 12 (1), 137–159.

Choi, Seung-Whan, & Luo, Shali. (2013). Economic Sanctions, Poverty, and International Terrorism: An Empirical Analysis. International Interactions, 39 (2), 217–245.

Coleman, James S. (1986). Social Theory, Social Research, and a Theory of Action. The American Journal of Sociology, 91 (6), 1309–1335.

Coleman, James S. (1990). Foundations of Social Theory. Cambridge, MA: Harvard University Press.

Commission of the EU. (2017). Restrictive measures (sanctions) in force. Regulations based on Article 215 TFEU and Decisions adopted in the framework of the Common Foreign and Security Policy. Last update on 2017-08-04.

Commission of the EU. (2018). EU Sanctions Map. Last update on 2018-02-10. Retrieved from https://sanctionsmap.eu/#/main (accessed on 2019-10-01).

Connolly, Richard. (2015). The impact of EU economic sanctions on Russia. In Iana Dreyer & José Luengo-Cabrera (eds.), On Target? EU Sanctions as Security Policy Tools (pp. 29–38). Paris: EU Institute for Security Studies.

Cooley, Alexander, & Heathershaw, John. (2017). Dictators Without Borders. Power and Money in Central Asia. New Haven: Yale University Press.

Coppedge, Michael. (1997). Modernization and Thresholds of Democracy: Evidence for a Common Path and Process. In Manus Midlarsky (ed.), Inequality, Democracy, and Economic Development. Cambridge: Cambridge University Press.

Cortright, David. (2007). Sanctions and Stability Pacts: The Economic Tools of Peacemaking. In Ira William Zartman (ed.), Peacemaking in International Conflict: Methods & Techniques. (pp. 385–418). Washington, DC: United States Institute of Peace.

Cortright, David, Gerber, Linda, & Lopez, George A. (2005). Implementing Targeted Sanctions: The Role of International Agencies and Regional Organizations. In Peter Wallensteen & Carina Staibano (eds.), International Sanctions: Between Words and Wars in the Global System (pp. 144–158). New York: Frank Cass.

Cortright, David, & Lopez, George A. (eds.). (1995). Economic Sanctions: Panacea or Peacebuilding in a Post-Cold War World. Cortright, Boulder, CO: Westview.

Cortright, David, & Lopez, George A. (2000a). Learning from the Sanctions Decade. Global Dialogue, 2 (3), 11–24.

Cortright, David, & Lopez, George A. (2000b). The Limits of Coercion. Bulletin of the Atomic Scientists, 56 (6), 18–20.

Cortright, David, & Lopez, George A. (2000c). The Sanctions Decade: Assessing UN Strategies in the 1990s. London: Lynne Rienner.

Cortright, David, & Lopez, George A. (2001). Assessing Smart Sanctions. Targeted Sanctions: Lessons from the 1990s. In Michael Brzoska (ed.), Smart Sanctions: The Next Steps (pp. 19–37). Baden-Baden: Nomos.

Cortright, David, & Lopez, George A. (eds.). (2007). Uniting Against Terror: Cooperative Nonmilitary Responses to the Global Terrorist Threat. Cambridge, MA: MIT Press.

Cortright, David, Lopez, George A., & Gerber-Stellingwerf, Linda. (2008). The Sanctions Era: Themes and Trends in UN Security Council Sanctions Since 1990. In Vaughan Lowe, Adam Roberts, Jennifer Welsh, & Dominik Zaum (eds.), The United Nations Security Council and War (pp. 205–225). Oxford: Oxford University Press.

Cox, Dan G., & Drury, A. Cooper. (2006). Democratic Sanctions: Connecting the Democratic Peace and Economic Sanctions. Journal of Peace Research, 43 (6), 709–722.

Dahl, Robert A. (1971). Polyarchy: Participation and Opposition. New Haven: Yale University Press.

Dahrendorf, Ralf. (2003). A Definition of Democracy. Journal of Democracy, 14 (4), 101–114.

Damrosch, Lori F. (1993). The civilian impact of economic sanctions. In Lori Fisler Damrosch (ed.), Enforcing Restraint: Collective Intervention in Internal Conflicts (pp. 274–315). New York, NY: Council on Foreign Relations Press.

Damrosch, Lori F. (1994). The Collective Enforcement of International Norms Through Economic Sanctions. Ethics and International Affairs, 8 (1), 59–75.

Daoudi, Munther S., & Dajani, Mohammad S. (1983). Economic Sanctions: Ideals and Experience. Boston: Routledge and Kegan Paul.

Dashti-Gibson, Jaleh, Davis, Patricia, & Radcliff, Benjamin. (1997). On the Determinants of the Success of Economic Sanctions: An Empirical Analysis. American Journal of Political Science, 41 (2), 608–618.

Davenport, Christian. (2007). State Repression and Political Order. Annual Review of Political Science, 10, 1–23.

Dehejia, Rajeev H., & Wood, Bernard. (1992). Economic Sanctions and Econometric Policy Evaluation: A Cautionary Note. Journal of World Trade 26 (1), 73–84.

Desai, Raj M., Olofsgård, Anders, & Yousef, Tarik M. (2009). The Logic of Authoritarian Bargains. Economics & Politics, 21 (1), 93–125.

Devakumar, Delan, Birch, Marion, Osrin, David, Sondorp, Egbert, & Wells, Jonathan. (2014). The Intergenerational Effects of War on the Health of Children. BMC Medicine, 12 (57), 1–15.

Di Palma, Giuseppe. (1990). To Craft Democracies: An Essay on Democratic Transitions. Berkeley: University of California Press.

Diamond, Larry. (1999). Developing Democracy: Toward Consolidation. Baltimore: The Johns Hopkins University Press.

Diamond, Larry. (2002). Thinking About Hybrid Regimes. Journal of Democracy, 13 (2), 21–35.

Diamond, Larry. (2008). The Democratic Rollback: The Resurgence of the Predatory State. Foreign Affairs, 87 (2), 36–48.

Diamond, Larry. (2011). The Impact of the Economic Crisis: Why Democracies Survive? Journal of Democracy, 22 (1), 17–30.

Diamond, Larry. (2015). Facing Up to the Democratic Recession. Journal of Democracy, 26 (1), 141–155.

Diskin, Abraham, Diskin, Hanna, & Hazan, Reuven. (2005). Why Democracies Collapse: The Reasons for Democratic Failure and Success. International Political Science Review, 26 (3), 291–309.

Dizaji, Sajjad F., & Bergeijk, Peter A. G. van. (2013). Potential Early Phase Success and Ultimate Failure of Economic Sanctions: A VAR Approach with an Application to Iran. Journal of Peace Research, 50 (6), 721–736.

Dos Reis Stefanopoulos, Alexandra, & Lopez, George A. (2014). From coercive to protective tools: The evolution of targeted sanctions. In Mónica Serrano & Thomas G. Weiss (eds.), The International Politics of Human Rights: Rallying to the R2P cause? London and New York: Routledge.

Doxey, Margaret. (1971). The Rhodesian Sanctions Experiment. Year Book of World Affairs, 25, 140–159.

Doxey, Margaret. (1972). International Sanctions: A Framework for Analysis with Special Reference to the UN and Southern Africa. International Organization, 26 (3), 527–550.

Doxey, Margaret. (1980). Economic Sanctions and International Enforcement. London: Macmillan.

Doxey, Margaret. (1996). International Sanctions in Contemporary Perspective. Basingstoke: Macmillan.

Doyle, Michael W. (1986). Liberalism and World Politics. The American Political Science Review, 80 (4), 1151–1169.

Dresden, Jennifer R., & Howard, Marc M. (2016). Authoritarian Backsliding and the Concentration of Political Power. Democratization, 23 (7), 1122–1143.

Drezner, Daniel W. (1998). Conflict Expectations and the Paradox of Economic Coercion. International Studies Quarterly, 42 (4), 709–731.

Drezner, Daniel W. (1999a). The Sanctions Paradox: Economic Statecraft and International Relations. Cambridge: Cambridge University Press.

Drezner, Daniel W. (2000). Bargaining, Enforcement, and Multilateral Sanctions: When Is Cooperation Counterproductive? International Organization, 54 (1), 73–102.

Drezner, Daniel W. (2003). The Hidden Hand of Economic Coercion. International Organization, 57 (3), 643–659.

Drezner, Daniel W. (2011). Sanctions Sometimes Smart: Targeted Sanctions in Theory and Practice. International Studies Review, 13 (1), 96–108.

Drury, A. Cooper. (1998). Revisiting Economic Sanctions Reconsidered. Journal of Peace Research, 35 (4), 497–509.

Drury, A. Cooper. (2001). Sanctions as Coercive Diplomacy: The U.S. President's Decision to Initiate Economic Sanctions. Political Research Quarterly, 54 (3), 485–508.

Drury, A. Cooper. (2005). Economic Sanctions and Presidential Decisions: Models of Political Rationality. New York: Palgrave Macmillan.

Drury, A. Cooper, & Li, Yitan. (2006). U.S. Economic Sanction Threats Against China: Failing to Leverage Better Human Rights. Foreign Policy Analysis, 2 (4), 307–324.

Drury, A. Cooper, & Peksen, Dursun. (2014). Women and Economic Statecraft: The Negative Impact International Economic Sanctions Visit on Women. European Journal of International Relations, 20 (2), 463–490.

Dyson, Tim, & Cetorelli, Valeria. (2017). Changing Views on Child Mortality and Economic Sanctions in Iraq: A History of Lies, Damned Lies and Statistics. BMJ Global Health, 2 (2), 1–5.

Early, Bryan R. (2011). Unmasking the Black Knights: Sanctions Busters and Their Effects on the Success of Economic Sanctions. Foreign Policy Analysis, 7 (4), 381–402.

Ehteshami, Anoushiravan. (2009). Machtstrukturen in Iran. Aus Politik und Zeitgeschichte (APuZ), 49, 9–14.

Elliott, Kimberly A. (1998). The Sanctions Glass: Half Full or Completely Empty? International Security, 23 (1), 50–65.

Epstein, David L., Bates, Robert H., Goldstone, Jack A., Kristensen, Ida, & O'Halloran, Sharyn. (2006). Democratic Transitions. American Journal of Political Science, 50 (3), 551–569.

Erdmann, Gero. (2011). Transition from Democracy. Loss of Quality, Hybridisation and Breakdown of Democracy. GIGA Working Paper Series, no. 161.

Eriksson, Mikael, & Wallensteen, Peter. (2015). Targeting Sanctions and Ending Armed Conflicts: First Steps towards a New Research Agenda. International Affairs, 91 (6), 1387–1398.

Escribà-Folch, Abel. (2012). Authoritarian Responses to Foreign Pressure: Spending, Repression, and Sanctions. Comparative Political Studies, 45 (6), 683–713.

Escribà-Folch, Abel. (2013). Accountable for What? Regime Types, Performance, and the Fate of Outgoing Dictators, 1946–2004. Democratization, 20 (1), 160–185.

Escribà-Folch, Abel, & Wright, Joseph. (2010). Dealing with Tyranny: International Sanctions and the Survival of Authoritarian Rulers. International Studies Quarterly, 54, 335–359.

Escribà-Folch, Abel, & Wright, Joseph. (2015). Foreign Pressure and the Politics of Autocratic Survival. Oxford: Oxford University Press.

Escribà-Folch, Abel, & Wright, Joseph. (2016). Sanctions, Autocratic Regimes, and Conflict. Comparative Democratization. Newsletter of the American Political Science Association, 14 (2), 12–15.

Farrall, Jeremy M. (2007). United Nations Sanctions and the Rule of Law. Cambridge: Cambridge University Press.

Fearon, James D. (1994). Domestic Political Audiences and the Escalation of International Disputes. American Political Science Review, 88 (3), 577–592.

Feaver, Peter D., & Lorber, Eric B. (2015). The Sanctions Myth. The National Interest. Retrieved from http://nationalinterest.org/print/feature/the-sanctions-myth-13110.

Filkins, Dexter. (2013). The Shadow Commander. The New Yorker, 2013-09-30. Retrieved from https://www.newyorker.com/magazine/2013/09/30/the-shadow-commander.

Foa, Roberto S., & Mounk, Yascha. (2016). The Danger of Deconsolidation. Journal of Democracy, 27 (3), 5–17.

Foa, Roberto S., & Mounk, Yascha. (2017). The Signs of Deconsolidation. Journal of Democracy, 28 (1), 5–15.

Fowler, Robert R. (2000). Report of the Panel of Experts on Violations of Security Council Sanctions Against UNITA (Fowler Report). Document S/2000/203. New York. Retrieved from http://www.un.org/ga/search/view_doc.asp?symbol=S/2000/203.

Freedom House. (2009). Freedom in the World Report 2009. Washington, DC: Freedom House.

Freedom House. (2018). Freedom in the World Report 2018. Washington, DC: Freedom House.

Friedman, Milton. (2002 [1962]). Capitalism and Freedom. Chicago: University of Chicago Press.

Fukuyama, Francis. (2005). "Stateness" First. Journal of Democracy, 16 (1), 84–88.

Fukuyama, Francis. (2013). What Is Governance? Governance, 26 (3), 347–368.

Fukuyama, Francis. (2015). Why Is Democracy Performing So Poorly? Journal of Democracy, 26 (1), 11–20.

Galbert, Simond de. (2015). A Year of Sanctions against Russia – Now What? A European Assessment of the Outcome and Future of Russia Sanctions. Retrieved from http://csis.org/publication/year-sanctions-against-russia-now-what (accessed on 2019-10-01).

Gallie, Walter B. (1956). Essentially Contested Concepts. Proceedings of the Aristotelian Society, 56, 167–198.

Galtung, Johan. (1967). On the Effects of International Economic Sanctions, with Examples from the Case of Rhodesia. World Politics, 19 (3), 378–416.

Gandhi, Jennifer. (2008). Political Institutions Under Dictatorship. Cambridge: Cambridge University Press.

Gandhi, Jennifer, & Przeworski, Adam. (2006). Cooptation, Cooperation, and Rebellion under Dictatorships. Economics & Politics, 18 (1), 1–26.

Gandhi, Jennifer, & Przeworski, Adam. (2007). Authoritarian Institutions and the Survival of Autocrats. Comparative Political Studies, 40 (11), 1279–1301.

Gasiorowski, Mark J. (1995). Economic Crisis and Political Regime Change: An Event History Analysis. American Political Science Review, 89 (4), 882–897.

Geddes, Barbara. (1999). What Do We Know about Democratization after Twenty Years? Annual Review of Political Science, 2, 115–144.

Geddes, Barbara. (2004). Authoritarian Breakdown. Working Paper. Retrieved from http://citeseerx.ist.psu.edu/viewdoc/download?doi=10.1.1.659.7165&rep=rep1&type=pdf (accessed on 2019-10-01).

Geddes, Barbara, Wright, Joseph, & Frantz, Erica. (2014). Autocratic Breakdown and Regime Transitions: A New Data Set. Perspectives on Politics, 12 (2), 313–331.

Gentile, Emilio. (2011). Totalitarian regimes. In Bertrand Badie, Dirk Berg-Schlosser, & Leonardo Morlino (eds.), The International Encyclopedia of Political Science (Vol. 8, pp. 2627–2633). Los Angeles et al.: Sage.

Gerschewski, Johannes, Merkel, Wolfgang, Schmotz, Alexander, Stefes, Christoph H., & Tanneberg, Dag. (2012). Warum überleben Diktaturen? PVS, Sonderheft, 47, 1–26.

Gershenson, Dmitriy, & Grossman, Herschel I. (2001). Cooption and Repression in the Soviet Union. Economics & Politics, 13 (1), 31–47.

Gibbons, Elizabeth, & Garfield, Richard. (1999). The Impact of Economic Sanctions on Health and Human Rights in Haiti 1991–1994. American Journal of Public Health, 89 (10), 1499–1504.

Gibney, Mark, Cornett, Linda, Wood, Reed, Haschke, Peter, Arnon, Daniel, & Pisanò, Attilio. (2017). The Political Terror Scale 1976–2016. Retrieved from http://www.politicalterrorscale.org/ (accessed on 2019-10-01).

Gilbert, Leah, & Mohseni, Payam. (2011). Beyond Authoritarianism: The Conceptualization of Hybrid Regimes. Studies in Comparative International Development, 46 (3), 270–297.

Giumelli, Francesco. (2010). New Analytical Categories for Assessing EU Sanctions. The International Spectator, 45 (3), 131–144.

Giumelli, Francesco. (2011). Coercing, Constraining and Signaling. Explaining UN and EU Sanctions after the Cold War. Colchester: ECPR Press.

Giumelli, Francesco. (2013). How EU Sanctions Work: A New Narrative. EU Institute for Security Studies, Chaillot Paper 129. Retrieved from http://www.iss.europa.eu (accessed on 2019-10-01).

Giumelli, Francesco. (2015). Understanding United Nations Targeted Sanctions: An Empirical Analysis. International Affairs, 91 (6), 1351–1368.

Giumelli, Francesco, & Ivan, Paul. (2013). The Effectiveness of EU Sanctions. An Analysis of Iran, Belarus, Syria and Myanmar (Burma). EPC Issue Paper 76.

Glassman, Ronald. (1991). China in Transition: Communism, Capitalism and Democracy. Westport: Praeger.

Gleditsch, Kristian S., & Ward, Michael D. (2006). Diffusion and the International Context of Democratization. International Organization, 60 (4), 911–933.

Gleditsch, Nils P., Wallensteen, Peter, Eriksson, Mikael, Sollenberg, Margareta, & Strand, Håvard. (2002). Armed Conflict 1946–2001: A New Dataset. Journal of Peace Research, 39 (5), 615–637.

Gordon, Joy. (1999). A Peaceful, Silent, Deadly Remedy: The Ethics of Economic Sanctions. Ethics & International Affairs, 13, 123–142.

Gordon, Joy. (2011). Smart Sanctions Revisited. Ethics and International Affairs, 25 (3), 315–335.

Gordon, Scott. (1999). Controlling the State: Constitutionalism from Ancient Athens to Today. Cambridge, MA: Harvard University Press.

Gorji, Ali. (2014). Sanctions against Iran: The Impact on Health Services. Iranian Journal of Public Health, 43 (3), 381–382.

Grauvogel, Julia, Licht, Amanda, & Soest, Christian von. (2014). Taking the Streets? Disentangling the Impact of Sanction Threats on Mass Protest. Working paper.

Grauvogel, Julia, Licht, Amanda A., & Soest, Christian von. (2017). Sanctions and Signals: How International Sanction Threats Trigger Domestic Protest in Targeted Regimes. International Studies Quarterly, 61 (1), 86–97.

Grauvogel, Julia, & Soest, Christian von. (2014). Claims to Legitimacy Count: Why Sanctions Fail to Instigate Democratisation in Authoritarian Regimes. European Journal of Political Research, 53 (4), 635–653.

Grauvogel, Julia, & Soest, Christian von. (2015). Sanctions can be Counter-Productive in Instigating Democratic Reform in Authoritarian Regimes. Blog Democratic Audit UK. Retrieved from http://www.democraticaudit.com/?p=10373 (accessed on 2019-10-01).

Grigoriadis, Theocharis. (2016). Religious Origins of Democracy & Dictatorship. Journal of Policy Modeling, 38 (5), 785–809.

Gunitsky, Seva. (2014). From Shocks to Waves: Hegemonic Transitions and Democratization in the Twentieth Century. International Organization, 68 (3), 561–597.

Gunitsky, Seva. (2015). Lost in the gray zone: competing measures of democracy in the former Soviet Republics. In Alexander Cooley & Jack L. Snyder (eds.), Ranking the World: Grading States as a Tool of Global Governance (pp. 112–150x). New York: Cambridge University Press.

Gurr, Ted R., & Harff, Barbara. (2016). Elite Leadership Characteristics.

Gurr, Ted R., Marshall, Monty G., & Asal, Victor. (2016). Minorities at Risk Discrimination.

Haass, Richard N. (1997). Sanctioning Madness. Foreign Affairs, 76 (6), 74–85.

Haass, Richard N. (1998). Economic Sanctions and American Diplomacy. New York: Council on Foreign Relations.

Haber, Stephen, & Menaldo, Victor. (2011). Do Natural Resources Fuel Authoritarianism? A Reappraisal of the Resource Curse. American Political Science Review, 105 (1), 1–26.

Habermas, Jürgen. (1996). Über den internen Zusammenhang von Rechtsstaat und Demokratie. In Jürgen Habermas (ed.), Die Einbeziehung des Anderen. Studien zur politischen Theorie (pp. 293–305). Frankfurt/Main: Suhrkamp.

Hadenius, Axel, & Teorell, Jan. (2005). Assessing Alternative Indices of Democracy. Working Paper, Committee on Concepts and Methods – Political Concepts No. 6 (2005).

Hadenius, Axel, & Teorell, Jan. (2007). Pathways from Authoritarianism. Journal of Democracy, 18 (1), 143–157.

Haggard, Stephan. (2016). Hard Target: Sanctions, Inducements and the Case of North Korea. Manuscript, 2016-08-22. East Asia Foundation.

Haggard, Stephan, & Kaufman, Robert R. (1997). The Political Economy of Democratic Transitions. Comparative Politics, 29 (3), 263–283.

Haggard, Stephan, & Kaufman, Robert. (2016). Democratization During the Third Wave. Annual Review of Political Science, 19, 125–144.

Haggard, Stephan, & Noland, Marcus. (2017). Hard Target: Sanctions, Inducements, and the Case of North Korea. Stanford, CA: Stanford University Press.

Hart, Robert A. (2000). Democracy and the Successful Use of Economic Sanctions. Political Research Quarterly, 53 (2), 267–284.

Hawkins, Darren, & Lloyd, Joshua. (2003). Questioning Comprehensive Sanctions: The Birth of a Norm. Journal of Human Rights, 2 (3), 441–454.

Hayek, Friedrich A. von. (1971). Die Verfassung der Freiheit [The Constitution of Liberty]. Tübingen: Mohr.

Hegre, Håvard, Oneal, John R., & Russett, Bruce. (2010). Trade Does Promote Peace: New Simultaneous Estimates of the Reciprocal Effects of Trade and Conflict. Journal of Peace Research, 47 (6), 763–774.

Heine-Ellison, Sofia. (2001). The Impact and Effectiveness of Multilateral Economic Sanctions: A Comparative Study. The International Journal of Human Rights, 5 (1), 81–112.

Herb, Michael. (2005). No Representation without Taxation? Rents, Development, and Democracy. Comparative Politics, 37 (3), 297–316.

Heritage Foundation. (2017). Index of Economic Freedom Report 2017. Washington, DC: Heritage Foundation.

Hovi, Jon, Huseby, Robert, & Sprinz, Detlef F. (2005). When Do (Imposed) Economic Sanctions Work? World Politics, 57 (4), 479–499.

Howard, Marc M., & Roessler, Philip G. (2006). Liberalizing Electoral Outcomes in Competitive Authoritarian Regimes. American Journal of Political Science, 50 (2), 365–381.

Hufbauer, Gary C., & Schott, Jeffrey J. (1985). Economic Sanctions Reconsidered: History and Current Policy. Washington, DC: Peter G. Peterson Institute for International Economics.

Hufbauer, Gary C., Schott, Jeffrey J., & Elliott, Kimberly A. (1990). Economic Sanctions Reconsidered. History and Current Policy. Second Edition. Washington, DC: Peter G. Peterson Institute for International Economics.

Hufbauer, Gary C., Schott, Jeffrey J., Elliott, Kimberly A., & Oegg, Barbara. (2007). Economic Sanctions Reconsidered. Third Edition. Washington, DC: Peterson Institute for International Economics.

Hultman, Lisa, & Peksen, Dursun. (2017). Successful or Counterproductive Coercion? The Effect of International Sanctions on Conflict Intensity. Journal of Conflict Resolution, 61 (6), 1315–1339.

Humphreys, Macartan. (2005). Natural Resources, Conflict, and Conflict Resolution: Uncovering the Mechanisms. The Journal of Conflict Resolution, 49 (4), 508–537.

Huntington, Samuel P. (1968). Political Order in Changing Societies. New Haven: Yale University Press.

Huntington, Samuel P. (1991). The Third Wave: Democratization in the Late Twentieth Century. Norman: University of Oklahoma Press.

Jeitschko, Thomas D., Linz, Susan J., Noguera, Jose, & Semykina, Anastasia. (2014). Economic Security and Democratic Capital: Why Do Some Democracies Survive and Others Fail? Journal of Behavioral and Experimental Economics, 50, 13–28.

Jentleson, Bruce W. (2000). Economic sanctions and post–cold war conflicts: Challenges for theory and policy. In Paul C. Stern & Daniel Druckman (eds.), International Conflict Resolution after the Cold War (pp. 123–177). Washington, DC: National Academy Press.

Jing, Chao, Kaempfer, William H., & Lowenberg, Anton D. (2003). Instrument Choice and the Effectiveness of International Sanctions: A Simultaneous Equations Approach. Journal of Peace Research, 40 (5), 519–535.

Jones, Lee, & Portela, Clara. (2014). Evaluating the "Success" of International Economic Sanctions: Multiple Goals, Interpretive Methods and Critique. Working Paper 3. London: Centre for the Study of Global Security and Development.

Kaempfer, William H., & Lowenberg, Anton D. (1988). The Theory of International Economic Sanctions: A Public Choice Approach. The American Economic Review, 78 (4), 786–793.

Kaempfer, William H., & Lowenberg, Anton D. (1992). Using Threshold Models to Explain International Relations. Public Choice, 73 (4), 419–443.

Kaempfer, William H., & Lowenberg, Anton D. (1999). Unilateral Versus Multilateral International Sanctions: A Public Choice Perspective. International Studies Quarterly, 43 (1), 37–58.

Kaempfer, William H., & Lowenberg, Anton D. (2000). A public choice analysis of the political economy of international sanctions. In Steve Chan & A. Cooper Drury (eds.), Sanctions as Economic Statecraft. Theory and Practice (pp. 158–186). London: Palgrave Macmillan.

Kaempfer, William H., & Lowenberg, Anton D. (2007). The political economy of economic sanctions. In Todd Sandler & Keith Hartley (eds.), Handbook of Defense Economics, Volume 2 (pp. 867–911). Amsterdam: North Holland.

Kaempfer, William H., Lowenberg, Anton D., & Mertens, William. (2004). International Economic Sanctions Against a Dictator. Economics & Politics, 16 (1), 29–51.

Kagan, Robert. (2008). The Return of History and the End of Dreams. New York: Alfred A. Knopf.

Kagan, Robert. (2015). The Weight of Geopolitics. Journal of Democracy, 26 (1), 21–31.

Kant, Immanuel. (2010 [1795]). Perpetual Peace. Translated by W. Hastie, 1891: Syracuse University Humanities Center.

Kapstein, Ethan B., & Converse, Nathan. (2008). Why Democracies Fail. Journal of Democracy, 19 (4), 57–68.

Karl, Terry L. (1995). The Hybrid Regimes of Central America. Journal of Democracy, 6 (3), 72–86.

Kálnoky, Boris. (2011). Iran ist einer der weltweit größten Heroinhändler. Die Welt, 2011-01-21. Retrieved from http://www.welt.de/politik/specials/wikileaks/article12265736/Iran-ist-einer-der-weltweit-groessten-Heroinhaendler.html.

Kelsen, Hans. (1925). Allgemeine Rechtslehre. Berlin/Heidelberg/New York.

Kelsen, Hans. (1963 [1929]). Vom Wesen und Wert der Demokratie. Aalen.

Kirshner, Jonathan. (1997). The Microfoundations of Economic Sanctions. Security Studies, 6 (3), 32–64.

Knight, W. Andy. (2004). Improving the effectiveness of UN Arms Embargoes. In Richard M. Price & Mark Zacher (eds.), The United Nations and Global Security (pp. 39–54). New York: Palgrave Macmillan.

Knutsen, Tommy A. (2016). Should Liberals Sometimes Prefer Dictatorships to Democracies? A Closer Look at the Hayek Thesis. Democratization, 23 (3), 375–394.

Krustev, Valentin L. (2010). Strategic Demands, Credible Threats, and Economic Coercion Outcomes. International Studies Quarterly, 54 (1), 147–174.

Kuran, Timur. (1995). Private Truths, Public Lies: The Social Consequences of Preference Falsification. Cambridge, MA: Harvard University Press.

Lacy, Dean, & Niou, Emerson M. S. (2004). A Theory of Economic Sanctions and Issue Linkage: The Roles of Preferences, Information, and Threats. The Journal of Politics, 66 (1), 25–42.

Lakatos, Imre. (1978). The Methodology of Scientific Research Programmes. Vol. 1: Philosophical Papers. Cambridge: Cambridge University Press.

Lam, San L. (1990). Economic Sanctions and the Success of Foreign Policy Goals: A Critical Evaluation. Japan and the World Economy, 2 (3), 239–248.

Lasswell, Harold D. (1958). Politics: Who Gets What, When, How. Cleveland: Meridian.

Lauth, Hans-Joachim. (2004). Demokratie und Demokratiemessung. Eine konzeptionelle Grundlegung für den interkulturellen Vergleich. Wiesbaden: VS Verlag für Sozialwissenschaften.

Lawson, Robert A., & Clark, Jeff R. (2010). Examining the Hayek-Friedman Hypothesis on Economic and Political Freedom. Journal of Economic Behavior & Organization, 74 (3), 230–239.

Lektzian, David, & Souva, Mark. (2003). The Economic Peace between Democracies: Economic Sanctions and Domestic Institutions. Journal of Peace Research, 40 (6), 641–660.

Lektzian, David, & Souva, Mark. (2007). An Institutional Theory of Sanctions Onset and Success. Journal of Conflict Resolution, 51 (6), 848–871.

Levitsky, Steven, & Way, Lucan. (2002). The Rise of Competitive Authoritarianism. Journal of Democracy, 13 (2), 51–65.

Levitsky, Steven, & Way, Lucan. (2010). Competitive Authoritarianism: Hybrid Regimes After the Cold War. Cambridge: Cambridge University Press.

Levitsky, Steven, & Way, Lucan. (2015). The Myth of Democratic Recession. Journal of Democracy, 26 (1), 45–58.

Licht, Sonja. (1995). The use of sanctions in former Yugoslavia: Can they assist in conflict resolution? In David Cortright & George A. Lopez (eds.),

Economic Sanctions: Panacea or Peacebuilding in a Post-Cold War World (pp. 153–160). Cortright, Boulder, CO: Westview.

Lijphart, Arend. (1977). Democracy in Plural Societies: A Comparative Exploration. New Haven: Yale University Press.

Lindberg, Staffan. (2006). Democracy and Elections in Africa. Baltimore: Johns Hopkins University Press.

Lindberg, Staffan. (2009). A theory of elections as a mode of transition. In Staffan Lindberg (ed.), Democratization by Elections: A New Mode of Transition (pp. 314–341). Baltimore, MD: Johns Hopkins University Press.

Lindsay, James. (1986). Trade Sanctions as Policy Instruments: A Re-Examination. International Studies Quarterly, 30 (2), 153–173.

Linz, Juan J. (1975). Totalitarian and authoritarian regimes. In Fred Greenstein & Nelson Polsby (eds.), Handbook of Political Science, vol. 3. Reading, MA: Addison Wesley.

Linz, Juan J. (1978). Crisis, breakdown, and reequilibration. In Juan J. Linz & Alfred C. Stepan (eds.), The Breakdown of Democratic Regimes (pp. 3–124). Baltimore & London: The Johns Hopkins University Press.

Linz, Juan J. (1994). Presidential or parliamentary democracy: Does it make a difference? In Juan J. Linz & Arturo Valenzuela (eds.), The Failure of Presidential Democracy: Comparative Perspectives. Vol. I. Baltimore: Johns Hopkins University Press.

Linz, Juan J. (1997). Democracy Today: An Agenda for Students of Democracy. Scandinavian Political Studies, 20 (2), 115–134.

Linz, Juan J., & Stepan, Alfred C. (1996). Problems of Democratic Transition and Consolidation: Southern Europe, South America, and Post-Communist Societies. Baltimore: The Johns Hopkins University Press.

Lipset, Seymour M. (1959). Some Social Requisites of Democracy. The American Political Science Review, 53 (1), 69–105.

Lipset, Seymour M. (1960). Political Man: The Social Bases of Politics. New York: Doubleday.

Lipset, Seymour M. (1994). The Social Requisites of Democracy Revisited. American Sociological Review, 59 (1), 1–22.

Loewenstein, Karl. (1969). Verfassungslehre. Übersetzt von Rüdiger Börner. Tübingen.

Lopez, George A. (2011). Sanctions. In Bertrand Badie, Dirk Berg-Schlosser, & Leonardo Morlino (eds.), The International Encyclopedia of Political Science (Vol. 7, pp. 2351–2354). Los Angeles et al.: Sage.

Lopez, George A. (2012). In Defense of Smart Sanctions: A Response to Joy Gordon. Ethics & International Affairs, 26 (1), 135–146.

Lopez, George A. (2013). Enforcing human rights through economic sanctions. In Dinah Shelton (ed.), The Oxford Handbook of International Human Rights Law. Oxford: Oxford University Press.

Lopez, George A., & Cortright, David. (1997). Economic Sanctions and Human Rights: Part of the Problem or Part of the Solution? The International Journal of Human Rights, 1 (2), 1–25.

Lopez, George A., & Cortright, David. (2010). Targeted sanctions, counterterrorism, and strategic peacebuilding. In Daniel Philpott & Gerard Powers (eds.), Strategies of Peace. Transforming Conflict in a Violent World (pp. 169–188). New York: Oxford University Press.

Lopez, George A., & Cortright, David. (2011). Sanctions as alternatives to war. In Christopher J. Coyne & Rachel L. Mathers (eds.), The Handbook on the Political Economy of War (pp. 534–570). Cheltenham: Edward Elger.

Luck, Edward C. (2006). UN Security Council: Practice and Promise. London: Routledge.

Lucretius (Titus Lucretius Carus). (1866 [1st cent. BCE]). De Rerum Natura. Libri Sex. Cambridge: Deighton Bell.

Lueders, Hans, & Croissant, Aurel. (2014). Wahlen, Strategien autokratischer Herrschaftssicherung und das Überleben autokratischer Regierungen [Elections, strategies of autocratic power maintenance and the survival of autocratic regimes]. Zeitschrift für Vergleichende Politikwissenschaft, 8 (3), 329–355.

Machiavelli, Niccolò. (1950 [1531]). The Prince and the Discourses. New York: The Modern Library.

Maeda, Ko. (2010). Two Modes of Democratic Breakdown: A Competing Risks Analysis of Democratic Durability. The Journal of Politics, 72 (4), 1129–1143.

Magaloni, Beatriz. (2006). Voting for Autocracy: Hegemonic Party Survival and Its Demise in Mexico. New York: Cambridge University Press.

Magaloni, Beatriz. (2008). Credible Power-Sharing and the Longevity of Authoritarian Rule. Comparative Political Studies, 41 (4/5), 715–741.

Magaloni, Beatriz, & Kricheli, Ruth. (2010). Political Order and One-Party Rule. Annual Review of Political Science, 13 (1), 123–143.

Major, Solomon. (2012). Timing Is Everything: Economic Sanctions, Regime Type, and Domestic Instability. International Interactions, 38 (1), 79–110.

Major, Solomon, & McGann, Anthony J. (2005). Caught in the Crossfire: "Innocent Bystanders" as Optimal Targets of Economic Sanctions. Conflict Resolution, 49 (3), 337–359.

Maravall, José M., & Przeworski, Adam (eds.). (2003). Democracy and the Rule of Law. New York: Cambridge University Press.

Marinov, Nikolay. (2005). Do Economic Sanctions Destabilize Country Leaders? American Journal of Political Science, 49 (3), 564–576.

Marshall, Monty G. (2018). Major Episodes of Political Violence (MEPV) and Conflict Regions, 1946-2016. Retrieved from http://www.systemicpeace.org/inscrdata.html (accessed on 2019-10-01).

Marshall, Monty G., & Elzinga-Marshall, Gabrielle. (2016). State Fragility Index and Matrix 2016. Retrieved from http://www.systemicpeace.org/inscr/SFImatrix2016c.pdf (accessed on 2019-10-01).

Marshall, Monty G., Gurr, Ted R., & Jaggers, Keith. (2017). Polity IV Project. Political Regime Characteristics and Transitions, 1800–2016. Dataset Users' Manual.

Marshall, Thomas H. (1950). Citizenship and Social Class and Other Essays. Cambridge: Cambridge University Press.

McDonald, Patrick J. (2004). Peace through Trade or Free Trade? Journal of Conflict Resolution, 48 (4), 547–572.

McDonald, Patrick J. (2007). The Purse Strings of Peace. American Journal of Political Science, 51 (3), 569–582.

McDonald, Patrick J. (2010). Capitalism, Commitment, and Peace. International Interactions, 36 (2), 146–168.

McGuire, Martin C., & Olson, Mancur. (1996). The Economics of Autocracy and Majority Rule: The Invisible Hand and the Use of Force. Journal of economic literature, 34 (1), 72–96.

McLean, Elena V., & Whang, Taehee. (2010). Friends or Foes? Major Trading Partners and the Success of Economic Sanctions. International Studies Quarterly, 54 (2), 427–447.

Mehlum, Halvor, Moene, Karl, & Torvik, Ragnar. (2002). Plunder & Protection, Inc. Journal of Peace Research, 39 (4), 447–459.

Meltzer, Allan H., & Richard, Scott F. (1981). A Rational Theory of the Size of Government. Journal of Political Economy, 89 (5), 914–927.

Merkel, Wolfgang. (1999). Systemtransformation. Eine Einführung in die Theorie und Empirie der Transformationsforschung. Opladen: Leske und Budrich.

Merkel, Wolfgang. (2004). Embedded and Defective Democracies. Democratization, 11 (5), 33–58.

Merkel, Wolfgang. (2010). Are Dictatorships Returning? Revisiting the 'Democratic Rollback' Hypothesis. Contemporary Politics, 16 (1), 17–31.

Merkel, Wolfgang. (2011). Transition. In Bertrand Badie, Dirk Berg-Schlosser, & Leonardo Morlino (eds.), The International Encyclopedia of Political Science (Vol. 8, pp. 2661–2663). Los Angeles et al.: Sage.

Merkel, Wolfgang. (2014). Is Capitalism Compatible with Democracy? Zeitschrift für Vergleichende Politikwissenschaft, 8 (2), 109–128.

Mertens, William G. (2000). Economic Sanctions in a Dictatorship Model. Discussion Papers in Economics. Working Paper 00-10. Center for Economic Analysis Department of Economics, University of Colorado at Boulder.

Miers, Anne C., & Morgan, T. Clifton. (2002). Multilateral Sanctions and Foreign Policy Success: Can Too Many Cooks Spoil the Broth? International Interactions, 28 (2), 117–136.

Milante, Gary. (2007). A Kleptocrat's Survival Guide: Autocratic Longevity In the Face of Civil Conflict. World Bank Policy Research Working Paper 4186. Development Economics Research Group, World Bank. Retrieved from http://elibrary.worldbank.org/doi/pdf/10.1596/1813-9450-4186 (accessed on 2019-10-01).

Montesquieu, Charles-Louis de Secondat, Baron de. (1995 [1748]). De l'Esprit des lois. Paris: Gallimard.

Moore Jr., Barrington. (1966). Social Origins of Dictatorship and Democracy: Lord and Peasant in the Making of the Modern World. Boston, MA: Beacon Press.

Morgan, T. Clifton, Bapat, Navin A., & Kobayashi, Yoshiharu. (2013). Threat and Imposition of Sanctions (TIES) Data 4.0. Users' Manual.

Morgan, T. Clifton, Bapat, Navin A., & Kobayashi, Yoshiharu. (2014). Threat and Imposition of Economic Sanctions 1945-2005: Updating the TIES Dataset. Conflict Management and Peace Science, 31 (5), 541–558.

Morgan, T. Clifton, & Schwebach, Valerie L. (1997). Fools Suffer Gladly: The Use of Economic Sanctions in International Crises. International Studies Quarterly, 41 (1), 27–50.

Morrison, Kevin M. (2014). Nontaxation and Representation: The Fiscal Foundations of Political Stability. Cambridge: Cambridge University Press.

Mousseau, Michael. (2013). The Democratic Peace Unraveled: It's the Economy. International Studies Quarterly, 57 (1), 186–197.

Møller, Jørgen, & Skaaning, Svend-Erik. (2011). Requisites of Democracy. Conceptualization, Measurement, and Explanation. London and New York: Routledge.

Møller, Jørgen, & Skaaning, Svend-Erik. (2013). Autocracies, Democracies, and the Violation of Civil Liberties. Democratization, 20 (1), 82–106.

Mueller, John E., & Mueller, Karl. (1999). Sanctions of Mass Destruction. Foreign Affairs, 78 (3), 43–53.

Munck, Gerardo L. (2001). The Regime Question: Theory Building in Democracy Studies. World Politics, 54 (1), 119–144.

Naghavi, Alireza, & Pignataro, Giuseppe. (2015). Theocracy and Resilience against Economic Sanctions. Journal of Economic Behavior & Organization, 111, 1–12.

Nephew, Richard. (2018). The Art of Sanctions. A View from the Field. New York: Columbia University Press.

Neuenkirch, Matthias, & Neumeier, Florian. (2015). The Impact of UN and US Economic Sanctions on GDP Growth. European Journal of Political Economy, 40 (1), 110–125.

Neuenkirch, Matthias, & Neumeier, Florian. (2016). The Impact of US Sanctions on Poverty. Journal of Development Economics, 121 (C), 110–119.

Nili, Shmuel. (2011). Democratic Disengagement: Toward Rousseauian Global Reform. International Theory, 3 (3), 355–389.

Nili, Shmuel. (2013). Rigorist Cosmopolitanism: A Kantian Alternative to Pogge. Politics, Philosophy and Economics, 12 (3), 260–287.

Nincic, Miroslav, & Wallensteen, Peter (eds.). (1983). Dilemmas of Economic Coercion: Sanctions in World Politics. New York: Praeger.

Nixon, Itai. (2012). Economic Sanctions and Autocratic Repression. Washington, DC: Georgetown University.

Nooruddin, Irfan. (2002). Modeling Selection Bias in Studies of Sanctions Efficacy. International Interactions, 28 (1), 59–75.

Nossal, Kim R. (1989). International Sanctions as International Punishment. International Organization, 43 (2), 301–322.

Nossal, Kim R. (1999). Liberal democratic regimes, international sanctions, and global governance. In Raimo Väyrynen (ed.), Globalization and Global Governance (pp. 127–150). Lanham, MD: Rowman and Littlefield.

O'Donnell, Guillermo, & Schmitter, Philippe C. (1986). Transitions from Authoritarian Rule. Tentative Conclusions about Uncertain Democracies. Baltimore: Johns Hopkins University Press.

O'Sullivan, Meghan L. (2003). Shrewd Sanctions: Statecraft and State Sponsors of Terrorism. Washington, DC: Brookings Institution Press.

Olson, Mancur. (1993). Dictatorship, Democracy, and Development. The American Political Science Review, 87 (3), 567–576.

Olson, Richard S. (1979). Economic Coercion in World Politics: With a Focus on North-South Relations. World Politics, 31 (4), 471–494.

Oneal, John R. (2003). Measuring Interdependence and Its Pacific Benefits: A Reply to Gartzke & Li. Journal of Peace Research, 40 (6), 721–725.

Oneal, John R., & Russett, Bruce M. (1997). The Classical Liberals Were Right: Democracy, Interdependence, and Conflict, 1950–1985. International Studies Quarterly, 41 (2), 267–293.

Oneal, John R., & Russett, Bruce. (1999a). Assessing the Liberal Peace with Alternative Specifications: Trade Still Reduces Conflict. Journal of Peace Research, 36 (4), 423–442.

Oneal, John R., & Russett, Bruce M. (1999b). The Kantian Peace: The Pacific Benefits of Democracy, Interdependence, and International Organizations, 1885–1992. World Politics, 52 (1), 1–37.

Osa, Maryjane, & Corduneanu-Huci, Cristina. (2003). Running Uphill: Political Opportunity in Non-democracies. Comparative Sociology, 2 (4), 605–629.

Ottaway, Marina. (2003). Democracy Challenged: The Rise of Semi-Authoritarianism. Washington, DC: Carnegie Endowment for International Peace.

Overland, Jody, Simons, Kenneth, & Spagat, Michael. (2005). Political Instability and Growth in Dictatorships. Public Choice, 25 (3/4), 445–470.

Özbudun, Ergun. (2011). Authoritarian regimes. In Bertrand Badie, Dirk Berg-Schlosser, & Leonardo Morlino (eds.), The International Encyclopedia of Political Science (Vol. 1, pp. 107–118). Los Angeles et al.: Sage.

Pape, Robert A. (1997). Why Economic Sanctions Do Not Work. International Security, 22 (2), 90–136.

Pape, Robert A. (1998). Why Economic Sanctions Still Do Not Work. International Security, 23 (1), 66–77.

Patterson, Ruairi. (2013). EU Sanctions on Iran: The European Political Context. Middle East Policy, 20 (1), 135–146.

Peksen, Dursun. (2009). Better or Worse? The Effect of Economic Sanctions on Human Rights. Journal of Peace Research, 46 (1), 59–77.

Peksen, Dursun. (2010). Coercive Diplomacy and Press Freedom: An Empirical Assessment of the Impact of Economic Sanctions on Media Openness. International Political Science Review, 31 (4), 449–469.

Peksen, Dursun. (2011). Economic Sanctions and Human Security: The Public Health Effect of Economic Sanctions. Foreign Policy Analysis, 7 (3), 237–251.

Peksen, Dursun. (2014). Economic Sanctions and Official Ethnic Discrimination in Target Countries, 1950–2003. Defence and Peace Economics, 27 (4), 480–502.

Peksen, Dursun. (2017). How Do Target Leaders Survive Economic Sanctions? The Adverse Effect of Sanctions on Private Property and Wealth. Foreign Policy Analysis, 13 (1), 215–232.

Peksen, Dursun, & Drury, A. Cooper. (2009). Economic Sanctions and Political Repression: Assessing the Impact of Coercive Diplomacy on Political Freedoms. Human Rights Review, 10 (3), 393–411.

Peksen, Dursun, & Drury, A. Cooper. (2010). Coercive or Corrosive: The Negative Impact of Economic Sanctions on Democracy. International Interactions, 36 (3), 240–264.

Peksen, Dursun, Peterson, Timothy M., & Drury, A. Cooper. (2014). Media-driven Humanitarianism? News Media Coverage of Human Rights Abuses and the Use of Economic Sanctions. International Studies Quarterly, 58 (4), 855–866.

Peterson, Timothy M. (2014). Taking the Cue: The Response to US Human Rights Sanctions against Third Parties. Conflict Management and Peace Science, 31 (2), 145–167.

Plattner, Marc F. (2015). Is Democracy in Decline? Journal of Democracy, 26 (1), 5–10.

Pond, Amy. (2015). The Political Economy of Market Liberalization. PhD Dissertation, Political Science, The University of Michigan.

Pond, Amy. (2017). Economic Sanctions and Demand for Protection. Journal of Conflict Resolution, 61 (5), 1073–1094.

Popper, Karl. (1963). Conjectures and Refutations: The Growth of Scientific Knowledge. London: Routledge & Kegan Paul.

Popper, Karl. (2002 [1959]). The Logic of Scientific Discovery. London and New York: Routledge.

Portela, Clara. (2010). European Union Sanctions and Foreign Policy: When and Why Do they Work? London: Routledge.

Portela, Clara, & Soest, Christian von. (2012). GIGA Sanctions Dataset Codebook. Retrieved from https://www.giga-hamburg.de/de/system/files/publications/giga_sanctions_dataset_codebook_soest-portela.pdf (accessed on 2019-10-01).

Przeworski, Adam. (1991). Democracy and the Market. Political and Economic Reforms in Eastern Europe and Latin America. Cambridge: Cambridge University Press.

Przeworski, Adam, Alvarez, Michael, Cheibub, José, & Limongi, Fernando. (2000). Democracy and Development. Political Institutions and Well-being in the World, 1950–1990. New York: Cambridge University Press.

Puddington, Arch. (2007). The Pushback Against Democracy. Journal of Democracy, 18 (2), 125–137.

Puddington, Arch. (2008). Is the Tide Turning? Journal of Democracy, 19 (2), 61–73.

Puddington, Arch. (2009). A Third Year in Decline. Journal of Democracy, 20 (2), 93–107.

Puddington, Arch. (2010). The Erosion Accelerates. Journal of Democracy, 21 (2), 136–150.

Putnam, Robert. (1993). Making Democracy Work: Civic Traditions in Modern Italy. New Jersey: Princeton University Press.

Ray, James L., & Russett, Bruce. (1996). The Future as Arbiter of Theoretical Controversies: Predictions, Explanations and the End of the Cold War. British Journal of Political Science, 26 (4), 441–470.

Rodong Sinmun. (2018-04-21). Resolution "On Proclaiming Great Victory of the Line of Simultaneous Development of Economic Construction and Building of Nuclear Force," 3rd Plenary Meeting of the 7th Central Committee of the Workers' Party of Korea, held in presence of Chairman Kim Jong Un. Retrieved from http://www.rodong.rep.kp/en/index.php?strPageID=SF01_02_01&newsID=2018-04-21-0019 (accessed on 2019-10-01).

Ross, Michael. (2001). Does Oil Hinder Democracy? World Politics, 53 (3), 325–361.

Ross, Michael. (2011). Replication Data for: Oil and Gas Pro- Duction and Value, 1932–2009. Retrieved from http://dvn.iq.harvard.edu/dvn/dv/mlross (accessed on 2019-10-01).

Rowe, David M. (2000). Economic sanctions, domestic politics and the decline of Rhodesian Tobacco, 1965–79. In Steve Chan & A. Cooper Drury (eds.), Sanctions as Economic Statecraft: Theory and Practice (pp. 131–157). Basingstoke: Macmillan.

Rueschemeyer, Dietrich, Stephens, Evelyne, & Stephens, John D. (1992). Capitalist Development and Democracy. Cambridge: Polity Press.

Russell, Bertrand. (2004 [1938]). Power. A New Social Analysis. London and New York: Routledge.

Russett, Bruce. (1993). Grasping the Democratic Peace: Principles for a Post-Cold War World. Princeton: Princeton University Press.

Russett, Bruce, & Oneal, John R. (2001). Triangulating Peace: Democracy, Interdependence, and International Organizations. New York: Norton.

Russett, Bruce, Oneal, John R., & Davis, David R. (1998). The Third Leg of the Kantian Tripod for Peace: International Organizations and Militarized Disputes, 1950–85. International Organization, 52 (3), 441–467.

Rustow, Dankwart A. (1970). Transitions to Democracy: Toward a Dynamic Model. Comparative Politics, 2 (3), 337–363.

Rutland, Peter. (2014). The Impact of Sanctions on Russia. Russian Analytical Digest 157, 2–7.

Sandschneider, Eberhard. (1995). Stabilität und Transformation politischer Systeme. Stand und Perspektiven politikwissenschaftlicher Transformationsforschung. Wiesbaden: Springer.

Sartori, Giovanni. (1987). The Theory of Democracy Revisited. New Jersey: Chatham House Publishers.

Schedler, Andreas. (2002). The Menu of Manipulation. Journal of Democracy, 13 (2), 36–50.

Schedler, Andreas. (2006). The logic of electoral authoritarianism. In Andreas Schedler (ed.), Electoral Authoritarianism: The Dynamics of Unfree Competition (pp. 1–26). Colorado: Lynne Rienner.

Schedler, Andreas. (2009). The New Institutionalism in the Study of Authoritarian Regimes. Totalitarismus und Demokratie: Zeitschrift für Internationale Diktatur- und Freiheitsforschung, 6 (2), 323–340.

Schmitter, Philippe C. (2015). Crisis and Transition, But Not Decline. Journal of Democracy, 26 (1), 32–44.

Schneider, Carsten Q., & Schmitter, Philippe C. (2004). Liberalization, Transition and Consolidation: Measuring the Components of Democratization. Democratization, 11 (5), 59–90.

Schumpeter, Joseph A. (1976 [1942]). Capitalism, Socialism and Democracy. London: George Allen & Unwin.

Selden, Zachary. (1999). Economic Sanctions as Instruments of American Foreign Policy. Westport, CT: Praeger.

Shagabutdinova, Ella, & Berejikian, Jeffrey. (2007). Deploying Sanctions while Protecting Human Rights: Are Humanitarian "Smart" Sanctions Effective? Journal of Human Rights, 6 (1), 59–74.

Shefter, Martin. (1994). Political Parties and the State: The American Historical Experience. Princeton: Princeton University Press.

Shin, Geiguen, Choi, Seung-Whan, & Luo, Shali. (2016). Do Economic Sanctions Impair Target Economies? International Political Science Review, 37 (4), 485–499.

Shirah, Ryan. (2012). Authoritarian Backsliding in New Democracies APSA 2012 Annual Meeting Paper.

Silitski, Vitali. (2010). Survival of the Fittest: Domestic and International Dimensions of the Authoritarian Reaction in the Former Soviet Union

Following the Colored Revolutions. Communist and Post-Communist Studies, 43 (4), 339–350.

Simoes, Alexander J. G., & Hidalgo, César A. (2011). The Economic Complexity Observatory: An Analytical Tool for Understanding the Dynamics of Economic Development. Workshops at the Twenty-Fifth AAAI Conference on Artificial Intelligence. Retrieved from http://atlas.media.mit.edu/en/resources/permissions/ (accessed on 2019-10-01).

Simons, Geoffrey L. (1999). Imposing Economic Sanctions: Legal Remedy or Genocidal Tool? London: Pluto.

Slavov, Slavi T. (2007). Innocent or Not-so-innocent Bystanders: Evidence from the Gravity Model of International Trade about the Effects of UN Sanctions on Neighbour Countries. World Economy, 30 (11), 1701–1725.

Smith, Alastair. (1996). The Success and Use of Economic Sanctions. International Interactions, 21 (3), 229–245.

Smith, Alastair. (1998). International Crises and Domestic Politics. The American Political Science Review, 92 (3), 623–638.

Smith, Benjamin. (2004). Oil Wealth and Regime Survival in the Developing World, 1960–1999. American Journal of Political Science, 48 (2), 232–246.

Snyder, Richard. (1998). Paths out of Sultanistic Regimes: Combining structural and voluntarist perspectives. In H. E. Chehabi & Juan J. Linz (eds.), Sultanistic Regimes (pp. 49–81). Baltimore, MD: The Johns Hopkins University Press.

Soest, Christian von, & Wahman, Michael. (2012). Sanctions and Democratization in the Post-Cold War Era. APSA 2012 Annual Meeting Paper.

Soest, Christian von, & Wahman, Michael. (2015). Are Democratic Sanctions Really Counterproductive? Democratization, 22 (6), 957–980.

Spaniel, William, & Smith, Bradley C. (2015). Sanctions, Uncertainty, and Leader Tenure. International Studies Quarterly, 59, 735–749.

Svolik, Milan W. (2008). Authoritarian Reversals and Democratic Consolidation. The American Political Science Review, 102 (2), 153–168.

Svolik, Milan W. (2009). Power Sharing and Leadership Dynamics in Authoritarian Regimes. American Journal of Political Science, 53 (2), 477–494.

Svolik, Milan W. (2012). The Politics of Authoritarian Rule. Cambridge: Cambridge University Press.

Tang, Min, Huhe, Narisong, & Zhou, Qiang. (2017). Contingent Democratization: When Do Economic Crises Matter? British Journal of Political Science, 47 (1), 71–90.

Tanneberg, Dag, Stefes, Christoph, & Merkel, Wolfgang. (2013). Hard Times and Regime Failure: Autocratic Responses to Economic Downturns. Contemporary Politics, 19 (1), 115–129.

Taubenfeld, Rita F., & Taubenfeld, Howard J. (1964). The Economic Weapon: The League and the United Nations. Proceedings of the American Society of International Law at Its Annual Meeting, 58, 183–205.

Teorell, Jan. (2010). Determinants of Democratization. Explaining Regime Change in the World, 1972–2006. Cambridge: Cambridge University Press.

The Telegraph. (2014-11-05). Turkey's President Moves into World's Biggest Palace Costing £384 Million. Retrieved from https://www.telegraph.co.uk/news/worldnews/europe/turkey/11210083/Turkeys-president-moves-into-worlds-biggest-palace-costing-384-million.html (accessed on 2019-10-01).

Tolstoy, Leo. (2014 [1878]). Anna Karenina. Translated by M. Schwartz. New Haven and London: Yale University Press.

Tostensen, Arne, & Bull, Beate. (2002). Are Smart Sanctions Feasible? World Politics, 54 (3), 373–403.

Trading Economics. (2018). North Korea Exports 2001–2018. Data from International Trade Center. Retrieved from https://tradingeconomics.com/north-korea/exports (accessed on 2019-10-01).

Tsebelis, George. (1990). Are Sanctions Effective? A Game-Theoretic Analysis. Journal of Conflict Resolution, 34 (1), 3–28.

Tucker, Joshua A. (2007). Enough! Electoral Fraud, Collective Action Problems, and Post-Communist Colored Revolutions. Perspectives on Politics, 5 (3), 535–551.

Tullock, Gordon. (1987). Autocracy. Boston, MA: Kluwer.

Ulfelder, Jay. (2007). Natural-Resource Wealth and the Survival of Autocracy. Comparative Political Studies, 40 (8), 995–1018.

Ulfelder, Jay. (2012). Democratic transitions. In Jeffrey Haynes (ed.), Routledge Handbook of Democratization (pp. 147–160). London and New York: Routledge.

Ulfelder, Jay, & Lustik, Michael. (2007). Modelling Transitions To and From Democracy. Democratization, 14 (3), 351–387.

United Nations Development Programme. (2011). Towards Human Resilience: Sustaining MDG Progress in an Age of Economic Uncertainty Retrieved from https://www.undp.org/content/dam/undp/library/Poverty%20Reduction/Towards_SustainingMDG_Web1005.pdf (accessed on 2019-10-01).

United Nations Development Programme. (2018). Human Development Data (1990–2015). Retrieved from http://hdr.undp.org/en/data# (accessed on 2019-10-01).

United Nations Security Council. (1992). S/RES/757 (Yugoslavia), 1992-05-30. Retrieved from http://www.un.org/en/ga/search/view_doc.asp?symbol=S/RES/757(1992) (accessed on 2019-10-01).

United Nations Security Council. (2016). S/RES/2270 (Democratic People's Republic of Korea), 2016-03-02. Retrieved from https://www.un.org/press/en/2016/sc12267.doc.htm (accessed on 2019-10-01).

United Nations Security Council. (2018). Consolidated United Nations Security Council Sanctions List. Retrieved from https://www.un.org/sc/suborg/en/sanctions/un-sc-consolidated-list (accessed on 2019-10-01).

UNSC Panel of Experts. (2017). Midterm Report of the Panel of Experts Submitted Pursuant to Resolution 2345 (2017), Submitted on 5 September 2017. S/2017/742.

UNSC Panel of Experts. (2018). Final Report of the Panel of Experts Submitted Pursuant to Resolution 2345 (2017), Submitted on 5 March 2018. S/2018/171.

U.S. Department of Treasury. (2018). Sanctions Programs and Country Information. Retrieved from https://www.treasury.gov/resource-center/sanctions/Programs/Pages/Programs.aspx (accessed on 2019-10-01).

Vanhanen, Tatu. (2003). Democratization. A Comparative Analysis of 170 Countries. London and New York: Routledge.

Vatansever, Adnan. (2015). Energy Sanctions and Russia: What Comes Next? Retrieved from http://atlanticcouncil.org/publications/issue-briefs/energy-sanctions-and-russia-what-comes-next (accessed on 2019-10-01).

Wallensteen, Peter. (1968). Characteristics of Economic Sanctions. Journal of Peace Research, 5 (3), 248–267.

Wallensteen, Peter. (2000). A Century of Economic Sanctions: A Field Revisited. Uppsala Peace Research Papers No. 1. Department of Peace and Conflict Research, Uppsala University. Retrieved from http://www.uu.se/digitalAssets/18/18601_UPRP_No_1.pdf (accessed on 2019-10-01).

Wallensteen, Peter, & Grusell, Helena. (2012). Targeting the Right Targets? The UN Use of Individual Sanctions. Global Governance, 18 (2), 207–230.

Wallensteen, Peter, Staibano, Carina, & Eriksson, Mikael. (2003). Making Targeted Sanctions Effective: Guidelines for Implementation of UN Policy Options. Results from the Stockholm Process on the Implementation of Targeted Sanctions. Uppsala: Department of Peace and Conflict Research, Uppsala University Retrieved from http://pcr.uu.se/digitalAssets/173/c_173853-l_1-k_final_report_complete.pdf (accessed on 2019-10-01).

Wantchekon, Leonard. (2002). Why do Resource Dependent Countries Have Authoritarian Governments? Journal of African Finance and Economic Development, 5 (2), 57–77.

Weber, Max. (2010 [1905]). The Protestant Ethic and the Spirit of Capitalism. Translated by Talcott Parsons. Lexington, KY: CreateSpace.

Wenar, Leif. (2008). Property Rights and the Resource Curse. Philosophy & Public Affairs, 36 (1), 2–32.

Weingast, Barry R. (1997). The Political Foundations of Democracy and the Rule of Law. American Political Science Review, 91 (2), 245–263.

Weisberg, Jacob. (2006). Thanks for the Sanctions. Slate, 2006-08-02. Retrieved from http://www.slate.com/articles/news_and_politics/the_big_idea/2006/08/thanks_for_the_sanctions.html (accessed on 2019-10-01).

Wenar, Leif. (2008). Property Rights and the Resource Curse. Philosophy & Public Affairs, 36 (1), 2–32.

Whang, Taehee. (2010). Structural Estimation of Economic Sanctions: From Initiation to Outcomes. Journal of Peace Research, 47 (5), 561–573.

Whang, Taehee, McLean, Elena V., & Kuberski, Douglas W. (2013). Coercion, Information, and the Success of Sanction Threats. American Journal of Political Science, 57 (1), 65–81.

Wintrobe, Ronald. (1990). The Tinpot and the Totalitarian: An Economic Theory of Dictatorship. The American Political Science Review, 84 (3), 849–872.

Wintrobe, Ronald. (1998). The Political Economy of Dictatorship. New York: Cambridge University Press.

Wood, Reed M. (2008). A Hand upon the Throat of the Nation: Economic Sanctions and State Repression, 1976-2001. International Studies Quarterly, 52 (3), 489–513.

Wood, Reed M., & Gibney, Mark. (2010). The Political Terror Scale (PTS): A Re-Introduction and a Comparison to CIRI. Human Rights Quarterly, 32 (2), 367–400.

Woodberry, Robert D. (2012). The Missionary Roots of Liberal Democracy. American Political Science Review, 106 (2), 244–274.

Woodward, Susan L. (1995a). Balkan Tragedy: Chaos and Dissolution after the Cold War. Washington, DC: Brookings Institute.

Woodward, Susan L. (1995b). The use of sanctions in former Yugoslavia: Misunderstanding political realities. In David Cortright & George A. Lopez (eds.), Economic Sanctions: Panacea or Peacebuilding in a Post-Cold War World (pp. 141–152). Cortright, Boulder, CO: Westview.

World Bank. (2014). Indicators of the Strength of Public Management Systems (ISPMS). Retrieved from http://siteresources.worldbank.org/PUBLICSECTORANDGOVERNANCE/Resources/285741-1361569244497/ISPMS_Indicators.xlsx (accessed on 2019-10-01).

World Bank. (2018a). Exports of Goods and Services (%of GDP). Retrieved from https://data.worldbank.org/indicator/NE.EXP.GNFS.ZS (accessed on 2019-10-01).

World Bank. (2018b). Fuel Exports (%of merchandise exports). Retrieved from: https://data.worldbank.org/indicator/TX.VAL.FUEL.ZS.UN?name_desc=false&view=chart (accessed on 2019-10-01).

Wright, Joseph. (2008). Do Authoritarian Institutions Constrain? How Legislatures Affect Economic Growth and Investment. American Journal of Political Science, 52 (2), 322–343.

Wright, Joseph, Frantz, Erica, & Geddes, Barbara. (2015). Oil and Autocratic Regime Survival. British Journal of Political Science, 45 (2), 287–306.

Wu, Wenbo, & Davis, Otto A. (1999). The Two Freedoms, Economic Growth and Development: An Empirical Study. Public Choice, 100 (1/2), 39–64.

Zakaria, Fareed. (1997). The Rise of Illiberal Democracy. Foreign Affairs, 76 (6), 22–43.

Zakaria, Fareed. (2003). The Future of Freedom: Illiberal Democracy at Home and Abroad. New York: Norton.

ZDF. (2017-09-04). Interview with Wolfgang Nowak, former Head of Planning at the German Federal Chancellery. heute-journal.

Development Economics and Policy

Series edited by Joachim von Braun, Ulrike Grote and Manfred Zeller

Vol. 1 Andrea Fadani: Agricultural Price Policy and Export and Food Production in Cameroon. A Farming Systems Analysis of Pricing Policies. The Case of Coffee-Based Farming Systems. 1999.

Vol. 2 Heike Michelsen: Auswirkungen der Währungsunion auf den Strukturanpassungsprozeß der Länder der afrikanischen Franc-Zone. 1995.

Vol. 3 Stephan Bea: Direktinvestitionen in Entwicklungsländern. Auswirkungen von Stabilisierungsmaßnahmen und Strukturreformen in Mexiko. 1995.

Vol. 4 Franz Heidhues / François Kamajou: Agricultural Policy Analysis – Proceedings of an International Seminar, held at the University of Dschang, Cameroon on May 26 and 27 1994, funded by the European Union under the Science and Technology Program (STD). 1996.

Vol. 5 Elke M. Förster: Protection or Liberalization? A Policy Analysis of the Korean Beef Sector. 1996.

Vol. 6 Gertrud Schrieder: The Role of Rural Finance for Food Security of the Poor in Cameroon. 1996.

Vol. 7 Nestor R. Ahoyo Adjovi: Economie des Systèmes de Production intégrant la Culture de Riz au Sud du Bénin: Potentialités, Contraintes et Perspectives. 1996.

Vol. 8 Jenny Müller: Income Distribution in the Agricultural Sector of Thailand. Empirical Analysis and Policy Options. 1996.

Vol. 9 Michael Brüntrup: Agricultural Price Policy and its Impact on Production, Income, Employment and the Adoption of Innovations. A Farming Systems Based Analysis of Cotton Policy in Northern Benin. 1997.

Vol. 10 Justin Bomda: Déterminants de l'Epargne et du Crédit, et leurs Implications pour le Développement du Système Financier Rural au Cameroun. 1998.

Vol. 11 John M. Msuya: Nutrition Improvement Projects in Tanzania: Implementation, Determinants of Performance, and Policy Implications. 1998.

Vol. 12 Andreas Neef: Auswirkungen von Bodenrechtswandel auf Ressourcennutzung und wirtschaftliches Verhalten von Kleinbauern in Niger und Benin. 1999.

Vol. 13 Susanna Wolf (ed.): The Future of EU-ACP Relations. 1999.

Vol. 14 Franz Heidhues / Gertrud Schrieder (eds.): Romania – Rural Finance in Transition Economies. 2000.

Vol. 15 Katinka Weinberger: Women's Participation. An Economic Analysis in Rural Chad and Pakistan. 2000.

Vol. 16 Christof Batzlen: Migration and Economic Development. Remittances and Investments in South Asia: A Case Study of Pakistan. 2000.

Vol. 17 Matin Qaim: Potential Impacts of Crop Biotechnology in Developing Countries. 2000.

Vol. 18 Jean Senahoun: Programmes d'ajustement structurel, sécurité alimentaire et durabilité agricole. Une approche d'analyse intégrée, appliquée au Bénin. 2001.

Vol. 19 Torsten Feldbrügge: Economics of Emergency Relief Management in Developing Countries. With Case Studies on Food Relief in Angola and Mozambique. 2001.

Vol. 20 Claudia Ringler: Optimal Allocation and Use of Water Resources in the Mekong River Basin: Multi-Country and Intersectoral Analyses. 2001.

Vol. 21 Arnim Kuhn: Handelskosten und regionale (Des-)Integration. Russlands Agrarmärkte in der Transformation. 2001.

Vol. 22 Ortrun Anne Gronski: Stock Markets and Economic Growth. Evidence from South Africa. 2001.

Vol. 23 Patrick Webb / Katinka Weinberger (eds.): Women Farmers. Enhancing Rights, Recognition and Productivity. 2001.

Vol. 24 Mingzhi Sheng: Lebensmittelkonsum und -konsumtrends in China. Eine empirische Analyse auf der Basis ökonometrischer Nachfragemodelle. 2002.

Vol. 25 Maria Iskandarani: Economics of Household Water Security in Jordan. 2002.

Vol. 26 Romeo Bertolini: Telecommunication Services in Sub-Saharan Africa. An Analysis of Access and Use in the Southern Volta Region in Ghana. 2002.

Vol. 27 Dietrich Müller-Falcke: Use and Impact of Information and Communication Technologies in Developing Countries' Small Businesses. Evidence from Indian Small Scale Industry. 2002.

Vol. 28 Wolfram Erhardt: Financial Markets for Small Enterprises in Urban and Rural Northern Thailand. Empirical Analysis on the Demand for and Supply of Financial Services, with Particular Emphasis on the Determinants of Credit Access and Borrower Transaction Costs. 2002.

Vol. 29 Wensheng Wang: The Impact of Information and Communication Technologies on Farm Households in China. 2002.

Vol. 30 Shyamal K. Chowdhury: Institutional and Welfare Aspects of the Provision and Use of Information and Communication Technologies in the Rural Areas of Bangladesh and Peru. 2002.

Vol. 31 Annette Luibrand: Transition in Vietnam. Impact of the Rural Reform Process on an Ethnic Minority. 2002.

Vol. 32 Felix Ankomah Asante: Economic Analysis of Decentralisation in Rural Ghana. 2003.

Vol. 33 Chodechai Suwanaporn: Determinants of Bank Lending in Thailand: An Empirical Examination for the Years 1992 to 1996. 2003.

Vol. 34 Abay Asfaw: Costs of Illness, Demand for Medical Care, and the Prospect of Community Health Insurance Schemes in the Rural Areas of Ethiopia. 2003.

Vol. 35 Gi-Soon Song: The Impact of Information and Communication Technologies (ICTs) on Rural Households. A Holistic Approach Applied to the Case of Lao People's Democratic Re- public. 2003.

Vol. 36 Daniela Lohlein: An Economic Analysis of Public Good Provision in Rural Russia. The Case of Education and Health Care. 2003.

Vol. 37 Johannes Woelcke. Bio-Economics of Sustainable Land Management in Uganda. 2003.

Vol. 38 Susanne M. Ziemek: The Economics of Volunteer Labor Supply. An Application to Countries of a Different Development Level. 2003.

Vol. 39 Doris Wiesmann: An International Nutrition Index. Concept and Analyses of Food Insecurity and Undernutrition at Country Levels. 2004.

Vol. 40 Isaac Osei-Akoto: The Economics of Rural Health Insurance. The Effects of Formal and Informal Risk-Sharing Schemes in Ghana. 2004.

Vol. 41 Yuansheng Jiang: Health Insurance Demand and Health Risk Management in Rural China. 2004.

Vol. 42 Roukayatou Zimmermann: Biotechnology and Value-added Traits in Food Crops: Relevance for Developing Countries and Economic Analyses. 2004.

Vol. 43 F. Markus Kaiser: Incentives in Community-based Health Insurance Schemes. 2004.

Vol. 44 Thomas Herzfeld: *Corruption begets Corruption*. Zur Dynamik und Persistenz der Korruption. 2004.

Vol. 45 Edilegnaw Wale Zegeye: The Economics of On-Farm Conservation of Crop Diversity in Ethiopia: Incentives, Attribute Preferences and Opportunity Costs of Maintaining Local Varieties of Crops. 2004.

Vol. 46 Adama Konseiga: Regional Integration Beyond the Traditional Trade Benefits: Labor Mobility contribution. The Case of Burkina Faso and Côte d'Ivoire. 2005.

Vol. 47 Beyene Tadesse Ferenji: The Impact of Policy Reform and Institutional Transformation on Agricultural Performance. An Economic Study of Ethiopian Agriculture. 2005.

Vol. 48 Sabine Daude: Agricultural Trade Liberalization in the WTO and Its Poverty Implications. A Study of Rural Households in Northern Vietnam. 2005.

Vol. 49 Kadir Osman Gyasi: Determinants of Success of Collective Action on Local Commons. An Empirical Analysis of Community-Based Irrigation Management in Northern Ghana. 2005.

Vol. 50 Borbala E. Balint: Determinants of Commercial Orientation and Sustainability of Agricultural Production of the Individual Farms in Romania. 2006.

Vol. 51 Pamela Marinda: Effects of Gender Inequality in Resource Ownership and Access on Household Welfare and Food Security in Kenya. A Case Study of West Pokot District. 2006.

Vol. 52 Charles Palmer: The Outcomes and their Determinants from Community-Company Contracting over Forest Use in Post-Decentralization Indonesia. 2006.

Vol. 53 Hardwick Tchale: Agricultural Policy and Soil Fertility Management in the Maize-based Smallholder Farming System in Malawi. 2006.

Vol. 54 John Kedi Mduma: Rural Off-Farm Employment and its Effects on Adoption of Labor Intensive Soil Conserving Measures in Tanzania. 2006.

Vol. 55 Mareike Meyn: The Impact of EU Free Trade Agreements on Economic Development and Regional Integration in Southern Africa. The Example of EU-SACU Trade Relations. 2006.

Vol. 56 Clemens Breisinger: Modelling Infrastructure Investments, Growth and Poverty Impact. A Two-Region Computable General Equilibrium Perspective on Vietnam. 2006.

Vol. 57 Meike Wollni: Coping with the Coffee Crisis. An Analysis of the Production and Marketing Performance of Coffee Farmers in Costa Rica. 2007.

Vol. 58 Franklin Simtowe: Performance and Impact of Microfinance. Evidence from Joint Liability Lending Programs in Malawi. 2008.

Vol. 59 Xiangping Jia: Credit Rationing and Institutional Constraint. Evidence from Rural China. 2008.

Vol. 60 Holger Seebens: The Economics of Gender and the Household in Developing Countries. 2009.

Vol. 61 Stephan Piotrowski: Land Property Rights and Natural Resource Use. An Analysis of Household Behavior in Rural China. 2009.

Vol. 62 Sebastian M. Scholz: Rural Development through Carbon Finance. Forestry Projects under the Clean Development Mechanism of the Kyoto Protocol. Assessing Smallholder Participation by Structural Equation Modeling. 2009.

Vol. 63 Jakob Rupert Friederichsen: Opening Up Knowledge Production through Participatory Research? Agricultural Research for Vietnam's Northern Uplands. 2009.

Vol. 64 Olivier Ecker: Economics of Micronutrient Malnutrition. The Demand for Nutrients in Sub-Saharan Africa. 2009.

Vol. 65 Julia Johannsen: Operational Assessment of Monetary Poverty by Proxy Means Tests. 2009

Vol. 66 Ephraim Nkonya / Nicolas Gerber / Philipp Baumgartner / Joachim von Braun / Alessandro De Pinto / Valerie Graw / Edward Kato / Julia Kloos / Teresa Walter: The Economics of Land Degradation. Toward an Integrated Global Assessment. 2011.

Vol. 67 S. Idriss Nazaire Houssou: Operational Poverty Targeting by Proxy Means Tests. Models and Policy Simulations for Malawi. 2013.

Vol. 68 Abdul Salam Lodhi: Education, Child Labor and Human Capital Formation in Selected Urban and Rural Settings of Pakistan. 2013.

Vol. 69 Evita Hanie Pangaribowo: Household Food Consumption, Women´s Asset and Food Policy in Indonesia. 2013.

Vol. 70 Dan Liu: China's New Rural Cooperative Medical Scheme. Evolution, Design and Impacts. 2013.

Vol. 71 Camille Saint-Macary: Microeconomic Impacts of Institutional Change in Vietnam's Northern Uplands. Empirical Studies on Social Capital, Land and Credit Institutions. 2014.

Vol. 72 Beatrice Wambui Muriithi: Commercialization of Smallholder Horticultural Farming in Kenya. Poverty, Gender, and Institutional Arrangements. 2014.

Vol. 73 Christian C. W. Grovermann: Assessment of Pesticide Use Reduction Strategies for Thai Highland Agriculture. Combining Econometrics and Agent-based Modelling. 2015.

Vol. 74 Dawit Diriba Guta: Bio-Based Energy, Rural Livelihoods and Energy Security in Ethiopia. 2015.

Vol. 75 Tigabu Degu Getahun: Industrial Clustering, Firm Performance and Employee Welfare. Evidence from the Shoe and Flower Cluster in Ethiopia. 2016.

Vol. 76 Abu Hayat Md. Saiful Islam: Impact of Technological Innovation on the Poor. Integrated Aquaculture-Agriculture in Bangladesh. 2016.

Vol. 77 Christine Husmann: The Private Sector and the Marginalized Poor. An Assessment of the Potential Role of Business in Reducing Poverty and Marginality in Rural Ethiopia. 2016.

Vol. 78 Qui Chen: Biomass Energy Economics and Rural Livelihood in Sichuan, China. 2018.

Vol. 79 Franziska Schünemann: Economy-Wide Policy Modeling of the Food-Energy-Water Nexus. Identifying Synergies and Tradeoffs on Food, Energy, and Water Security in Malawi. 2018.

Vol. 80 Till Ludwig: Consumption Choices. The effects of food production, markets and preferences on diets in India. 2019.

Vol. 81 Tobias Lechner: Collateral Damage Autocracy? On the Impact of Economic Sanctions on the Political System. 2020.

www.peterlang.com

www.ingramcontent.com/pod-product-compliance
Ingram Content Group UK Ltd.
Pitfield, Milton Keynes, MK11 3LW, UK
UKHW021009120926
8556IPUK00029B/287